OUR CRIME WAS BEING JEWISH

OUR CRIME WAS BEING JEWISH

Hundreds of Holocaust Survivors Tell Their Stories

Anthony S. Pitch

Foreword by Michael Berenbaum

Skyhorse Publishing

Skyhorse Publishing books may be purchased in bulk at special discounts for sales promotion, corporate gifts, fund-raising, or educational purposes. Special editions can also be created to specifications. For details, contact the Special Sales Department, Skyhorse Publishing, 307 West 36th Street, 11th Floor, New York, NY 10018 or info@skyhorsepublishing.com.

Skyhorse® and Skyhorse Publishing® are registered trademarks of Skyhorse Publishing, Inc.®, a Delaware corporation.

Visit our website at www.skyhorsepublishing.com.

10 9 8 7 6 5 4 3 2

Library of Congress Cataloging-in-Publication Data is available on file.

Cover design by Laura Klynstra

ISBN: 978-1-5107-6014-1
Ebook ISBN: 978-1-63220-854-5
Printed in the United States of America

Throughout the text, the acronym USHMM stands for the United States Holocaust Memorial Museum in Washington, DC. The RG tags indicate the record group number of the statements. The views or opinions expressed in this book, and the context in which the text and images are used, do not necessarily reflect the views or policy of, nor imply approval or endorsement by, the United States Holocaust Memorial Museum. Readers are urged to visit this museum for a greater visual insight into the Holocaust or to visit its website, http://www.ushmm.org/.

In loving memory of my parents, Chummy and Ivor,
and my brothers, Warwick and Leonard,

and

for my grandchildren, Kayla, Maya, and Eli.

Learn from the suffering and wisdom of survivors
and the triumphant heritage of endurance.

FOREWORD

◆

WHEN CONTEMPLATING HOW TO SHAPE the final exhibit at the United States Holocaust Memorial Museum, in essence how to transition between the world of the Holocaust and our world, we felt compelled to hear the voices of those who had made the transition themselves, the survivors who were denizens of that world of horror and evil, yet who emerged to live in our world. We were mindful of Elie Wiesel's admonition, "Only those who were there really know." Yet we had to disregard the second part of his warning, "and those who were there can never tell."

So we shaped a final film, *Testimony*, that was linked by disparate, seemingly unrelated testimonies of survivors, and fragments of memories. No single story told the whole; no survivor spoke for anyone other than his or her self and his or her own experience. But the accumulated testimonies, person by person, story by story, gave full-throated voice to the entirety of the events we now call the Holocaust. They successfully communicate to the visitors what it was like to be in the inner chambers of hell, in its anguish and pain, in its courage and fortitude, in its humiliation and degradation, but also in its humanity, however weak or compromised, however corrupt or decent that may be.

Anthony Pitch concludes his preface to *Our Crime Was Being Jewish* with the following words, ". . . There is no chronological order to the stories, as a reflection of the survivors' shattered lives. Likewise there is no index, because many who should have been included were silenced by murder."

Pay attention to Pitch's subtle, deliberate method; the book is fragmented, deliberately so. He has refused to impose an order of the fragments of testimonies. Pitch does not use chronology as his organizing principle, nor does he employ geographic groupings of experiences, region by region. Insights build on insights and the compiler—one can neither quite call him an author nor an editor, yet he surely is both—adds not a word to the testimonies that have been given. He presumes that fragment after fragment will not yield a fragmented understanding, but something far more integrated.

And he is right.

Some readers may be frustrated for they crave organization and order, but Pitch has transmitted the chaos and disorder of the manner in which the people who experienced life and death in the ghettos and forests, in the death camps and partisan units, went on living and suffering as those around them were murdered.

We experience so much and yet Pitch resists labels and ordering. One can read of spiritual resistance as Norbert Wollheim recalls asking his fellow inmate standing on the roll call how he could pray, only to be struck by his reply that he was thanking God that He did not make him like the murderers on site. But Wollheim's testimony is not joined by other such testimonies. It stands alone, as others had different experiences. The outsider may seek to join them together, to impose categories, to insist on labels.

One can sense the anguish of what the great literary historian Lawrence Langer calls "choiceless choices," as Cecilie Klein-Pollack recounts her arrival at Auschwitz. A prisoner conveyed vital information, life and death information: The old, the young, and parents with children were being sent to die, automatically, unalterably. Her mother absorbed this information and acted quickly, boldly. She asked for her grandchild, telling her daughter that old women would be treated better if they had young children. And when sent off with her young grandson to certain death, she admonished Cecilie, "Take care of your sister," who she knew would be shattered by the loss.

Pitch presents the testimony. He offers no commentary and he expects—demands—that his reader understand all that is being said and will find the necessary commentary within the person's own soul.

One reads of the thin reed that separated those who had the capacity to go on with life, knowing full well that tomorrow would be worse than today, that more suffering and humiliation was in store for them, and those who, facing the very same reality, succumbed in body or spirit, or in both, and knowingly or unknowingly gave up.

Reading this book recalled for me the cliché that the devil is in the details. Because Pitch presents so many different testimonies, which offer the most specific details on life and death, loss and destruction, we, his readers, become intimate with the devil—for some, too uncomfortably intimate.

Pitch has sensitively and oh so wisely chosen fragments of testimonies primarily from the vast collection of oral histories available at the United States Holocaust Memorial Museum. From time to time he adds testimonies from other sources, and every once in a while from a book or a document. He has stayed with the testimonies of the victims and their liberators; we see their killers and tormentors almost exclusively through the eyes of those they victimized, not from their memoirs or documents and only rarely through their post-war testimony.

I too have probed the archives and read the books that Pitch has devoured. I am even familiar with the people whose testimonies he quotes, and thus I am all the more impressed not only by his research, but by his exquisite, excruciating taste. He has chosen so very well. Readers should be grateful.

Read the words of those who were there. They really do know something that even those of us who draw close to the gates of this inferno cannot fully know. You cannot but agree with Wiesel, and yet you must also disagree because they do tell us so much if only we are willing to listen. I trust their words and I have come to trust Pitch's choices.

Before you is a wonderful tool. Go read it!

Michael Berenbaum, PhD
Director of the Sigi Ziering Institute at the American Jewish University; former project director of the US Holocaust Memorial Museum, overseeing its creation; and former president and CEO of the Survivors of the Shoah Visual History Foundation

PREFACE

◆

THIS BOOK WAS PROMPTED BY revolting anti-Semitism in France, epitomized by the antics of a so-called comedian. He ridicules the Holocaust in a skit named *Shoananas*, and makes fun of a Frenchman, who was kidnapped, tortured, and murdered, only because he was Jewish. Yet his audiences roar with laughter. Ignorance of history cannot be justified by his birth long after the Holocaust. He is just the latest in a long line of anti-Semites, spanning thousands of years, who have targeted Jews for the "crime of being Jewish."

For this book I studied countless interviews with survivors that are held by the United States Holocaust Memorial Museum (USHMM), in Washington, DC; the University of Southern California Shoah Foundation; the Institute for Visual History and Education in Los Angeles; testimony before the International Military Tribunal at Nuremberg; the Eichmann trial in Jerusalem; hearings before the US House of Representatives; and the content of a handful of books by those who lived to write about the Holocaust. The selected stories give an instant understanding of the broad range of atrocities committed by anti-Semites; they will leave the reader limp. But they will also show how Jews have always defied the odds, bequeathing a triumphant heritage of endurance. The stories in this book testify to that everlasting resilience.

"You heard everybody say, 'We've got to survive and tell the world what is going on.'"

—*Ruth Webber, Survivor*

People who say the Holocaust is a hoax cannot answer an elderly survivor who asked me, "If the Holocaust never happened, then where is my family?"

Inside this book are the searing, poignant, and shocking memories of those who lived to recall it, compiled for those too naive to believe them. Consider a dumbfounded inmate who asked why his friend was praying, only to be told he was thanking God for not making him like the murderers on site—or the prisoner sitting on a latrine when brushed by a man hanging above him. "If you go in the swimming pool, you expect to get wet. When you're there, you expect to see hangings." A child tells of finding a hiding place between piles of corpses. A GI who liberated the prisoners of Buchenwald said it was worse than a dream as he walked around inmates who seemed "in a trance." A puzzled woman saw her dead friend on a pile of corpses; the friend was wearing what seemed like a white jacket when it should have been blue. On closer inspection, it looked white because of the level at which it was covered in lice. A cantor "with a beautiful tenor voice" could not take it anymore and ran to the electrified fence to commit suicide. Five boys about to be hanged didn't give the Germans a chance when they jumped off the stools and hanged themselves. The tattooed number on a woman's forearm was thought by Texans to be a reminder of a good time at a summer camp. Jews on the way to Birkenau lit Friday night candles made from margarine and blanket threads. Slave laborers thought they were lucky to have numbers tattooed on their forearms instead of on their cheeks or foreheads. With their hair shaved off, sisters standing side by side could not recognize each other. Women barricaded themselves indoors to prevent rape by Russian liberators who said, "We liberated you, but now you don't want to love us?" A young woman tells of being strapped down while doctors took unknown parts for experiments that left her unable to have children.

These experiences are told by the survivors of the Nazi concentration camps of World War II. Their words are evidence of innocents made barren by monsters devoid of feeling. Inside are accounts of men, women, and children physically and mentally deformed by the acts of Germans run amok. These are the testimonies of slaves, whose burden was to lead guiltless people into the gas chambers and then incinerate their corpses.

No one can dispute the chilling words of the commandant of Auschwitz, who told a postwar courtroom before he was hanged, that millions were killed during his reign of terror. Inmates, telling their stories within, wept when recalling how they had seen babies burned alive, and parents and siblings led off to their deaths under the whips of guards and the snaps of ferocious dogs. Within these pages are the damning testimonies from the International Military Tribunal at Nuremberg, better known as the War Crimes Trials, and later from the trial of Adolf Eichmann. Here are the details of those who sobbed while telling courts in Germany and Israel of their travails during the Holocaust. Personal narratives inside this book describe sights so grotesque that the storytellers would not have believed they happened if they had not seen them with their own eyes. It would have been incomprehensible to imagine that atrocities took place on such a scale.

As the brutalized survivors grow old and pass away, they take with them their branded forearms and chests, and painful memories of murdered loved ones, brutally killed by the Nazis through guns, gas chambers, and hangings, or too emaciated from starvation or disease to escape their doom. But their sufferings live on through their writings and documented verbal accounts. Horrific though they may be, stretching disbelief beyond the frontiers of understanding, they remain the best evidence of what the war was like, what it *felt* like. Their words share experiences that images and statistics cannot. To remember their suffering and indignities is to strengthen the heritage of endurance. Those who lived to talk about the horrors have added immeasurably to a history of survival under persecution.

The Nazis implemented their "Final Solution" with all the power of the State. No one from the top down stood apart to shout, "Stop!" They killed without compunction, believing they were ridding themselves of vermin. The survivors proved their staying power, and their right to hold their heads high. Triumphantly, so long as there are people who can read, the survivors' messages will live on forever. Their writings will rivet and inspire future generations. These are the words of those who were the objects of terror. They lived it. They saw what took place. They came out alive. These are their stories.

In the words of a lady who spoke to a man about to escape from a French train bound for Auschwitz, where she was condemned to the incinerator, "You must do it! If you get out maybe you can tell the story. Who else will tell it?"

English was a foreign language for most of the survivors, so slight modifications have been made to correct the grammar and wordage of many remembrances. No changes alter the meaning, thoughts, or intentions of those from whom all can learn.

The spelling of survivors' names matches those in the records of the USHMM. The maiden names of some survivors are included. All names are spelled in English. Some of them may have been changed by survivors after the war. Spellings of places and people involved in the war utilize the most common English spellings of them.

Keep in mind that there is no chronological order to the stories, as a reflection of the survivors' shattered lives. Likewise there is no index, because many who would have been included were silenced by murder.

—Anthony S. Pitch

GLOSSARY*

***

Aliya. Immigration to what would become Israel.

Anschluss. Union of Germany and Austria.

Appel. German for "roll call."

Appellplatz. German word for the location of a roll call.

Auf. German shorthand for "get up!"

Bracha. Blessing.

Daven. Pray.

Führer. German for "leader," the title assumed by Adolf Hitler.

Gestapo. German police.

Hanukkah. Festival of Lights. Jewish commemoration of successful revolt against Antiochus IV, second century BC.

Haeftling. German for "prisoner" or "inmate."

Halakha. Religious ruling.

***

*Words not denoted as German or Polish are Hebrew or Yiddish. Exclamation points are added to convey in written English the use of the words as commands in their original language.

Hatikvah. Preeminent Zionist song that became the Israeli national anthem.

Hinlegen. German for "lie down!"

Huepfen. German for "jump!"

Judenrat. German for "Jewish council."

Kapo. A concentration camp prisoner, often a vicious felon, in charge of supervising other prisoners.

Kaddish. Jewish prayer for the dead.

Kindertransport. Children's transport.

Kristallnacht. Night of broken glass, November 9–10, 1938. Nazi destruction of Jewish synagogues, shops, and homes; killings and the sending of Jews to concentration camps.

Mezuzah. Parchment-inscribed biblical prayers fixed to Jewish house doorposts.

Meshuga. Crazy.

Muselmann. Prisoner on the verge of death.

Pesach. Jewish holiday of Passover, commemorating freedom from Egyptian bondage.

Raus. German for "out!"

Reich. The German empire controlled by the Nazis.

Rollen. German for "roll over!"

Rosh Hashanah. Holy day of Jewish new year.

Saujuden. German for "Jewish swine."

Schnell. German for "quick!"

Shema. Beginning of Jewish prayer, "Hear, O Israel, the Lord our God, the Lord is One."

Shmata. Rag.

Sonderkommando. Jews forced to aid with the disposal of gas chamber victims.

Swinia. Polish for "swine" (f).

Tefillin. Religious phylacteries worn on head and arm by biblical command.

Torah. First five books of Hebrew Bible, given to Moses as divine law.

Wasser. German for "water."

Yom Kippur. Day of Atonement, holiest day of Jewish calendar.

Zhid or zhidki. Polish or Russian for "Jew" or "Jews."

I commanded Auschwitz until December 1, 1943, and estimate that at least 2.5 million victims were executed and exterminated there by gassing and burning and at least another half a million succumbed to starvation and disease, making a total dead of about three million. This figure represents about 70 percent or 80 percent of all persons sent to Auschwitz as prisoners, the remainder having been selected and used for slave labor in the concentration camp industries.

—*Rudolf Höss, Nuremberg trials, vol. 11, 4/15/1946;*
The Avalon Project, Yale University

I must state that I consider this murder, this extermination of the Jews, to be one of the most heinous crimes in the history of mankind.

—*Adolf Eichmann, Eichmann trial, session 95, 7/13/61;*
Nizkor Project, League for Human Rights of B'nai Brith Canada

If the Holocaust never happened, then where is my family?

—*Leon Reich, survivor;*
telephone conversation with the author, April 2014

My mother gave me a loaf of bread when we arrived at Auschwitz, but I told her I was young and was going to work. If they made me work, they would feed me. She had two small children with her and I did not know if they would die, so she would need the bread more than me. I didn't kiss her. I couldn't do it. I ran away from her, like my father did. Mengele made the selection, telling people to go left or right. They disappeared. Forever.

—*Andrei Rosenberg; USHMM, RG-50.030*0416*

There will be denials that this ever happened, so you had better know that not only did it happen, but there aren't any words to describe the real agonies, the real tortures, the wasted lives, and the ruined lives of the families that came back. I hope my children will never feel this pain. I tried to protect them. I tried not to talk about it, but now that they are adults, they have to assume the responsibility and pass on this legacy from generation to generation. It isn't only our children. It should be everyone's children, for you must remember them forever. They must not die in vain. And this must never be repeated again. If you let those cowards write these books, because they don't want to assume the responsibility for what they did to us, then we have lost. They're marching again in Austria with swastikas. How does that make a survivor feel? We may not be here much longer, but it is you that must prevent it. You can only prevent it if you're not going to be afraid to read the books that we leave behind, to watch our movies that we leave behind. If you are not going to be afraid of a little sadness, then we have accomplished something. When somebody comes over to me after I speak in a school and tells me proudly, "I cannot read this book. I cannot go to a movie to see anything to do with the Holocaust because it's too sad," don't expect me to give you a pat on your shoulder. If we could live it, you can watch it.

—*Cecilie Klein-Pollack in an interview with Sandra Bradley for the USHMM film* Testimony, *RG-50.042*-0018*

On my left forearm, in black ink, is my number 57779, with an upside down triangle underneath, representing a Jew. From that day on we had no names, only our numbers. The tattoo is so ugly, and since they put it on me, I cannot look at it. It always reminds me of the horrible place called Auschwitz and the loss of my whole family. I seldom wear a short-sleeved blouse.

—*Joyce Wagner, author of* A Promise Kept: To Bear Witness

Mauthausen [concentration camp in] Austria was a slaughterhouse for human beings when we liberated it on May 5, 1945. I was with the Eleventh Army Division, C Battery, 492nd Armored Field Artillery Battalion. It was such a horror that I chose not to discuss it for about thirty years. I do not want this overshadowed by the repugnant neo-Nazi groups who say this thing did not happen. There were facilities to kill, process, and cremate the bodies. To kill, they generally used gas chambers and then threw the bodies in to cremate them. That is why I was so horrified. There were four to five gas-fired furnaces. The Nazis had many marched out before we got there, to get them out of our hands. We saw some on the road about three days before, in their gray and white striped uniforms and the word *Jude* on their chests. They were emaciated, weighing about 60–70 pounds, covered in filth, smelling, in poor shape, and couldn't move. We gave them our C and K rations, but some of them went into convulsions. Then our medical people fed them intravenously.

—*Dix Lathrop; USHMM, RG-50.234.0119*

I became a [Norwegian] flight attendant and flew all those horrible people into Nuremberg [for the War Crimes Trials]. I met some of the worst people on earth. The ones flying in were there to be tried. I remember a lady by the name of Eve Montbeliesse. She was really a terror. She had gloves on. They were made from human skin and had a man's nipple on top of the glove. It's just not explicable how you feel about people like that. You can't imagine it. It upsets me to this day.

—*Anita Simons; USHMM/National Council of Jewish Women, Sarasota-Manatee section, RG-50.154*0024*

When we arrived at Auschwitz in April 1945, we waited in the dark when suddenly lights shone on our freight train, and the Nazis shouted at us to get out. We jumped out, holding babies and infants, and they shoved us forward. The smell was awful, like people burning. We saw fire belching out of tall chimneys but never thought it must be Jewish flesh. Two Jews told us in Yiddish to give up the children and save ourselves. They said we would die with the babies and children if we held onto them. The majority of people clung to them anyway. Mengele stood there deciding who should live and who would die. My father hugged me and said, "Yitzhak, be strong and don't give up. We will meet again." I have never forgotten those words. One of my brothers and I, sixteen years old, were separated from my parents, two sisters, and two other brothers, who were sent to the right. My brother Yaacov was able to work and was therefore on the left with me [but] snuck through to be with the family on the right. As we walked through the shower room, I saw hundreds of tall barrels full of gold teeth, fillings, and glasses. They had been taken from all those sent to the gas chamber.

—*Irving Schaffer; USHMM, RG-50.106*0122*

My friend, the cellist, ended up in Stutthof and so did his sister, where she died. But in his words, he had to unload a truck with several others at one point, and he was told that if it took longer than thirty minutes he would be shot. We didn't have watches, but being a concert cellist he played in his mind the Saint-Saëns cello concerto, which he knew took twenty-three minutes. So they unloaded the truck in time.

—*Henry Bermanis; USHMM, RG-50.030*0341*

In 1942, a distant relative of ours came back to our town, Będzin, Poland, and told us he was on his way to Auschwitz when he had escaped by jumping out of the train. My parents and I heard him telling about Auschwitz, that they were killing Jews there. I was nine years old. When he left, I heard my father and mother speaking angrily. They said he was lying. It could not be that this was happening. It's a pity he said such things, which were not true, because he was frightening everybody. This was their attitude. I think this is probably the basis for Jews not doing more to defend themselves because it seemed so unreal, so impossible. People may not like Jews, but nobody would think about massacring them. Afterward, I returned to Auschwitz. At the time it was deserted. They opened the museum much later. The only thing I found was in the gas chambers. The word "revenge" had been written in blood.

—*Saul Merin; USHMM, RG-50.030*0539*

We said good-bye to our families as about one hundred SS with machine guns marched out 250 men. In stalls normally housing horses, a man asked about our wives. The SS commander said, "I'll tell you about your wife." He took out his gun and shot him. Three days later the SS commander said we could write home and our loved ones could join us. Mine and others came, but two weeks later, in September 1943, men and women were separated at 5:00 a.m. The commander said the women would follow to the railroad station. That's the last time I saw my wife or my parents. The women never came. After days in crammed cattle cars, with no food or water, the SS opened the doors, and as they restrained German shepherds they shouted, "Get out you dirty Jews! Get out! Run! Run! Run! Get out! Get out! Run!" We saw a gate and it read "TREBLINKA."

—*Henry Robertson; USHMM, RG-50.233*0111*

They stuffed forty women into each cattle car, destination unknown. We were herded in like cattle. From a pharmacy I had obtained Luminal, a powdered sedative that taken in large dosages could result in death. I had put twenty-five dosages secretly into my pocket. It was worth gold in the ghetto. Panic erupted when the train started and I had no water, so I split the Luminal into three, giving a portion to my friend Sonia, a third for me, and the rest I traded for water. But I bent down and spilled the water. However, I got some more from that same person. Before we arrived at Majdanek concentration camp, at night, pandemonium set in when an eyewitness said they were taking the men to be burned. There was a doctor from Łódź in our cattle car, who cut her veins on the arms and legs. Everyone ran toward her to have their own veins sliced. She obliged by sharpening her knife on the cattle car's metal. She managed to cut open the veins of about thirty women, not all of whom died. I didn't want to die then, even though I was scared of being beaten, so those of us who had not had our veins slashed stayed apart as a group, and I gave my Luminal to a victim already bleeding. When morning came, a detail of inmates came in and stemmed the blood of some who'd been cut. People now wanted to live, but the female doctor died from the poison. On the walk from Lublin to Majdanek, we were joined by those who had been doctors at the hospital. They secretly gave out cyanide and every few yards someone fell dead, including some of the physicians.

—*Cyla (Tsilah) Kinori; University of Southern California Shoah Foundation, the Institute for Visual History and Education, VHA interview code 22398*

There were hundreds of people in two lines. I was on one side, which was to be taken to work, and the other went to the ovens. My mother hid a little diamond ring and small earrings in her mouth. They may have been the first present she got from my father. Quickly, I said, "Mom, give me the earrings." I gave them to a German woman and said, "Let's go over there." She didn't answer, so I took a chance and took my mother by one hand, my sister by the other, and my aunt followed behind. We went over to the other side. They knew something was going on, but they didn't know what. They just shot in the air. In that way we walked away from the selection at Auschwitz.

—*Eva Rosencwajig Stock; USHMM, RG-50.030*0225*

At the end of 1942, I was in Birkenau when they brought us to a clinic, told us to climb on chairs, and place our sexual organs on a machine. Then they ordered us down again. My penis had black patches on both sides. Four months later, in Auschwitz, they brutally removed sperm from all of us. A day later, they injected us in our spines, which completely numbed the lower parts of our bodies. Then they tied our hands and took us to the place where they would operate. They removed testicles on one side. I had a terrible pain for four or five days in the infirmary. Later I was in the coal mining camp of Janina, near Auschwitz. I had worked my full shift from 6:00 a.m. when they woke me at 2:00 a.m., put me in a car, and drove [me] to an infirmary, like the other young men. There they removed the other testicle from me and about one hundred men. Only a few survived. I was seventeen.

—*Witness A, Eichmann trial, (in camera); Vol. V, Nizkor Project,*
League for Human Rights of B'nai Brith Canada

I remember the date because January 6 was a Polish Catholic holiday, and that's when they annihilated the rest of the Jews from the Copernicus school. I personally witnessed it. I was working in a factory in Minsk, but had documents from the underground allowing me to be on the streets after the 7:00 p.m. curfew, when we carried out our resistance activities. That morning we heard shooting, put on our factory fire brigade helmets, and raced to help put out the fire. The remnants of Minsk's Jewish population was housed in the Copernicus school, now on fire, with smoke belching out. The roof was on the verge of collapse. Uniformed Germans, Latvians, security, and Polish police were shooting at the windows, aiming to kill anyone trying to escape. I saw partially burned bodies on the ledges of windows. Next to the school were two piles of bodies, six or seven feet high. A mother tried to throw her child out the window when someone shot her dead. A few steps from me a German, six feet plus, weighing about 250 pounds, took a little Jewish girl by the hand, led her to a wall, sat her down, even corrected her posture, and then moved back a few steps and shot her in the head. That atrocity stayed with me for many, many, many years after the war. At a moment like that, one is ready to do anything. But what could I do? Anything I did then would have resulted in all of us being killed. I could only pay them back through my acts in the underground. Too often, one hears the Holocaust never happened. Well, here is one eyewitness who saw what was going on and what happened.

—Steven Galezewski; USHMM, RG-50.030*0377

I was twenty-one years old when my friend and I decided to escape from the train carrying one thousand Jews from Drancy [internment camp], near Paris, to Auschwitz. For the journey lasting many days, we were given a triangular bit of cheese, a stale piece of bread, but no water. A single bucket was there to relieve ourselves. Many in the crowded cattle car urged us not to try to escape because the guards would take revenge on the group. An elderly woman on crutches spoke out in our favor. "You must do it! If you get out maybe you can tell the story. Who else will tell it?" she insisted. We tried to pry apart the bars, but our belts slipped off. Then we dipped our sweaters in human waste on the bottom of the car. We kept twisting the wet sweaters tighter, like a tourniquet. The human waste dripped down our arms. Finally there was just enough room for us to squeeze through. It was night when we jumped to our freedom. Of the one thousand people with me, only five survived the war.

—Leo Bretholz speaking to Committee on Foreign Affairs, US House of Representatives; 112C 1S, 11/16/2011, made possible by a grant from Jeff and Toby Herr, RG-50.549.02*0016

In the last days of December 1941, SS Franz Murer, a.k.a. the Butcher of Vilnius, gave a present to the ghetto: a carload of shoes belonging to the Jews executed at Ponary was brought into the ghetto. He sent these old shoes as a gift to the ghetto. Among them I recognized my mother's.

—Abram Suzkever, Nuremberg trials, vol. 8, 2/27/1946; The Avalon Project, Yale University

They took us to Auschwitz in April 1944 and selected us. "You go to the left, you go to the right." My father and mother went to the left. The next day I didn't have parents. I said to myself, *"If I cannot get out of here, I will kill myself."* I was leaning against a corner and didn't see who came from behind. It was a kapo, who hit me twice over my head with a truncheon.

—Anthony Lazar; USHMM, RG-50.233*0066

There was a German called Schillinger at Birkenau who was very cruel. Randomly, he would make us jump like rabbits or roll over in the mud. He inflicted so many punishments it was unbelievable. One day a transport arrived from Poland. The Germans had earlier told these Jews that whoever had papers for Latin America, but missed the ship, should bring all their valuables and they would travel there. The Jews believed them, but they were brought to Auschwitz instead. Schillinger started to argue with a man and woman. They accused him of duping them. They had said one thing and done something else. Schillinger punched the man. Very quickly the woman grabbed his revolver and shot him dead. As reprisals, the Germans took all of them to the gas chamber. It happened on Yom Kippur and we prayed to a merciful God for taking Schillinger away from us.

—*Froim (Erwin) Baum; USHMM, RG-50.030*0016*

When we got to Auschwitz, they pushed my mother and my older sister to one side because they looked fairly young, but pulled my little brother out of her hand. My mother heard him cry, so she ran back to him and pleaded with the Germans to let her go with her youngest son. They did, but first they beat her up and then kicked her. She was screaming and yelled at us that if we survived we must tell the world what was happening to us. "Try to survive!" she implored.

—*Helen Lebowitz Goldkind; USHMM, RG-50.106*0139*

I gave birth to a beautiful girl, whom the midwife said she would wash. But there was no hot water, no clothes, no diapers, no soap—nothing. I wrapped the baby in my prisoner's clothes and a blanket, now soaked with blood. In the morning Mengele checked the baby and ordered my breasts bound with a makeshift bandage. I was forbidden to breast-feed. The nurse bound my breasts and the baby cried terribly. A woman working in the depot stole a nightgown and gave it to me as a present. From it I made four diapers. We were given bread and soup. I put some bread in a piece of the diaper and dipped it in the soup. That's what I fed my baby. I was filled with milk, but I didn't dare unbind my breasts. The baby cried nonstop, but her cries lessened each passing day. Mengele came in daily to check on the baby. He talked politely to me and then left. I lay there for six or seven days, my belly swollen and wounds on my body. Mengele came in and said, "Tomorrow you will be ready. I will take you and the baby." I knew the baby and I would be sent to the gas chamber, but I was young and wanted to live, so I cried and could not sleep. I was screaming in the evening when suddenly a Czech doctor came in. She was a prisoner like me and asked matter-of-factly what I was screaming about. I told her we would be sent to the gas chamber the next day. She said, "I will help you." When she came back she said, "I brought you something. Give it to your baby. It's a syringe." When I asked what was in it she again said casually, "Morphine. It will kill your baby." I was amazed. "You want me to kill my baby!" She spoke with the voice of an angel, saying she had to save me. I told her to administer the syringe, but she refused, citing her Hippocratic oath and telling me the baby could not survive, and she had to save me. I finally injected my baby. It took a long time but she stopped breathing and they took her away. I did not want to continue living. In the morning Mengele asked for the girl but I told him she had died during the night. He ran outside, where they collected the dead bodies, but didn't find her tiny corpse. When he returned, he said I was lucky because I would leave Auschwitz in the next transport. I didn't care. I didn't want to live after what I had done.

—*Ruth Elias; USHMM/Massuah Institute for the Study of the Holocaust, Fortunoff Video Archive for Holocaust Testimonies at Yale University, RG-50.120.0036*

All of a sudden we were free and everybody danced in the street because the Germans were planning to make ovens in Theresienstadt like Auschwitz, but they ran out of time. Soup and bread were given out everywhere, just as it was on corners during the depression. I saw a little boy, about twelve, approach a group of hundreds of captured Germans. He carried a whip like a baseball bat and told them to wear only one shoe and walk barefoot with the other. They did as he said. If one of them said a single word, the little boy struck him hard. I told him it was a miracle how only six days earlier, I was watching inmates marching.

—*David Davis (né Davidovicz); USHMM, RG-50.030*0347*

It was winter in January, and even though it was snowing heavily and freezing, we had to strip and run naked to another barrack. They gave us striped cotton uniforms that were not warm, and which we wore in all seasons. Then it became really tough as we worked through rain and snow. I was in my third camp at Markstadt, working on bridges over the autobahn. We worked very hard, yet they still beat us with whips that were rubber hoses with wire inside. When they laid into victims, they really felt it. I was so desperate for food one night that when everyone was asleep I went near the kitchen to rummage in the dumpster for potato peels or anything to eat. A night guard spotted me and I hurried back to the barrack, thinking I was not followed. But they came in and asked who was out there. I was afraid that if I didn't own up they would beat up all of the approximately three hundred people in the barrack. So I got up and they beat such hell out of me that I didn't think I would be able to get up in the morning. However, the supervisor came in and asked who had been out the night before. Again I was afraid he would take it out on everybody, so I went up to him. He beat me mercilessly so that I could barely walk. I knew that if I went to the infirmary, I wouldn't get out alive. That was for certain. So I just pulled myself together and went to work. I had, as it is said, nine lives.

—*Solomon Klug; USHMM, RG-50.030*0109*

We learned to recognize Jews as an inferior race and no good when I grew up Catholic in Germany. I had a problem understanding that because I played with Jewish children and there was nothing wrong with them. Suddenly they became outcasts and had Stars of David on their clothes. I was an altar boy and asked the priest why all the anti-Jewish sentiment if Jesus was Jewish. He said I was not supposed to ask such questions. Doubt, he said, was not a very Christian thing to do. I should accept things as they were. He called me son, which I hated because I knew he couldn't have a son. One day I threw a book on the altar steps, ran away, and didn't go back. I was twelve. We had often tried to start a fire in the synagogue, a gorgeous, massive building, but when I saw people throwing things through the window I asked why the SS and SA did this to poor people. It didn't make any sense. I remember Kristallnacht very vividly. The Jews were told to leave. It was like an uncontrolled revolution. The mob took over, with many people looking for an opportunity to do ridiculous, violent, nasty things. It was obligatory to join the Hitler Youth, but it was like going to camp, marching, singing, and playing. I became a star swimmer. My father didn't like the kind of pigs they recruited, unqualified men becoming leaders. But I was tough enough to find out things for myself, and we were too young to have ideological convictions. We didn't like these crummy guys becoming leaders. We used to put condoms on their bikes, deflate the tires, and steal the saddles. But I was anti-authority. The gestapo caught me and I was sent to a camp near Ravensbrück.

—*Walter Meyer; USHMM, RG-50.030*0371*

13

At 4:00 a.m. I was summoned by the Russian general. "We have captured an important man. He has to live." I operated on him. It was my first operation on a German officer. Should I refuse to operate? My medical profession prevailed. But I took revenge in a certain sense. He was a young, very handsome general. He was in shock. I gave him a transfusion. As he came out of shock I told him, "You know what blood you got? From a Russian soldier. You know who's going to operate on you? I. I am a Jew." It was a very difficult operation, lasting four hours. We crossed the river and took Sandomierz, Poland. He had given all the secrets of the artillery's location. I didn't see him or hear from him again.

—*Ari Falik; USHMM/Manuscript Archives and Rare Book Library, Emory University, RG-50.010*0032*

I had been in Auschwitz only three days when I saw naked people walking toward the gas chambers. I thought I was dreaming. I couldn't understand it. Then the SS came and looked at our tattoo numbers. When they had gone, I asked why they looked at numbers. The women looked at me like I was crazy and said, "Don't you know? If they don't like the number, they pick you out and you join the others. It's called selection."

—*Ilse Marcus; USHMM, interview with Rosalyn Manowitz on the experiences of survivors who were members of Hebrew Tabernacle Congregation, RG-50.150*0026*

In Ravensbrück I was still a preteen, but so embarrassed at being naked that I tried to cover myself, even though I was not yet developed. A woman with a truncheon yelled at me to walk with my hands by my side, and I complied. I walked by a stationary train

14

and was thinking of falling under it when an older woman asked my name and kind of adopted me. We were in the middle bunk and she had her arms around me, but she didn't move. I tried to wake her, telling her we had to get out of bed. Some women must have seen what I was doing and said, "Oh my God! She's dead." I lay on her, and I also wanted to die. The other women wouldn't let me, and pulled me off. I don't remember how long I was in that barrack, but I heard a baby cry. A woman whispered to me that I had to keep it secret. They were going to try and hide the mother and newborn. I thought, *I wonder if I will ever have children of my own. Would it ever happen?* However, I was petrified and repeated the Shema Israel over and over. I went into my own private little world when I said the prayer. Then I was taken to Bergen-Belsen.

—*Eva Brettler; USHMM, RG-50.030*0546*

In July 1944, people were shoved into some kinds of barracks and there were many more guards on the towers. Somehow word got around that this was the end. We would be killed. The night before we were taken to Auschwitz; some young fellows and strong women tried to break out. There was a wooden fence with wire on top. They pulled out a few planks and whoever seized the opportunity ran toward it. Guards opened fire and brought dogs. A heap of bodies lay at the opening. The hole was very narrow and by the time they got going, it was already too late. Only a few made it out. One of them was my brother-in-law. A woman shot in the legs was left to die. Her agonizing cries went on all night long. She begged to be killed and kept yelling that her legs were shot off. But they did not kill her because she would be a lesson to others. In the morning we were put on the train for Auschwitz.

—*Regina Gelb; USHMM, made possible by a grant from Jeff and Toby Herr, RG-50.549.02*0013*

We had to peel potatoes and were very hungry, so we tried to take some for ourselves. The man who sat next to me, a Czech, had taken six or seven potatoes, and I was less adept so I took only one. We were searched and discovered. The numbers on our arms were written down and at roll call; the person who kept the report suddenly called out our numbers. "Sentenced to death for sabotage. Death by hanging. The sentence is to be carried out immediately." The Czech was hanged, but not like people are normally hanged, being placed on a box which is then kicked away. He was hoisted up. It was a very painful death. Then it was my turn. When I already had the cord around my neck, the camp commandant asked, "Is he the one who had only one potato?" An SS man said, "Yes. Let's suspend him for a couple of hours with his hands up." I believe that at that moment, I would have by far preferred to be hanged properly. My hands were tied behind my back and I was suspended like that. Nature, thank God, is far more merciful than people; I immediately lost consciousness after this incredible pain, and I don't know how long I was suspended there. I have no idea. When I came to I was lying on the floor of the machine shop and a doctor was trying to replace my arms, which had been dislocated. He gave me compressors the whole night long. The next day I had to carry on working in the transport detail. My friends did everything they could to give me lighter jobs, but it was very difficult.

—*Alfred Oppenheimer; Eichmann trial, session 68, 6/7/1961, Nizkor Project, League for Human Rights of B'nai Brith Canada*

We went through five years of torture for no reason at all—only because we were born Jewish.

—*Abraham Lewent; USHMM, RG-50.030*0130*

I know of no crime in the history of mankind more horrible in its details than the treatment of the Jews. Nazi party precepts, later incorporated within the policies of the German State, often expressed by the defendants at bar, were to annihilate the Jewish people.

—*Major William Walsh, assistant trial counsel for the US at the Nuremberg trials, vol. 3, 12/13/45; The Avalon Project, Yale University*

They posted a guard outside homes, where no one could enter or leave for three days; then they collected all the Jews from suburban Budapest and told them they could take only a little food and clothing, but no jewelry. It was the worst part of exile. We were in the open air for a week, with nothing. There were no facilities. We couldn't wash ourselves and slept on the ground. If you had a blanket, you were lucky. There were one or two wells for drinking water. There wasn't any rain, but it was hell. Then the Germans put us in cattle cars with so many people that we traveled with those who died. One bucket was to drink from and the other to defecate in and urinate. My father told me he never thought my first trip abroad would be like this, even though I was then in my twenties. We arrived at Auschwitz, where babies and the elderly were immediately selected and sent to be killed. They never even entered the camp. Everyone took a shower, and that's when the Germans saw the naked girl who had worn an orthopedic shoe because one leg was shorter than the other. They took her away because of the gammy foot and killed her. She was only eighteen, and a nice girl.

—*Eva Muhlrad Rozsa; USHMM, RG-50.233*0117*

17

During the war I went on davening. I davened every day. Somehow in Buna, that was Auschwitz 3, a pair of tefilin was smuggled in. Menashe and I got up every morning and stood in line just to say the bracha. I think about this today and I say it was crazy. According to halakha we didn't have to do it. But it was a shelter. It was a link to my home, to my childhood.

—*Elie Wiesel; USHMM/William B. Helmreich's book* Against All Odds: Holocaust Survivors and the Successful Lives They Made in America, *RG-50.165*0133*

Crematorium 3's crew refused to obey orders and barricaded themselves inside the living quarters. They put their straw mattresses to the torch and exchanged fire with the SS guards, using small weapons in their possession. The guards got reinforcements, and when it was over the crematorium was a gutted shell with several hundred prisoners dead. But the crew of crematorium 1 thought the uprising had begun. After throwing their German kapo into the burning furnace, they cut barbed wire enclosing the crematorium and dispersed to the Vistula River. The SS gave chase and every single one of the several hundred prisoners was hunted down and killed. Several days later, the crew of crematorium 2 was gassed and all that remained of the approximately fifteen hundred strong Birkenau Sonderkommandos was the crematorium 4 crew of less than one hundred men. The three crematoriums were then blown up and dismembered. Number 4 was left intact until final evacuation of the Auschwitz-Birkenau camp. In the sudden evacuation, the remaining Sonderkommandos managed to get intermingled with the general camp population and share their fate and survival chances. I was told after the war that about thirty or forty of them survived the death marches.

—*Philip Goldstein; USHMM, RG-50.233*0037*

At liberation I didn't feel any elation because I was still in Bergen-Belsen, lying on the floor of something which looked like a very big barn. There were still mountains of skeletons around me, yet they were actually people, who had once been human beings. Then there were others with diarrhea or typhus running aimlessly to the latrine and back. So nothing changed, in a way. They were saying the English Army was approaching, but we should not go to the gate too quickly because we might be shot. Then they opened the gates and they came in. When you have been incarcerated for such a long time, you cannot change. Once we were lucky. My whole family had arrived together in Auschwitz, but now I realized that I would never see my parents again because there was no way they could have survived the horrors. I just hope that their deaths were not painful. So I started thinking about my family and all those people who had perished.

—*Estelle Klipp (née Estella Gippsa Weingarten); USHMM, made possible by a grant from Jeff and Toby Herr, RG-50.549.02*0059*

An individual crawled on his hands and knees out of one group at Dachau and said, "Thank God. Americans!" I told him to come with me. My objective was Munich. I was taken to a castle. Inside was a piano. He asked if he could play, which he did. He was a genius. The next day he came to my headquarters and asked if he could leave for his home nearby to see if anyone from his family was alive. I never saw him again.

—*Ralph Miles; USHMM/University of California, Los Angeles, RG-50.005*0043*

On April 24, they evacuated the camp again [near Dachau] and everybody had to go out. One son left his father because he couldn't go on anymore. He was completely emaciated. There were times that fathers took a piece of bread away from their children because they couldn't control their hunger anymore. There were times when they were biting the flesh of dead people. It didn't take long before they were gone. We were just like wolves. There was no dignity anymore. There was nothing left in us anymore. We heard the allies had bombed a train not far away and nobody survived. That night we ran into the forest and hid in case the Germans came. It was very quiet. A boy came running back and said, "Let's go out! I saw an American tank in the camp!" We were liberated by a completely black regiment. We had never seen a black person before. They were giants. The white captain said not to be scared and to come out. They would give us food. So we came out.

—*Sarah Schwimmer; USHMM/Gratz College Hebrew Education Society, RG-50.462*0099*

There is no merit in being a survivor. No one should be proud at all. One can be satisfied. One can be happy to have survived, or satisfied to have shown resistance and courage. But to be proud? The Bible says pride cometh before the fall. Survivor's guilt is nonsense. What kind of guilt? Did they do anything wrong that they survived? They should be happy that they survived. You know, there are many false stories. There's a whole mythology about the survivor and the survivor's children. The children are influenced by having learned about what happened to the parents, naturally. But why should anybody be guilty about surviving? Why? It's ridiculous.

—*Ernest Koenig; USHMM, made possible by a grant from Jeff and Toby Herr, RG-50.549.02*0003*

I volunteered to be a barber at Treblinka. They took us to the gas chamber area as they were rushing victims there with shouts and yells. They forced them to sit down and we had to remove their hair with only five cuts. This was one of the worst times for me at Treblinka. It was my last contact with living victims. A woman grabbed my arm and asked if the young would live. I couldn't tell her otherwise, so I said they would. She said, "Now I can die assured that my son will live and take revenge." We collected the hair for the German military industry. I had some ghastly moments as a barber. A woman begged me not to cut her hair hurriedly. I slowed down, but a whip struck my face and head. Nobody could help her blind daughter behind, so she got to the gas chamber shouting hysterically, laughing, and screaming, "Don't cry! Let's show the murderers that we are not afraid to die! Don't give them the satisfaction of seeing you look sad!"

—Chil Rajchman; USHMM, RG-50.030*0185

It was strange to be back in Budapest after the war. We didn't know who survived and who had not. A school friend and the Russians were searching for Hungarian Nazis, who were responsible for most of the atrocities. But we still didn't have peace. There were bombed-out buildings and very little food. The Russians took as much as they could. They dismantled hotel toilets and sinks. They went wild. Those so-called soldiers had never seen anything closely resembling comfort or luxury. They took rings off fingers and watches from people's arms. Some of them wore five or six watches. They always said to give whatever you could. It was a strange world.

—Francis Akos; USHMM, made possible by a grant from Jeff and
Toby Herr, RG-50.549.02*0021

After Theresienstadt and Auschwitz, I went to school in Kosheetza, Czechoslovakia. It was quite an experience. I was eight, and apart from one other boy, I was the only Jew in my whole school. To this day I'm really sad to say I find it so difficult to understand why we were so disliked. We looked just like the rest of the kids. We did not appear Jewish in any way. We didn't wear hats or yarmulkes or have long hair or anything like that. My only mark was my tattoo number. That branded me as a Jew. I don't think this other fellow had a number from any camp, but he was Jewish, and they knew it. Maybe he looked more Jewish than I did, if there's such a thing. Even at that age, the boys, who were eight, nine, or ten, were out there to beat us up. Every day after school, they waited for us. We had to run, not for our lives, because we were not old enough to really do that kind of harm to each other, but we had to run because we were going to be beaten up.

—*Rene Slotkin; USHMM, made possible by a grant from Jeff and Toby Herr, RG-50.549.02*0008*

I picked up a knife during our escape from Sobibór, which was probably brought in by a rabbi because written in Polish on the pearl handle was Kosher for Pesach. A Ukrainian was thrown off his bike, and another guard was so puzzled that he held his rifle like a truncheon and didn't know what to do. A Soviet Army officer jumped on a table and said something I'll always remember: "The time has come to take revenge. Let's stand up and fight our way out! If anyone survives, he should remember to tell the world the story of Sobibór." Somebody yelled "Hoorah," followed by another. Then everybody yelled "Hoorah! Hoorah!" and ran. Bullets whistled past me as escapees fell down. I ran through empty gates between two fences and had only one more to penetrate, but I couldn't cut it with my knife. Suddenly, a man with an ax cut through the fence, and as they were shooting at us, others scrambled over the top. Their combined weight collapsed the fence, which fell on me. I thought my time was up. But the barbed wire didn't go too deep into my clothes because I wore a leather coat stolen from a storeroom. I slipped out of the coat and ran, falling down a few times and thinking I was shot, but I wasn't. Mines exploded around me, but I reached the forest with about eighty others. Until the end of the war, I worked as a courier with Polish partisans.

—*Thomas Blatt; USHMM, RG-50.030*0028*

Sometimes we survivors of the Holocaust are very well off. We raised children. But there are no uncles, aunties, grandfathers, or grandmothers. You do everything by yourself. You start a new life. The brain is a computer and you can never forget it. But life goes on. Life is life. You lose loved ones and friends to death, but life is life. Yet there is always the feeling of being cut off from your roots.

—*Victor Mintz; USHMM/Jewish Community Relations Council, Anti-Defamation League of Minnesota and Dakotas, RG-50.156*0041*

One night at Allendorf, where I worked, as a teenager, in the munitions factory, I was in the tunnel alone when a German soldier tried to rape me. I fought him off. He could not complain because Aryans were not supposed to dirty themselves by touching a Jewish subhuman. I never walked in the tunnel alone again.

—*Agnes Tennenbaum; USHMM/USHMM/Phoenix Holocaust Survivors' Association in affiliation with Cline Library of Northern Arizona University, RG-50.060*0055*

They rounded up the children and elderly and marched us to a wooded area. We saw men digging a deep hole. They told us all to line up and I noticed they had machine guns. They opened fire on us. Women toppled into the grave. Others were screaming and trying to escape, but there was nowhere to run to because of the rifles and machine guns. I tumbled into the pit like everybody else and others fell on me. I must have lost consciousness for a while. When I came to, there were other people on top of me. I wasn't sure if I was dead or alive. I had a wound in my back where a bullet had grazed it. I felt something sticky and saw it was blood. There were no Germans around so I climbed out. It was easy because it was even ground. I ran into the woods and sat down in the thick undergrowth. It was daylight and I couldn't go out into the clearing. Then I heard a man approach with a German shepherd. I thought it was the end. The dog stuck his head under the branches but continued on. To this day I don't understand what happened because they were trained to hunt people. I stayed there until it was dark; then I returned to the barrack where I lived with my stepmother. Everybody wanted to know what had happened. Another little girl had come back, and most of the people from the barrack were missing. The next day we two children hid under a bunk until everybody came back at night. Then all of us were marched out.

—*Esthy Adler; USHMM, RG-50.030*0004*

The trains from Łódź to Auschwitz were loaded with people. We expected we would be killed. At unloading there were SS men but also Jewish Sonderkommandos getting us out. We asked them where we were and where we were going. They said this was the Day of Reckoning, the Day of Judgment.

—*Paula Szmajer Biren; USHMM, funded by a grant from Carole and Maurice Berk, RG-50.030*0500*

One day a very nice woman told the SS that she had among her children a very talented girl, a ballet dancer. "Would you like to see this girl dance?" They said yes. So she told the girl to dance. She was one of the most beautiful children that I have ever seen. She was about fourteen years old. As she was dancing, tears ran down her cheeks because I'm sure she remembered the applause of an audience while her parents watched and got so much pleasure from seeing their daughter dance with such talent. When it was over, they took this child with them. We never expected to see her again, but a few days later they brought her back and we didn't recognize her. She had been tortured. She had been raped. She was in a daze and didn't even know she had to get up in the morning to attend roll call. If you did not attend, you were beaten to death. The SS caught her. It takes a long time for somebody to die when you are beaten to death, and all I remember was praying to God that she would die quickly. She was screaming to God. She was screaming for her mother. Nobody could help her. When she was dead, they took her to the gas chamber.

—*Cecilie Klein-Pollack in an interview with Sandra Bradley for the USHMM film* Testimony, *RG-50.042*-0018*

The conspiracy or common plan to exterminate the Jew[s] was so methodically and thoroughly pursued that despite the German defeat and Nazi prostration, this Nazi aim largely has succeeded. Five million seven hundred thousand Jews are missing from the countries in which they formerly lived, and over 4.5 million cannot be accounted for by the normal death rate, nor by immigration; nor are they included among displaced persons. History does not record a crime ever perpetrated against so many victims or one ever carried out with such calculated cruelty.

—*Robert Jackson, chief US prosecutor at the Nuremberg trials, vol. 2, 11/21/45; The Avalon Project, Yale University*

On the long march from Warsaw to Dachau, my brother and I were helping an older gentleman who happened to be a rabbi. We carried him for a long time. He could no longer walk and we dragged him a little bit, but he just fell down. We were not allowed to bend down and help him; otherwise, they would kill us too. So as we walked on, we heard a shot.

—*William Klein; USHMM, RG-50.106*0123*

When we got to Auschwitz from the Łódź ghetto in 1944, I was fourteen. My mother was standing on the other side, and it was very painful for me as a youngster because the woman had to undress completely right there. All the women had to undress as the men stood on the other side. As we walked toward the selection, I waved to my mother. It was very painful for me to see my mother naked, but I'm sure everybody felt the same way. I raised only one question with my father, "Where's God?" His answer to me was, "This is the way God wants it, and this is the way it's going to be." He knew he was going to the crematorium. That's the last time I saw them. It's very disturbing and very painful. There are nights that I don't sleep, wondering what went through their minds before their deaths. It didn't take very long to know you're going to the gas chamber. It took a minute and a half, two minutes. You began to choke. The screaming and the hollering, it's still ringing in my ears. It doesn't go away. It'll never go away. The older you get, the more it works on you, the more guilty you feel that you're alive. You miss them much more.

—*Sam Bankhalter in an interview with Sandra Bradley for the USHMM film* Testimony, *RG-50.042*0005*

I definitely thought I was a privileged prisoner. I had just become a teen-ager and I spoke passable German. The kapos hid me from selections, especially in the fall, when things got severe. They protected me. One time, I hid in a latrine up to my mouth in excrement. I had to look for a barrack and take a shower with my clothes on to get rid of the smell.

—*Steven Fenves; USHMM, RG-50.030*0494*

Joe Gould, the Jewish manager of world heavyweight boxing champ James J. Braddock, told this story on his deathbed to a friend, Budd Schulberg. He said he was in the gym in 1936 when he took a tele-phone call from Max Schmeling, then the German contender for the crown. Schmeling said he was in the office of the German Minister of Propaganda, Dr. Joseph Goebbels, who wanted to talk to him about matching the two for a title fight. "We're very anxious to arrange a championship match between your fighter and our fighter, in Ber-lin, and we want to know what your conditions are," said Goebbels. Gould replied, "Well first, I want five hundred thousand dollars in a New York bank before we leave." Goebbels answered, "That's no problem." Then Gould said, "And also, we want one judge to be American, with an English referee." Goebbels paused. "Just a min-ute, I'll have to ask Mr. Schmeling." He came back and said, "Mr. Schmeling says that's OK, too." Then Gould said, "And we want first class passages and first class accommodation for ten people in your best hotel." Goebbels agreed. "That'll be alright. Is there any other condition?" Gould replied, "Well, there's just one more. We'd like you to release all the Jews from your concentration camps." There was no public explanation for [the] cancellation of the fight.

—*Budd Schulberg; USHMM, RG-50.030*0502*

When I was ten years old in the summer of 1937, my maternal grand-father decided to take me to Europe. He used to refer to Hitler as, "That very bad man who is going to make this world change." He felt that Hitler was going to precipitate an enormous war. He wanted me to see Europe as it was. He could never go back to Russia as long as the communists were there. My father, an admiral in the British Royal Navy, and my mother, a Czarist refugee, decided I would have one gigantic history, geography, and sociological lesson. We went everywhere. In Warsaw, a cosmopolitan city, we saw a Jewish woman try to go into a shop. A man hollered at her that he didn't want any dirty Jews in there. I didn't understand what he was saying but grandfather did. He went up to her in the street and asked her what she was trying to buy. She told him. Grandfather then told her to wait at the corner and he would go and get it for her. He went into the store, got it, and came back out. I asked him why he did that and he said, "Because he doesn't have the right to refuse to sell those things if he's in business. I wanted to see if he really didn't have the things because he told her he didn't have what she wanted. He was lying." Grandfather, in full view of the man who came out to watch him, walked over and handed the woman the things. He refused her money. Then he walked back and spat at the man, who didn't dare do anything. Grandfather asked me, "Why was it wrong for that man to push the woman out of his shop? Do you think those people deserve to be treated like that?"

—*Leigh Fraser; USHMM/Gratz College Hebrew Education Society,*
RG-50.462*0060

When you were a muselmann, it meant you were ready for the heap. You were not going to be around too long. People avoided that person. They didn't even help them. You couldn't give them food or anything, except watch them go down the tubes. I became a little rougher, less sympathetic during those months, but that went away after the war. I became a human being once again.

—*Alan Kalish; USHMM/Jeff and Toby Initiative for Rescuing the Evidence, RG-50.562*0002*

My unit was stationed in Majdanek, in a Polish Army under Soviet command, when a court found five guards guilty of atrocities against the Jewish and Polish people and sentenced them to death. The execution was performed in Majdanek and was very simple. I was a second lieutenant when my company was assigned to put up a barrier between the witnesses, hundreds of thousands of citizens, and the place of execution. Gallows were put up and the guardsmen, with their hands and legs tied, were made to stand on the beds of trucks. On command, the trucks accelerated and the victims dropped down and were hanged. Only four were executed because the fifth guard hanged himself in his cell.

—*Steven Galezewski; USHMM, RG-50.030*0377*

Internees capable of work at once marched to Auschwitz or to the camp at Birkenau. Those incapable of work were undressed completely and surrendered their valuables. Steps were taken to keep them in doubt that they were going to their deaths. Doors and walls bore inscriptions to the effect that they were going to undergo a delousing operation or take a shower. This was made known in several languages. Death by gassing set in within three to fifteen minutes.

—*Auschwitz Commandant Rudolf Höess at the Nuremberg trials, vol. 11, 4/15/46; The Avalon Project, Yale University*

One of the Belsen overseers in the woods was giving an inmate hell. The prisoner responded in Dutch, "Man, you're crazy." It turned out that the SS man was a Dutchman, and boy, he beat the living daylights out of him. When we came back that evening, the sergeant was there and we all had to stand to attention. He demanded to know if anything had happened that day. This turkey said, "Yes, sergeant, this man said I'm crazy." The sergeant replied, "That man was right. Detail dismissed," and we got sent on. But it varied. Some of them would drop a cigarette butt and walk away. Others would drop the cigarette butt and wait for you to pick it up and then step on your fingers. You never knew.

—*Alexander Rosenberg; USHMM/Holocaust Survivors in Kentucky Interview Project, made possible by a grant from Jeff and Toby Herr, RG-50.549.05*0012*

I worked very close to the railway, which led to the crematorium. Sometimes in the morning, I passed near the buildings the Germans used as a latrine, and from there I could secretly watch the transport. The children were separated from their parents in front of the crematorium and were led separately into the gas chamber. Women carrying children in their arms, or in strollers, or those who had older children, were sent into the crematorium together with their offspring. The children were thrown in alive. Their cries could be heard all over the camp. It is hard to say how many there were. Our estimates of the number of children executed could only be based on the number of children's strollers, which were brought to the storerooms. Sometimes there were hundreds of these, but at other times they sent thousands.

—*Severina Shmaglevskaya, Nuremberg trials, vol. 8, 2/27/1946; The Avalon Project, Yale University*

The only official I got to know was a non-Jewish kapo, who told us, "You have arrived at hell on Earth. Nobody in his wildest dreams would have imagined that such a place exists. I have been in prison since 1938." He was an Austrian with a hard, weather-beaten face, and he gave us basic ideas on how to stay alive. "Don't trust anybody. Don't trust your best friend. Look out for yourself. Be selfish to the point of obscenity. Just be aware of one thing—try and stay alive from one minute to the other. And never let your guard down. Never try to relax. Always try to find out where the nearest guards are and what they are doing. Don't volunteer for anything. If you get sick, you might as well forget it. There is no worse place than to go to the infirmary. You get less food and no treatment, and you will be a goner in no time. Keep your strength up. Work as little as you can. Walk a fine balance between not working, and working hard enough so as not to arouse the suspicion of the guards. Conserve your strength." It was a terrible existence.

—*Fred Baron; USHMM/Jewish Community Relations Council, Anti-Defamation League of Minnesota and Dakotas, RG-50.156*0005*

The soup came in a single pot, but there were no spoons; so five people took turns taking a single swallow. I don't know what was in the soup, but there was no water. Thirst burned our hearts out at Auschwitz. Because August was hot outside, we would lie like snakes in the sand. No water. Then to the bathroom, a whole block away. It was a place with holes in the ground. You had to take so many minutes and no more; otherwise, you were beaten about the head with a piece of wood.

—*Rose Fine; USHMM/Gratz College Hebrew Education Society, RG-50.462*0006*

31

My friend and I believed that things could only get worse for the Jews in Germany after Hitler rose to power. He said the Jews thought of it like rain. They opened an umbrella and waited for it to stop and then closed it. I told the Jews this would not happen. Now that the Nazis had power they would not give it up, and nobody could stop them. My father, a retired rabbi living in Berlin, said that he had never done wrong to anyone, so why would they harm him? Kristallnacht happened on my birthday, November 10, 1938. The night before, I heard glass shattering at a Jewish store across the street from our house. A few minutes later, I heard another crash from a Jewish grocery in the next street. People were looking out of their windows and crying as I went out to see for myself. The next morning, many of the synagogues were burning, according to a prearranged plan. Someone called from a friend's house and said they were getting out because the gestapo was rounding up Jewish men and taking them to concentration camps. They had to sign away their houses and businesses. Some of them got out by paying through the nose. My father still continued to believe that these were aberrations. Shanghai was the only place I could go without a visa. Many Jews thought it was an immoral place and bad for their health. I got there six weeks before the outbreak of war. My father said I was merely out to see the world, an adventurer. My parents arrived a year later, when my father told me, "If it wasn't for your mother, I wouldn't have left Germany."

—*Walter Silberstein; USHMM/Gratz College Hebrew Education Society, RG-50.462*0069*

I spent the second night after my escape from the train to Auschwitz sleeping between two cows. When we used to go on trips through farm country with the kids, the smell of manure came in from the open window and it was a good feeling. I felt sheltered and invigorated because I slept between two cows. I felt that nobody could find me. I heard them chewing the cud and the smell was so nice. I felt protected. I was in a good, pastoral surrounding, and it was peaceful.

—*Leo Bretholz; USHMM, made possible by a grant from Jeff and Toby Herr, RG-50.549.02*0016*

My childhood essentially ended when the German armies marched into Poland on September 1, 1939. It is a very emotional date. I was eleven years old. Fear paralyzed many of us during the years of very brutal Nazi occupation, a feeling of total helplessness in which there was not much we could do about it. I am a Catholic and saw and heard that my friends from school, together with their parents, were killed or murdered. I cowered when a man in uniform, with a gun in his hand, told me to do things and I had to obey him. There was a sense of injustice and outrage at power being imposed on you against your will. I witnessed situations in which I stood there and couldn't do anything while people were brutalized by others. When I handled American claims for property lost in Poland, I was in Warsaw and reached survivors who operate the Jewish Historical Institute. From them I obtained a number of unique publications, such as witness accounts of the liquidation of the Sosnowiec ghetto, which you couldn't find in a library. I brought all of these back with me and donated them to the US Holocaust Memorial Museum when it opened. That's how my cooperation started with the museum.

—*Wallace Witkowski; USHMM, RG-50.106*0108*

My grandson's birthday has the same numbers as the tattoo given to his grandfather at Auschwitz. It is so strange.

—*Rachelle Perahia Margosh; USHMM, made possible by a grant from Jeff and Toby Herr, RG-50.030*0486*

We were taken out of the ghetto to the cattle cars by Hungarian gendarmes as we sang songs of hope. We were herded into a little cattle car about a third of the size of an American railroad car usually used to transport cattle or grain. Whoever didn't make it with the family in the same car was cut off. They just slammed the doors. There was barbed wire on the little bit of opening on the top of the car. The situation worsened by the minute. People looked for somewhere for the elderly to sit down, but there was no place. If you sat down, you couldn't get up because you were squeezed in like sardines. The journey lasted about three days. There was no water. If anyone had something to eat, we had to share it with others. Suddenly, we saw people taking care of their needs in the cars. The stench got worse every minute. There were people who converted to Christianity in the hope that they would be spared, but they were the first suicides. Death in the car, sickness, heart attacks. Those on medication couldn't take it. It was just indescribable. I can't recapture moments of it myself because if I do I go crazy. You saw your whole family languishing, bowel movements, these kind of things. It was a terrible scene. People who wanted to say their prayers started to chant, but others said they could not say them in that unclean place, which was against the law. They were very tough moments. We stood on the shoulders of others to look out. Someone said they saw a lot of people who would notify the authorities, but it was just a dream. Others reported that the bystanders laughed. Then we arrived at Birkenau. We smelled the stench of what we later knew to be burning flesh and bones. We had come face to face with reality.

—*Bart Stern in an interview with Sandra Bradley for the USHMM*
film Testimony, *RG-50.042*0025*

The journey by train was probably the worst experience. It was terrible. It took four, five, six, seven days—I don't know. There were no sanitary facilities in the car. Everybody did what they had to do wherever they could. A young woman I know went crazy. She was screaming all the time. Then we arrived at Dachau.

—Raphael Aronson; USHMM, RG-50.030*0289

My mother, brother, and I spent a lot of time hiding in many deep Berlin subway stations during air raids. When asked why I wasn't in the Hitler Youth uniform, I said it was being cleaned. I was caught in a streetcar without my Hitler Youth ID, had to drop my pants in front of everyone, and of course I was circumcised and therefore Jewish. They arrested me, tied my hands behind my back, and took me to the basement of SS headquarters. I was only twelve, but they tortured me for two days, knocking out my teeth and beating me, but they didn't get any information out of me. They put me in a cattle car to Dachau, crammed with captives and a whole bunch of corpses on the floor. There was nothing to eat, no water, and no sanitation facilities. It was the worst hell I've ever been in. During an air raid, someone opened the door and the strong jumped out. At a nearby camp, half the Russian prisoners were killed, but the others overpowered the soldiers and killed all the Hitler Youth they were training. I took off the Hitler Youth uniform of a kid my size and put it on, but the Russians wouldn't let me follow them. I found the old autobahn and flagged down a Mercedes carrying two SS officers, who told me they were on their way with a message for Hitler in Berlin. They said to jump in. I was German and talked like one, but they didn't know I was Jewish. They were waved through every roadblock because they had a sticker on the windshield. They dropped me off where my family had agreed to meet every day if we got separated. My mother almost fainted when she saw me in the uniform of the Hitler Youth. Soon the Russians came in.

—Fred Taucher; USHMM, RG-50.106*0143

A friend on the bottom bunk at Auschwitz gave me a piece of bread, an apple, and some cake. He said he had sneaked out at night and got it from the Sonderkommando in barrack 13, who worked in the crematoriums. I said I would go there the next day, but he described the dangers. Floodlights go back and forth. When the floodlights came by, you had to lie flat on your stomach so they didn't see any movement. If you were caught in those floodlights, you were finished because the Germans shot you. Thank God I made it. They asked if I spoke Yiddish. I said I'm a Jewish guy and I speak Yiddish, because the other kid didn't and they couldn't communicate with him, so they used their hands. They didn't have a problem with me. Everybody hugged me. I was the youngest kid; they were already big guys, like twenty-five, twenty-six, thirty years old. When I asked what was a crematorium, because I thought it was a factory, they explained, but cautioned me not to think they had it so good. They gassed and burned Jewish people and then dragged out the dead bodies and pulled out their gold teeth, which the Germans sold. After the gassing, all the victims' food remained and they were allowed to take it to the barracks. But in six months, they would all be cremated and replaced because the Germans said they knew too much, and it might leak out. I told them I didn't know the whereabouts of my mother, my father, and my two brothers. A fellow sat down and said my parents must have gone up to the sky. If they would have gone where I went, I would have met them inside eventuall—not in one day, but two days, or maybe next week or in two weeks, or three or four. But I never heard from them again. Never ever again. They said to take whatever fruit I wanted and gave me two bags. They warned me to be careful. Now I knew that the crematoriums were there. That's where people said they were going to bathe. There were showers inside, but instead of water, gas came out. That's how a lot of people died.

—*Sholom Rosencheck; USHMM, RG-50.030*0529*

Here's Weimar, where Goethe lived and died. He was perhaps the most distinguished intellectual to come out of Germany, the equivalent of England's Shakespeare, I suppose. So here's the irony of it. Here's the same area that could produce such a genius, and the degradation we saw in Buchenwald concentration camp. It was almost indescribable how these people could be caught up in that kind of thing. I've pondered it many times since, how thin that veneer of civilization is and how quickly even we could slip into that type of horror.

—Arthur Johnson; USHMM/Jewish Community Relations Council, Anti-Defamation League of Minnesota and the Dakotas, RG-50.156*0024

Had I not been in Auschwitz, had I not been a witness, had I not seen what I have seen, I'm not sure I could believe it. It's compulsory to teach the Holocaust, and at one New Jersey high school, a teacher was very upset with two students who said it was made up; it never happened. They made fun of it. I was told that these two students would be right in the front of the auditorium. Their attitude was such that I knew it meant trouble. So I made eye contact with them and said, "I understand that there are some people here who believe and are convinced, that this never happened." They perked up. Then I said, "I can understand it. If I had not been there, I wouldn't believe it either." From then on, I didn't have a problem with them. It disarmed them. What I saw was totally incomprehensible to any normal human being. I really think it's beyond a civilized person's comprehension.

—Ursula Pawel; USHMM, made possible by a grant from Jeff and Toby Herr, RG-50.030*0488

We must annihilate the Jews, wherever we find them, and wherever it is possible, in order to maintain the structure of the Reich as a whole. We have now approximately 2.5 million of them in the Government General, perhaps with the Jewish mixtures and everything that goes with it, 3.5 million Jews. We cannot shoot or poison those 3.5 million Jews; but we shall nevertheless be able to take measures which will lead, somehow, to their annihilation.

—*Hans Frank, Governor-General, Poland, Kraków, 12/16/41,*
Nuremberg trials, vol. 1, chapter 12; The Avalon Project,
Yale University

When the train stopped at Auschwitz, the Germans were screaming, "Raus! Raus! Raus!" We had to jump out of the cattle cars very quickly. My legs were entangled with people who I thought were sleeping because I started on the floor, but when we came to the destination I could touch the roof. I was lying on top of other people. When I freed myself and jumped out I saw that quite a few were dead and never left the car because they had suffocated.

—*Henry Greenbaum; USHMM, RG-50.106*0128*

It was a beautiful sunny morning that May 10, 1940, when I woke up, but I couldn't understand why it sounded as if there was a thunderstorm. The sky was blue, yet it sounded as if there were explosions. It was very strange, but people went to work. Then word got out that the Germans were invading. Those who had money and cars drove south, but my parents had no means so we tarried for two or three days. We had only just moved into an apartment, from the rented attics where my parents stayed and the small room downstairs where I lived. We had shared the kitchen and bathroom with others.

It was a very difficult life for them, and there wasn't much for me. Their big expense was a cold box with ice cubes instead of an electric refrigerator. I was the only Jewish person on the staff of the president of the touring club. He was an unusual person and told me not to stay. He suggested that whether we had the means or not, we should carry what we could and take the first train south. He said we should go to Paris and see what could be done afterward. This was very influential with my parents and we left by train for Paris.

—*Vera Glasberg; USHMM, RG-50.030*0561*

They were very thin and emaciated, the skinniest people I have ever seen. When we moved into the Dachau area, I was a reconnaissance corporal, in jeeps and armored cars in advance of other units. A lot of civilians coming out of the camp were Jews in their blue- and white-striped uniforms, which had particular significance for me. The first thing they did was look for food. They rummaged in the garbage cans and everywhere else. Most of the soldiers gave them their rations. The most amazing thing to me was that some of them were able to walk because they looked dead. There was a lot of emotion and confusion at that point because they were being freed. Lots of them were wandering the countryside while we hunted for SS men. We knew that the SS had escaped into the forests, and we had captured lots of weapons, pistols, and small arms, which we turned over to the refugees, telling them to go and look for Germans. They would go into the forests and pretty soon we'd hear shots, which was OK with us. We advanced quite rapidly, mopping up, because the war was effectively over.

—*William Kamman; USHMM/Jewish Community Relations Council, Anti-Defamation League of Minnesota and Dakotas, RG-50.156*0027*

The Germans didn't know whether to kill us or not toward the end of the war. So they marched us from one place to another, including Danzig. While many Germans fled with their horses, I could hardly walk. We women had open wooden shoes and I had paper around one foot. We had stolen some turnips and got diarrhea. Everybody felt sick and I weighed about 80 pounds. For weeks we walked, staying in barns and churches. Suddenly, we heard Russian, but were too tired to react. They arrived with tanks and shot all the Germans, which was beautiful. At the next village, we found others in our group who were hysterical. They said they had been raped by the Russians, so we all dressed up as though we were sick and ugly old women. We only had to say we had typhoid and they ran away.

—*Vera Oppenheim; USHMM/Rosalyn Manowitz on survivors' experiences, for Hebrew Tabernacle Congregation, RG-50.150*0029*

A young woman came in with a turban tightly wrapped around her head, which she said was itching. We removed it and saw her head so covered with lice that it resembled a giant anthill, where ants come out after it's kicked apart. You couldn't even see her hair. We cut off her hair, disinfected the scalp, and burned the turban outside. It was creepy. I've never seen anything like it. The Germans had been inoculated against typhus, but after the war, some of them contracted it by being forced to handle corpses. Toward the end at Bergen-Belsen, so many people were dying but nothing could be done for them. Once in a while, doctors would try and do something for them, but I don't think this was so much an effort to save them as it was an opportunity for the doctors to learn.

—*Rita Kerner Hilton; USHMM, RG-50.030*0002*

I heard on the radio that George Lincoln Rockwell [leader of the American Nazis] was going to speak at the Mall in Washington, DC. I had survived Auschwitz and other concentration camps, so I went to see the rally. I had sworn I would not be like the Jews in Europe, who prayed when the gestapo burst in. Jewish organizations had said this was America and it was freedom of speech. When I saw it, I couldn't believe that there were swastikas in America. Park police had roped them off, but the leader spoke into a microphone while his troops surrounded him with crossed arms, like the gestapo. I had my hand on the rope and was trying to reason with a marine turned Nazi. I asked him why he was doing this, and didn't the world suffer enough for what Hitler did? He asked who was I to talk like that. I [pointed to my tattoo and] replied, "You see this number? I got this in Auschwitz!" He said, "You big liar. How much did you pay to have this put on? We are going to build bigger and better gas chambers than Hitler had." When he said that, I jumped over the rope and started a riot. For the first time in my life, I was able to beat up a Nazi. He jumped on top of me and put his fingers in my eyes, but I tore his ear off. A policeman took me off as I told him he was breaking my arm. He told me to shut up, that I'd done enough damage already. So I was booked and paid a fine. The Nazi party called my house and said they would kill me, my wife, and children. I had friends come over to be with the kids while I was at work in Duke Zeibert's restaurant. The best criminal lawyers offered to defend me for free. The judge looked at me and said I had had enough of the Nazis and suffered too much. I should go downstairs and get back my money. He said we should make believe it never happened. People wanted me to give them permission to kill the Nazis, but I said no. I didn't want to be a martyr. I would have no part of breaking the laws of the United States.

—*David Yegher; USHMM, RG-50.233*0142*

From the Łódź ghetto, we went to Auschwitz. It was a cattle train for transporting cows and horses. People were shoved into the wagons. If you didn't go in, you were hit with the side of a weapon. That's hard, and they didn't care. They hit your head or your leg, or they hit a child. It was merciless. They didn't care how many people—men, women, children, everything—got stuffed in; then they locked the doors. It was summer and hot. People died from lack of air, oxygen, or thirst. In the morning, we looked around and there were dead bodies, so there was no hope.

—*Frances Davis; USHMM, RG-50.030*348*

I was selling nightgowns to a gentile stranger in the Przemyśl, Poland, ghetto when she suddenly said, "My God, you are so young and pretty! I feel sorry for you. If you want to hide, come to me." I was flabbergasted. I said, "Do you realize what you are saying? If you are caught, they will kill you." She replied, "I don't care. I'm not afraid." Her husband worked in the ghetto, but they lived on the other side of the city, quite a distance from us. In November 1942, rumors circulated that the Germans would take many of us. My husband, Julian, worked as a physician and decided we would leave the ghetto. He bribed a Jewish policeman, who probably bribed the other one, and they let us out. The most amazing thing is that we hid there for twenty-two months until August 1944. Our room was entered only through the kitchen where they lived, especially in winter because it was warmed by a stove. We could not sneeze, cough, make loud sounds, or get sick. The room had a window overlooking a field, but I wouldn't stand there, afraid that someone might spot me. There was no toilet in the apartment. If we wanted to use the facilities, we had to go down half a flight of stairs. When the war was almost over, there was a terrible fight between the German and Russian armies. The entire household went down to the basement except us. We sat in the pantry and Julian kept his hands over my ears, so I wouldn't hear the shooting. Suddenly it stopped, and I asked Julian, was I crazy or did I hear Russian words? At that moment, the lady opened the door and said, "You are free! The Russians are here. You can go out!"

—*Lena Jurand; USHMM, RG-50.106*0109*

We children had been hidden by Christian families while my mother worked for the Belgian Resistance. Close to being liberated, my mother was in Namur, searching for me, when there was an Allied air raid. She was the only one in the building to survive, but her leg was severed, and though taken to a hospital, she nearly died from loss of blood. My foster parents found her and I went to see her, but she had aged twenty years. She was white as a sheet and her hair had turned gray. But she came out of it. She had false papers and had escaped four times from captivity. She was absolutely heroic. She had moved around a lot and told me she wouldn't have done it if she had known my father had been killed. My sister was almost two when taken in by a Christian family who had become very attached to her in the almost three years she was with them. They had really raised her, and that is the sad part, which happened over and over again. She had become part of their family and they didn't want to give her up. But she was my mother's child and she wanted her back, so it became a battle. Fortunately, my father's brother had come to Belgium as an American soldier and found us at the time my mother was having a hard time. So my uncle used his influence with US officials to get my sister back. But my mother was in essence a stranger to her, though she was with me and other children, which made things a lot easier.

—*Daniel Goldsmith; USHMM/Gratz College Hebrew Education Society, RG-50.462*0106*

43

Stutthof was a horror. It was our first acquaintance with an extermination camp as opposed to the labor camps or concentration camps in Latvia. It was a place to kill a lot of people and starve them into being vulnerable to diseases so that they would die. It was not designed as a mass killing installation, but as a mass death installation. It was not designed to be survived. There was no work. There was just dying. Anything to destroy you. One young Russian inmate broke down and took a hammer and smashed his German guard over the head with it. He killed him. He was executed that night, and we had to stand and watch him hang.

—*Henry Bermanis; USHMM, RG-50.030*0341*

We had to undress completely, which was very unusual because in those days in Europe, women didn't undress in front of strangers. Men shaved us in every place and sprayed us with disinfectant. Then they gave us soap initialed RJF. Later, we discovered it was German for Pure Jewish Fat. It had been made from victims. Everything was utilized at Auschwitz. We had barely soaped and rinsed ourselves when they barked, "Schnell! Schnell!" We had to dress in clothes thrown on the floor. You can imagine how I felt seeing my mother in that place, but as soon as we got there, she was no longer my mother. She was the child and I was the mother because she couldn't function there. If the shoes didn't fit, you were doomed because you were on your feet most of the time. There was nowhere to sit down. Many people died because they didn't have the right shoes. Feet swelled up and hurt, and it was impossible to continue, but my shoes fit. Then once again the shouts of "Schnell! Schnell!" They painted the back of our clothes with red stripes so we couldn't escape. It was ridiculous. Girls tattooed us because we lost our names the minute we arrived. Everyone was called out by their tattooed number. My mother was such an aesthete that she checked out each girl to see who gave the neatest tattoo. I never saw a nicer tattoo, if you can call it nice.

—*Susan Eisdorfer Beer; USHMM, RG-50.030*0326*

I was sick with diarrhea at one of the eight camps I was in and spoke to myself saying, "Ossie, it's all over. It's finished." I couldn't keep it in any more. A Polish doctor remarked, "What's happened to you? You look so pale." Having no medication to take for diarrhea is pretty bad. I told him I couldn't keep it in and was giving up. He wouldn't let me succumb. He said they needed me for my languages. I would have to negotiate with them because I had studied fermentation in Hamburg and knew German. "You cannot die," he said. He only had two pills for the entire camp, but they would stop diarrhea, and he gave them to me. It was my most memorable experience because they put an end to my diarrhea, but he died three days later.

—*Oscar Baron; USHMM/National Council of Jewish Women,*
Sarasota-Manatee section, RG-50.154*0004

One day five boys stole some cigarettes destined for the German Army. They were caught and put in a little room with no windows for a week. I don't know how those boys survived without water, without food, without anything. But when we came to the square, we saw five gallows and little stools. They took the boys out and put the nooses around their necks. I've seen people die next to me, but I've never seen anybody young having a noose around the neck. They started to read out why they were being hanged. But those five boys didn't give them a chance. They jumped off the stools and killed themselves. They didn't wait for the Germans to kill them.

—*Zygmund Shipper; USHMM, funded by a grant from the Lerner*
Family Foundation, RG-50.030*0526

In the Polish ghetto, we had only one egg for dinner and there were my parents, my younger sister, and I. We sat down and discussed whether we should divide it into four. Alternatively, one person could eat it all and then the others would have a turn at eating one whenever we got it. We decided that one person would have it, to be stronger, and I was chosen to be first. It looked to me like one of the world's delicacies. As I ate, I looked up and saw my parents and sister, Dina, looking at me with hungry eyes. I remember their eyes as if it happened yesterday. Maybe this can illustrate how starved we were. There was certainly not enough bread, nor even substitute coffee or tea. We couldn't even get those.

—*Saul Merin; USHMM, RG-50.030*0539*

The first troops who came by were yellow Mongolians, with slit eyes, and one step away from being wild animals. I knew a sixteen-year-old girl who was raped several times before she died. Once they came to our apartment. They had never seen a flush toilet. They flushed, and we showed them how to use it. A Mongolian got so aggravated, thinking it was a bomb or something, that he took out his gun and shot it. They had come in to rape us, looking for women or gold or whatever. We were then fluent in Russian and told them we had venereal disease. They also had a craze for wristwatches, which they had never seen in their lives. They robbed a lot of people for their watches, and wore six, eight, or ten of them from their knuckles to their elbows. They walked into a man's apartment and saw a big grandfather clock, and told him to take it apart and make ten or fifteen watches. He said it was not possible, so they shot the clock and the man because they didn't believe him. The Russians loved fur and thought they were buying real seal furs. But they were rabbit furs, which we had died black, and would fall apart in two years. After the war, Budapest looked horrible. So many houses were burned or bombed out. We had no bridges. I had

46

some flour and we started selling blintzes on the street. Then I graduated to perfume. The Russians knocked the head off the bottle and drank it. Later I got smart and showed them how to unscrew it. So from one bottle of perfume we made two, filling them up with water.

—Pearl Herling; USHMM/Gratz College Hebrew Education Society, RG-50.462*0109

Thirty-eight years after I entered Landsberg, in advance of six US divisions, my wife and I were among about five hundred people in a West Coast hall when we heard two couples talking next to us with German accents. My wife learned that all four had survived concentration camps. She told them that I was involved in liberating a few. One woman asked where I had been. I told her the first one we entered was Landsberg. It was like a shock. She jumped out of her chair and came over to me almost hysterically. She grabbed my shoulders and yelled, "I've found my liberator!" She was crying and screaming. She hugged and shook my shoulders. Her husband led her back to her seat, but she kept leaning over and touching me. It was pitiful. About an hour later, we got up to leave and were walking out when she caught up to us and clutched my arm. She was a short five feet and I was a tall six feet. She looked up at me and was sort of whimpering. It was obvious that she was reliving the moments of liberation. She wouldn't let go. It lasted just a few minutes; then her husband came over and calmed her down. She must have been a girl of eighteen or nineteen at liberation. You could see from her reaction how terribly scarred she was.

—Philip Solomon; USHMM/Gratz College Hebrew Education Society, RG-50.462*0021

People were dying like flies as we marched in the snow from Dachau. There were about two thousand of us. If you walked a little out of line, a dog would bite you. There was no escape. I had lost my wooden shoes and ran barefoot. We thought they were going to kill us, but we went anyway. They put us in a ditch, ready to fire machine guns, and we thought they were going to shoot us. Luckily, there was a bombing raid and it snowed so heavily that we couldn't see. In the morning, the Germans were leaving and white flags flew over the houses. People were so hungry that some ate a dead horse. I didn't. We walked into a small town. We didn't know what was going on. We were afraid. Then we heard people screaming and the Americans came.

—*Israel Gruzin; USHMM, RG-50.030*0088*

On the day of liberation in 1945, it was quiet and eerie because we knew the Russians were closing in near Kraków. We didn't know where to go and were debating it when a hand grenade was thrown into the house and hit my hand. My little finger was severed in half and my thumb hung by a piece of skin. The palm of my wounded hand was bloodied and shredded. We screamed and I blacked out. The same hand grenade killed the lady with whom we lived during the war. My mother grabbed my baby sister and me, twelve, and fled outside. The house crumpled, but the street was deserted and quiet, so we walked to the hospital at the end of the road. They said my arm might have to be amputated because they didn't have any penicillin. However, the nuns saved my hand by stretching it, even though it was in splints, which might prevent it from growing back bent. Meanwhile, my mother was diagnosed with cancer. As they didn't want us to be orphans, they told me to convince her to have a breast removed, which she did. In the interim, we lived with a neighbor. We had posed as Catholics, and my mother had not allowed

48

me to use our surname of Litman, using Litinska instead; otherwise, they would kill us. Nobody in Jarosław knew us, nor that we had come from Kraków. My mother's friend had married a Catholic and she infuriated me by saying my hand was wounded because I had become a Catholic without being baptized. The Jewish Agency thought we were posing as Jews to get out of Poland, but eventually people who knew us from Kraków insisted we were indeed Jewish.

—Halina Litman Peabody; USHMM, RG-50.106*0152

The only time I remember my mother really breaking down and crying was when she heard a rumor that they would be sent to Poland. That frightened her. Even though Jews didn't know exactly what was happening there, they knew that Poland was the last resort. My mother and father had promised that we would never under any circumstances separate, yet it was decided that I, eleven years old, should stay. They felt that by separating, there was a chance that I could get out. A lady at the French camp said they had no room for me, and I would have to leave with them. I was so relieved, but my mother was terribly distressed. Then later, the same lady said they'd take me and I could stay. I said good-bye to my parents in a great hurry and they said, "Don't worry. We'll see you again." That was the last time I saw them. The adults literally had to subdue me. I was totally out of my mind. It was horror and pain. My mother and I wore the same dress. It's a print that I will never forget. It was a deep purple with little yellow lines. I have a photo of us together, wearing the same dresses. For days I was frantic, asking people, "Did you see a lady wearing this dress?"

—Sonja Samson; USHMM/Gratz College Hebrew Education Society,
RG-50.462*0121

When I got to Auschwitz, they had all kinds of ways of killing people, and they were especially cruel at the subcamp of Buna. Kapos would lay prisoners down on their stomachs. Then they would take a broom or a shovel, step on it, and break the guy's neck. At night, we had to bring in the dead. We put the corpses in a small two-wheeled cart. If somebody died, he had to be laid out during the roll call, so we laid out the dead person for them to begin the count. How else would they know that nobody had escaped?

—*Jack Bass; USHMM, RG-50.562*0001*

It was common practice to remove skin from the backs and chests of dead prisoners. I was commanded to do this on many occasions. It was chemically treated and placed in the sun to dry. After that, it was cut into various sizes for use as saddles, riding breeches, gloves, house slippers, and ladies' handbags. Tattooed skin was especially valued by SS men. Sometimes we did not have enough bodies with good skin. The next day, we would receive twenty or thirty bodies of young people who would have been shot in the neck or struck on the head so that the skin would be uninjured. We frequently got requests for the skulls or skeletons of prisoners. In those cases, we boiled the skull or the body; then the soft parts were removed and the bones were bleached, dried, and reassembled. In the case of skulls, it was important to have a good set of teeth. It was dangerous to have good skin or good teeth.

—*Franz Blaha, affidavit 1/9/46, Nuremberg trials, vol. 5, 1/11/46;*
The Avalon Project, Yale University

I have a note which says, "I remember times when death was a luxury." I used to carry it in my pocket, and if I got a little upset over something, I just used to touch my pocket and feel as happy as can be because then I didn't have any problems. If you saw dead people, you walked by and said, "Boy, you don't have to suffer anymore." Dying was not easy, even in a concentration camp. Hunger was a terrible death. Sickness was a terrible death. When you went into the crematorium, you had no choice. You went in there and a couple of seconds later you were dead. But people who died slowly... I remember times when death was a luxury. You literally envied people who were dead. I felt like that many times because you no longer had to go through the ordeal. You didn't have to suffer. It was over. So dying was a luxury.

—*Sam Bankhalter in an interview with Sandra Bradley for the* USHMM *film* Testimony, *RG-50.042*0005*

Carrying mountains of bricks and stone from one place to another was not enough to satisfy them. They did anything to kill us. How can a human being survive on a piece of bread? The worst thing was if you divided the bread into three pieces, you would still finish it. But you would die from hunger unless you divided that piece of bread. You needed strong willpower to divide it because we were so hungry. When an inmate died in her bunk, everyone jumped up to look for the bread. They fought over it. I would not steal from my mother. They gave us cold soup that was nothing but colored water. Some girls washed their hair with the soup. And the bread was heavy and black. You didn't have anywhere to hide it because inmates would be on the lookout.

—*Gina Schweitzer Beckerman; USHMM, RG-50.030*0259*

One afternoon, we watched a huge fire from the farmer's house where we were hiding, and everyone tried to guess what was burning. I thought a public school was alight. A lady called Anna Kobinska went to find out what was going on, and when she came back to the cellar where we took refuge, she hugged and kissed us and said, "I'm not going to let you go. Stay with me. Whatever will happen to you will also happen to me, and vice versa." She now lives near Kraków and we correspond, and I send her Christmas gifts. She went to a church and reported back to us that a mother had tried to hide her baby in a crib, but it cried, they were discovered, and they shot the infant. She said the Jews were rounded up and shoved into a warehouse, where machine guns slaughtered many before the structure was torched with gasoline. A girl of twelve, whom we knew, ran out after her parents were shot, and the commandant's brother-in-law caught her and threw her back in the fire. She escaped the flames, but again he snatched her and threw her back. Once more she fled, only this time she was on fire. A beautiful girl called Merka, in her twenties, was told to strip. A German touched her naked body, she slapped him, and they shot her. They wanted to retaliate against her father, but someone mistakenly pointed out his brother. They poked out his eyes before executing him. A son, Micha, survived and joined the partisans, when just out of his teens. Every time he shot a German he would say it was revenge for killing his parents, sister, and brother. But people in the Resistance later told us he was shot and killed.

—*Rachel Hochhauser; USHMM/Gratz College Hebrew Education Society, RG-50.462*0086*

My mother was hidden by my physician father's patient for five weeks, standing in a small wardrobe, though let out at night for a short time. At the same time, the Germans took my grandmother and my mother's sister with other Jews to the Ukrainian police cellars.

The commandant, who was executed after the war, had an aversion to old people. I gave him my mother's fur and asked him to release my aunt and grandmother. He released my aunt, but told me, "the old one must die." I gave my grandmother poison and she knew she had to die. She said to me, "One mother can raise ten children, but ten children cannot save one mother." She took a day to die because she shared the poison with another lady. Then they gave her body to my uncle and me, and we carried it to the Jewish cemetery. With a penknife, I marked her name and date of death on a nearby tree.

—*Raoul Harmeli; USHMM/Gratz College Hebrew Education Society, RG-50.462*0084*

I decided when I went to Germany, seven years after the war, that I would visit the warden of the prison where I spent about a year, and kill him. I had made up my mind to say, "Do you remember me? May I refresh your memory?" And then I would kill him. I knocked on the door and a lady opened it. I said, "I've come to see Dr. Soikner." She said, "Well, I'm very sorry, but he's no longer here. He moved to Hamburg." That changed the whole thing. I was not about to take the train to Hamburg because it was a long way. I forgot about it. But I never understood how one man could be so evil to another. This man had no right whatsoever to be so cruel, so sadistic, to a boy of sixteen. He didn't beat me personally, but he ordered that I be beaten, and placed in a little cell with nothing but two slices of bread daily for four weeks. This was the ultimate cruelty. He was a sadistic man. I still dream about him once in a while. I do a lot of scribbling with a pencil, and I see myself drawing his profile. I say, "Dammit, why do I do this?" I hated him passionately. It was like putting an eagle in a cage. What would have happened if I had killed him? Would I have had sleepless nights? I don't know. It never happened.

—*Walter Meyer; USHMM, RG-50.030*0371*

Dr. Elkous was in charge of the hospital at Landsberg concentration camp. In Kovno, Lithuania, he was a dedicated doctor and was prominent in the medical society. He didn't do anything other than read medical books and study medicine. He went to the same Jewish school as my father. He went to the German authorities and said he needed medication and equipment. They said they'd take care of it, but weeks passed by and nothing happened. So Dr. Elkous told them he needed bed linen[s] to meet the needs of more and more sick people, and if he didn't get it the same day, he would go on a hunger strike. He didn't get it, went on a hunger strike, and died about ten days later.

—*Raphael Aronson; USHMM, RG-50.030*0289*

In the entire universe of evil, which was Nazi-occupied Europe, there was no place that could match the hell of Birkenau in its first year of existence. We didn't even know upon arrival that Birkenau had just started to become the crown jewel of the Nazi killing machine of European Jewry. Birkenau belonged to a different universe of evil. That unique hell was a slaughterhouse rather than a concentration camp. Time was not conceived in terms of months or years, but in terms of days. If one survived the day, one achieved the unlikely. If one survived a month, one achieved the impossible. We walked the three kilometers from Auschwitz to Birkenau on May 1, 1942, and there were one thousand young and middle-aged men in our transport. Within one month, most of them were dead. By the end of about two months, most of those still alive were the ones who survived the camp. There were fifteen of us. From March 1942 until March 1943, there were no crematoriums in Birkenau. The gassing took place in an abandoned farmer's cottage while the burial, and later on the burning of the bodies, took place in adjacent pits surrounded by woods. The Sonderkommando crews were subject to periodic liquidations. The approximately five hundred-strong crew was murdered in 1942. The first job of the new crew was to dispose of the bodies of their predecessors. By fall of 1944, when Birkenau no longer functioned as a mass killing machine, the SS began the process of thinning out the ranks of the Sonderkommando. The first victims were several hundred men from the crew of crematorium 3. They were brought for disinfection and that was the first time that I came face to face with, and talked to, members of the Sonderkommando. They were told that they were being transferred to another camp. The disinfection process was used as a subterfuge to lull them into believing the deception. They weren't deceived, and were aware of their situation. From the disinfection, they were taken to Auschwitz, where they were put to death in the old gas chamber.

—Philip Goldstein; USHMM, RG-50.233*0037

The last time I saw my mother and younger brother was on June 26, 1943, in the Środula ghetto, Poland. I had long braids and it was raining, but she wore a jacket. She put it around me, so I wouldn't get wet. I didn't want to leave her, but she pushed me away. She said, "Somebody has to live to tell the story." I didn't want to leave them, but they pulled me away. Then she went off with my brother. She was a young woman. Later I found out my father had been shot. After liberation from an ammunition factory in Ludwigsdorf, Germany, I was seventeen and on a train headed for Poland. I was sitting with a priest and some girls and didn't have anywhere to rest my head, so I rested it on his lap. He started talking about the Jews. I sat up and said, "I'm Jewish and I was in a concentration camp. You'd better close your mouth because you don't know what you're talking about." He threw me down, got up, and went out.

—Zelda Piekarska Brodecki; USHMM, RG-50.030*0041

We had been force-marched to a labor camp a few miles from where we lived on the outskirts of Zloczow, Poland, when I got shot in the leg by crazy, drunk Germans in the middle of the night. They just shot people. My leg was amputated. When I got home, I cannot describe how my parents felt when they saw me without a leg. There was a doctor in the ghetto who was from Kraków. He was very gentle and promised to come the following week, but he didn't. He died of typhus. I wondered why I didn't get an infection because they didn't have sterilized gauze, but somehow, when you have to live, you live.

—Sophie Roth; USHMM/Gratz College Hebrew Education Society,
RG-50.462*0096

Hitler wanted to eliminate the Jews, but our revenge is by saying, "Look, we are here!" He wanted to do away with us. I would have died, and eventually we wouldn't have anybody left. I would be helping him out. Well, here we have two survivors, and we have three wonderful daughters and eight grandchildren. I'm very proud of my kids. They are, so to speak, following in the footsteps of their forefathers. My husband and I went back to Auschwitz thirty years after it was liberated, to confront it. We came back and I was addressing students, when one of them said, "You were telling us you went through such a terrible period in your life, and now you're saying you are married and have three children. How come you brought children into this world?" I stopped and thought about it, and said that even though I hadn't considered the fact, it was the natural thing to do. "But now that you ask me, I would have given Hitler a victory [if I didn't have children], because that's what he started out to do." The questioner said it had always bothered him, but now he saw my point. "You're right," he said. "Thank you for explaining it. I never thought of it."

—Regina Gutman Spiegel; USHMM, RG-50.106*0116

At the end of April 1945, we were liberated from Allach, a satellite camp of Dachau, by the Forty-Second Division, the Rainbow Division. The American soldiers killed quite a few Germans. They lined them up against a wall and killed them. I saw it happen. An American general saw it and went berserk. He kicked a soldier and a machine gun, and stopped them from firing it. They killed about seventeen guards, maybe more.

—William Lowenberg; USHMM, RG-50.549.01*0024549

At first my work was to load the clothes of people murdered after arrival by cattle cars. When I had been at Treblinka two days, my mother, sister, and two brothers were brought to the camp. I had to watch them being led away to the gas chambers. Several days later, when I was loading clothes on the freight cars, my colleagues found my wife's documents, and a photograph of my wife and child. That is all I have left of my family. Only a photograph.

—Samuel Rajzman, Nuremberg trials, vol. 8, 2/27/1946; The Avalon
Project, Yale University

I was seventeen at Zershe concentration camp when a man I think was a dentist took me to his quarters. He said he was going to pull a tooth and I could cry out, but nobody would hear me. Without an anesthetic or anything he pulled out a tooth. I wanted to stand up, but he ordered me to sit. He said if I yelled out or cried, he would kill me. Then he pulled out another tooth. I don't know why. He took out five from one side and three from the other. Now I have implants and a bridge.

—Aleksander Laks; USHMM, RG-50.637*0003

The line between a human being and an animal is very small. It doesn't need much. That I have learned. It does not need much. It is not difficult to be a human being in a human surrounding; otherwise, it doesn't need much. Believe me, no animal could be worse off than what I saw in Auschwitz. A wild beast in the jungle couldn't be worse.

—*Ilse Marcus; USHMM/Rosalyn Manowitz account of experiences of survivors who were members of Hebrew Tabernacle Congregation, RG-50.150*0026*

My brother took care of the horses for the SS at Theresienstadt. Every night they would get a lump of sugar after they were groomed. My mother was very sick and he tried to get lumps of sugar to her, but he was caught by one of the German policemen. He was taken to the punishment center, where everyone was tortured to death. Nobody survived. But he came back to the camp about three days later, so brutally beaten and tortured that we hardly recognized him. We understood he came back because he was needed for the horses. He was especially good with them and some of the SS got him out. But he looked terrible. A few lumps of sugar were good for horses, but not for his mother. On September 7, 1943, my parents were already in one cattle car bound for Auschwitz and my brother in another. I was boarding when an SS called my number and took me off the transport. Afterward, I learned from people coming back, whom we knew before at Theresienstadt, that my mother was taken to the gas chamber. My father and brother perished from beatings, malnutrition, and starvation.

—*Alice Bogart; USHMM, RG-50.233*0008*

I want the six million to be remembered as brave, courageous people who died for one reason only, that they were born of a different race. Their loss is a loss for all humanity. If anybody comes to the museum and sees the mementos that we left behind, whether it's a little shoe, a letter, our Torah, or prayer book, remember these are our precious valuables. Remember, from these books, that we are gone. And remember the agony of the survivors, who had to live with these memories, and could never touch them, could never have them back. We hope that future generations will never know our pain, and that everyone will stand up to any form of persecution. I taught my children love and not hate. But I could never forget. I could never forgive.

—*Cecilie Klein-Pollack in an interview with Sandra Bradley for the USHMM film* Testimony, *RG-50.042*-0018*

I had turned seven in December 1944, and we were liberated on a death march the following month. Nobody knew our destination, but we had a very hard time. It was winter and there was snow on the ground. They killed anyone who fell out of line or couldn't keep up. They were shot or pushed, and that was the end of them. That kept up for a very long time when all of a sudden our German guards disappeared. They were gone, and we were surrounded by Russian soldiers dressed in white. That was liberation. The Russians took us to a food warehouse and there was a frenzied stampede for anything we could get our hands on. I, being very little, couldn't really get through to anything, except I do remember very distinctly being able to grab hold of a gold can of something. It turned out to be sauerkraut.

—*Rene Slotkin; USHMM, made possible by a grant from Jeff and Toby Herr, RG-50.549.02*0008*

We didn't get anything to eat for days and were bitterly cold and hungry, but you could forget that if you were blessed with imagination. I planned a party [for] after the war and my dilemma for almost an entire day was whether I should have a blue or a red velvet dress. I couldn't decide. I really liked the color blue much better as a color, but I knew that red looked better on me. You could occupy your mind and hang your thoughts on trivia of that nature. If, unfortunately, you were a realist, you didn't have much of a chance. I felt I was lucky because I never faced reality.

—Gerda Klein; USHMM, RG-50.042*0001

We pulled up in the station and 280 British prisoners of war marched down. We saw barbed wire and men in pajamas digging trenches. I was a corporal and said to one of the guards, "Who are they?" He said, "Juden!" I said, "Pardon?" He said, "Jews!" as if we should have known. It was Auschwitz. The first thing we noticed was a terrible smell and the Jews told us it was the crematorium. We didn't know what they were talking about, but after a while, we realized what was going on. It was astonishing. We just couldn't believe they were burning Jews, but we knew they were right. It shook us rigid. We couldn't understand it. We thought if ever they got desperate, they'd put us in there. It was a genuine scare. We had some food parcels and didn't eat the German rations, so I had a piece of sausage and gave it to a Jew called Josef. Days later, he gave me a ring he had made from a steel pipe. I stuck it on my finger and it's been there ever since. About a week later, he disappeared. His mate said, "Gas chamber. Kaput." If a Jew got in the way of a certain high-ranking officer, he would kick him. Twice I saw him take out his luger and shoot two Jews. We were disgusted and would have mobbed him, but what could we do against armed Germans? If a kapo saw us talking to one of them he would go straight to the Jew and belt him with a truncheon. One day they didn't bring our soup, so we had the cabbage water the Jews ate. It was terrible and I spat it out. That's all the Jews lived on.

—*Ron Jones; USHMM, RG-50.030*0709*

The worst part of sharing a bunk in Auschwitz was to get up in the middle of the night to empty your bladder. Then you became aware of just how cold it was. When the container was full of urine you had to go outside and empty it. We didn't know how long we would last, or how it would end. We tried to find out from other prisoners what was happening in the rest of the world. How long would Hitler last? By the second half of 1943, there were more and more rumors that the tide of war had turned against him, and it was only a question of time before Hitler was beaten. Would he survive us, or would we survive him?

—*Gert Silberbard Silver; USHMM, RG-50.562*0010*

We talked about home, and we dreamed about having a loaf of bread to eat, and thinking maybe, maybe there's a chance that we would live through this, and there would be an end. We talked about a lot of recipes and things we used to eat at home. Once it got out of hand we would say, "Stop! Stop! We are starving! We can't take this anymore. It's too much!" All we thought about was food. How to survive. How to fill our stomachs.

—*Fela Warschau; USHMM, RG-50.030*0303*

I survived Neuengamme concentration camp near Hamburg because the fellow in charge of my barracks found out that I played the violin, and suddenly there was a violin. I played it for him, and he liked it. He really saved my life because prisoners were taken to the gas chambers of Bergen-Belsen and Auschwitz. Music helped me a lot. After the war, I went to my old apartment, not knowing whether my mother or father were alive, but they were. Everything was very difficult in those early months, but there was a craving in Budapest for some culture. We were musicians, yet we played in our overcoats because there was no heating. It was a strange situation. It was basically a Russian occupation. We went through all kinds of horror stories. But I practiced and played, and got back into the swing of things. I was the youngest concertmaster they ever had in the Budapest Philharmonic. But some of us felt that the world was open for talented, good instrumentalists, so I left. I was concertmaster in Gurterburg, Sweden. They treated me very nicely, and I made some good friends when I became concertmaster of the Berlin opera house for almost four years. I didn't have any bad feelings about being back in Germany. I considered it rehabilitation, a kind of restitution. Now we are at my second home, the orchestra hall in Chicago, where I have been assistant concertmaster for the past forty-four years.

—*Francis Akos; USHMM, made possible by a grant from Jeff and Toby Herr, RG-50.549.02*0021*

At Auschwitz I slept on the floor of the barrack. It was not a problem for the simple reason that I had slept on the floor at home in Czechoslovakia. We were a big family and we had only three rooms, a kitchen, bedroom, and a living room that was also a dining room. Only my mother and father, and my oldest sister, slept in beds.

—*William Klein; USHMM, RG-50.106*0123*

My tattoo number is 25702. When I came to this country [the United States] and I went on the train, people moved away. They thought I came from Sing Sing [prison]. They had never seen that. If I have a number, I must be a criminal, so they just moved away. They didn't want to see it. Even now, if I go in the hospital, they ask, "What is that? Were you in camp? Did you have a good time?" They didn't know it was from a concentration camp. I never cover it up. Never. You can't cover it up if you wear short sleeves. No, I never cover it up. It doesn't bother me. You get used to things. When my granddaughter was two, three years old, I told her it's a telephone number. I never talked about it. It's too painful, and for children, they would never understand it either. It's impossible. They found out, but on their own. They went to the library and found out. But I never talked about it.

—Lonia Mosak; USHMM, made possible by grant from Jeff and Toby Herr, RG-50.549.02*0045

A lady close to forty was chosen to get water for the tea. She had a bit of a blanket wrapped around her waist. The way to the kitchen was plastered with small stones and we didn't have any shoes. We had to walk barefoot. Coming back, the blanket poked out of her dress, and a German female told her to bend over. She took a stick and beat her until mucus came out of her mouth. Then she stepped on her neck with boots. All because she took a piece of the blanket.

—Rose Fine; USHMM/Gratz College Hebrew Education Society, RG-50.462*0006

Prisoners behaved like animals. They would kill for a little soup. If they saw food, they would grab it. In Birkenau, I had friends who were so aggressive that they would poke in the garbage bin and then wake me up and say they had made soup from potato peels or whatever. Others would put their heads in the huge pots of liquid and some solids. They had turned laborers into animals. It was unbelievable how people in those circumstances behaved. They were fighting for their lives. They didn't know any better. I was never aggressive because I'm not a big eater and I was never that hungry that I would go for somebody's food. Sometimes I traded my little bit of soup for a thin slice of bread and a tiny piece of margarine, which gave me energy. All the supervisors were mean. We were afraid to talk to them, but we were more scared of their dogs, which they let loose on us. Lithuanians in black uniforms were more cruel than the Germans and Poles. They wanted to show more loyalty to the führer than the Germans themselves. They were terrible people. They hated the Jews—couldn't stand our guts. We were afraid of Lithuanians more than anybody else.

—*Rose Szywic Warner; USHMM, RG-50.030*0270*

My outfit was part of the US Forty-Second Division and I saw the railroad cars with bodies in the boxcars. They had not removed the corpses. It was something that I wish I hadn't ever seen and hope I never see again. Unless you see something like that, it is unbelievable. Everybody in my outfit was very angry about it. If we could have gotten to them, I believe we would have done the same to them as they had done to the prisoners.

—*Roy Dodd; USHMM/Archives and Rare Book Library,*
Emory University, RG-50.010*0026

In 1942 the Germans decreed that Jews could not attend any school in Belgium, so I stayed home in suburban Brussels. In the summer, I had been attending a camp, even after the priest was shot for allowing Jews to attend. One day a friend of my mother's stopped me at our apartment door and said not to go in because the Germans were there. They had already taken my mother away. I trusted him because I'd seen him many times. We took a train to a Catholic convent in Louvain. It was probably an orphanage because quite a few children were not Jews. The Benedictine sisters gave me a Christian name, Christiane DeGraaf, but I knew many of the children were Jewish because although we all wore black dresses, when we filed into the chapel every morning, the Jews had to sit in the back during Mass. We were told to be quiet until it was over, when we all went to breakfast before school. We never left the convent grounds during the two and a half years I was there. Every time the SS came to search, the nuns would rush to the classrooms and tell us to run quietly away from the officers. I was only nine and we were all afraid, though quiet. It sounds fantastic, but about three hundred of us, of all ages, went up and down the stairs. I retained warm feelings for Catholics in general and nuns in particular because they took care of us under enormous stress. They spanked and punished us and were strict, but they did take care of us. When I went back with my husband about thirty years later, there were still a couple of nuns there who had looked after us. They reminisced like crazy, saying, "Do you remember how the SS used to come!" My American grandchild is named after my mother.

—*Rose Meyerhoff; USHMM/Jewish Community Relations Council, Anti-Defamation League of Minnesota and Dakotas, RG-50.156*0040*

When I attended the war crimes trials, I was horrified to meet the finality of evil face-to-face. Absolutely stupefied. I really can't find any words to have those monsters stand up and then pretend to be innocent and state it was never their fault. They said they were German soldiers and had to follow orders. They were terrified. These people, who could do things to other people without compunction, were terrified when they themselves were confronted with death. They were groveling. The lawyers were wonderfully ethical. Everything was aboveboard and fair.

—*Sheila Baxter; USHMM/National Council of Jewish Women,*
Sarasota-Manatee section, RG-50.154*0006

To begin with, the sounds were spaced out; then they came more frequently until they became a continuous crying that we all identified as the crying of a newborn baby. The man who had heard it first went to see where exactly the noise was coming from. Stepping over the bodies, he found the source of those little wailings. It was a baby girl, barely two months old, still clinging to her mother's breast and vainly trying to suckle. She was crying because she could feel that the milk had stopped flowing. He took the baby and brought it out of the gas chamber. We knew it would be impossible to keep her with us. Impossible to hide her or get her accepted by the Germans. And indeed, as soon as the guard saw the baby, he didn't seem at all displeased at having a little baby to kill. He fired a shot, and that little girl who had miraculously survived the gas was dead. The head of the largest pediatric hospital in Rome told me it was not impossible that the child, as she suckled, was insulated by the strength with which she was sucking at her mother's breast, which would have limited the absorption of the deadly gas.

—Inside the Gas Chambers: Eight Months in the Sonderkommando of Auschwitz *by Shlomo Venezia, translated by Andrew Brown and published by Polity Press in association with the USHMM*

The Nazis walked in and said they needed people to harvest on a farm not far from Birkenau. They took some men from our barrack, but didn't take me because I was too small. Someone told me, "Sol, put some straw in your shoes. You'll get a little taller." That's what I did. Then a German walked in and said, "We need one more," because one of them was sick and not healthy enough to work. The German looked at me and took me away. I got to work on the farm.

—*Sol (Shaya) Lurie; USHMM, RG-50.030*0141*

I stood next to a wall when the Warsaw ghetto uprising flared, knowing my father and the man I would marry were inside. A Christian woman next to me said it was very good they were burning the Jews, but the Germans were spoiling her Easter. This wasn't a single opinion. It was the voice of the people. On another occasion, a woman came to my furnished room and asked what happened to the Jewish woman who had lived there before. She asked for my papers and asked if I was also Jewish. I said I'd never met the other woman and I was not Jewish. Anyway, she said, I would have to accompany her to the gestapo. It was during the curfew, but she was a Polish woman working for the gestapo. During the long walk, I offered her money and my watch if she would let me go. She refused. However, soon she suffered tremendous pain and rang the bell at a pharmacy. She told the owner I was Jewish and he too would be killed unless he helped her. He gave her the medication and we continued to walk. A quarter of a mile from the gestapo, she demanded my money and watch in return for my freedom. I complied and wanted to commit suicide. I had nothing to lose. But I thought I could not give up, as I was young. Then I met a Jewish friend acting as governess for a Christian family in a small town. One was deaf and the other blind, and I pretended to be a Christian, wearing a big cross and knowing all the Catholic prayers by heart. I got the job.

—*Romana Koplewicz; USHMM, RG-50.106*0120*

There was a well-organized school in the ghetto in Tarnów, where children went on learning just as if they were in their regular school. One day the Germans loaded the entire school into trucks, teachers and pupils. Prepared for that eventuality, the teachers distributed poisoned chocolates to the kids, allowing them to believe they were going on a picnic. The truck stopped in the woods near a convent in a forest a few miles away, where Shmuel [Braw] believes that the Nazis intended to shoot everyone. The soldiers opened the doors to find everyone dead already. My daughter was in that transport," Shmuel said in a soft, barely audible voice. So were his twin nephews, the only children of his brother, who lacked Shmuel's ability to smell out danger.

—*A Typical Extraordinary Jew: From Tarnow to Jerusalem by Calvin Goldscheider and Jeffrey M. Green*

The tents at Bergen-Belsen blew away in a huge storm, but the barracks had windows. I saw a person walking without hair and wearing a crazy blue-striped dress. I couldn't believe it was me. I stood and looked at my reflection. I touched my face and my hair. That's the first time I saw myself. I was like a person shown a picture of a baby, who says, "That's me?" That's the way I was. It was a shocking experience.

—*Rita Kerner Hilton; USHMM, RG-50.030*0002*

The bunkers at Bialystock ghetto in Poland were under the floor and we could not escape because the door was jammed. If a child started to cry, everyone in the bunker was in danger. They told the mothers either to get out or shut the child's mouth. So they covered the children's mouths with pillows. But how long could they do this? The Germans stayed longer than a second. When this raid was over after a few days, they removed four hundred corpses of children who had been smothered to death.

—*Cyla (Tsilah) Kinori, University of Southern California Shoah Foundation, The Institute for Visual History and Education, VHA interview code 22398*

The toilets at Gurs and Rivesaltes concentration camps in France were huge cylindrical cans. You walked up wooden scaffolding to cans that you defecated into. It was a strange experience, certainly coming from a private bath, central heating, and all the rest of it. But the most unsettling experience was having diarrhea or stomach cramps. I looked down and couldn't tell if it, the feces, was from me, or from someone beside me.

—*Sonja Samson; USHMM/Gratz College Hebrew Education Society, RG-50.462*0121*

The Sonderkommando told of an old rabbi who was with a group of people taken to the gas chambers. The rabbi started to sing and asked them all to sing. "We are dying as martyrs. Don't be afraid to die," he said. Then they sang and danced before entering the gas chamber. The Sonderkommando were in a special block and we saw them every day. They said people were completely misled. They told us that victims were taken to the showers to be cleaned, and food would be there for them when they came out. When they entered the showers an SS man threw in a can of Zyklon B. For three or four minutes they heard people shouting; then everything was silent. They opened the doors and everybody was dead, holding on to each other. The scene was incredible. Mothers held their children tightly.

—*Sigmund Strochlitz; USHMM, RG-50.030*0397*

My father and his fellow doctors got together in Berlin after Hitler came to power and he said, "Let the Nazis get in. They won't last long. The German people won't stand for it." My father had a sign downstairs on the wall facing the street, which the Nazis painted over reading, "Germans resist. Don't buy health care from the doctor." For a while they even posted a guard there. My father had an offer to work in a hospital in Brazil, but he argued, "What would I do there? I don't know any Portuguese and I don't know anybody there. Let's sit it out." So, unfortunately, he never went. While I was in school, he was arrested and taken to a police prison, accused of performing an illegal abortion. A relative of my mother, who was a well-known lawyer in Berlin, was permitted to go to the prison, but he returned and told us my father had hanged himself with a belt. It was very unlikely that the German police would allow a prisoner to have a belt or shoelaces, but that was the explanation. He definitely wasn't the suicidal type.

—*Roger Bryan; USHMM, Gratz College Hebrew Education Society, RG-50.462*0076*

After the war, I went back to Poland, knowing none of my family was left, but still hoping. I was eleven when the war started, and my father owned a candy factory and a restaurant before the Germans confiscated them. People recognized me and I heard one say to the other, "The Jew is still alive. She lives." I knocked on the door of our house and a lady asked me what I wanted. I asked for a glass of water and told her I would tell her who I was and what I wanted. She hesitated until I said, "This is the house where I was born and lived with my parents." She asked where my parents were. If I had told her I was Jewish she would have thrown me out, so I said they were working on a farm. She went away to get a drink. I ran up to the attic, where my father had taken my mother, brother, and myself to hide gold coins in case something happened. I lifted a brick, as he had done, and found the coins. I heard her coming and ran down. Everything was ours, the furniture, paintings, chandelier, even a yellow credenza that my mother had bought for the kitchen. When she asked if my parents would return and take everything back, I said on the contrary, they would help her. I didn't know what to tell her, but it was wonderful to be back and close to my parents. Later I sent her something from America, but she wanted more, even to support her trip to the United States, which I couldn't afford.

—*Sonia Brodecki; USHMM, made possible by a grant from Jeff and Toby Herr, RG-50.549.02*0071*

At Stutthof we were infected with lice, and mice or rats rattling around under the straw, but as soon as it got light, they got away, so we lived with them. People got sick and many died. Out of one thousand women on the work detail, maybe one hundred were left. I had intestinal problems and my legs were covered with boils, oozing puss. We got through, but it lasted from August 1944 until January 1945. Then we heard that the Russians were closing in, so in January we began the death march toward Germany, walking by day and night. I had diarrhea and everyone was sick. Those unable to walk any more were shot. One morning we woke up in an empty barn and found our SS guards had fled. But our joy was short-lived. Five of us stayed together and we moved into a deserted farmhouse. Then Russian soldiers came in and would not believe that we were Jews from a concentration camp. They thought we were gentiles and Nazis. The soldiers were after us young women. They wanted to rape us, but somehow we managed to evade them by hiding under the beds or in the cellar. When we saw them approaching we hid in the barn or somewhere else. We learned a few words of Russian, but it didn't really help. It was hard.

—*Ilse Sauer; USHMM, RG-50.030*0273*

They transported us to an ammunition factory in Germany where there was a men's camp further out. To get their soup, they had to go into the women's camp to reach the kitchen. Someone hollered to me, "Sonja, I just saw one of your brothers!" I ran out and cried. Unbelievably, it was one of my brothers! But there was this SS woman, over six feet tall and the meanest, most horrible person you can imagine. She got hold of me and said I had it too good. I had made contact with men. I told her, "That was my brother!" It didn't matter. They never hit in the middle of the barrack, instead shoving me against the wall to increase my pain, and then slamming my face and knocking out my teeth. She beat me until I fell down. I couldn't take it anymore. I just lay there. It didn't bother her. "Now you know never to make a movement to anybody!" she shouted, as she walked away.

—*Sonja Gottlieb Ludsin; USHMM, RG-50.030*0262*

We had roll call three times a day, depending on how many people were in the camp. They could last one, three, five hours, or half a day if nobody was around to count. We had to stand up in any weather. Sometimes they would count us inside the barrack if it was raining, probably because the Germans or kapos didn't want to get wet. Most often, it was outside. In the brutal sun of August, it can be very muggy and unbearable in southern Poland. That was the bottom of the hill. In the fall, there was a lot of rain and it was like a swamp. In the winter, there was plenty of snow, in which we stood in rows of five. It was dreadful. In the morning, they gave us black water that they called coffee. At lunch, they brought soup that was like the coffee and given out from large barrels. I suppose they cooked a few potatoes in it, with some peels and cabbage. If we found a leaf of cabbage we were lucky. We never got the potatoes, which were either eaten on the way by the kapos, or by those who worked in the kitchen. For supper, we were given perhaps a quarter of a pound of bread. Sometimes there was a little bit of margarine or jam, or a slice of salami. That's all we lived on. You had to eat it right away because if you left it anywhere, you would never see it again. There was a tremendous amount of stealing. It was better to sleep with your shoes on, or else you wouldn't find them in the morning. Someone would have taken them. You wouldn't know who it was. Someone was always watching what you were wearing.

—*Simone Horowitz; USHMM/Gratz College Hebrew Education Society, RG-50.462*0087*

A group arrived at Auschwitz for the selection. There was a mother and her beautiful young daughter whom I saw with my own eyes. They separated the mother from the daughter. The daughter started to cry and ran toward her mother. A man grabbed her hair and threw her back. She ran back to her mother screaming that she wanted to stay with her. "Wherever my mother goes, I want to be with her!" They told her the mother was going to be gassed and she would not be joining her. She pleaded to go with her. The man grabbed his pistol, pulled it out, and shot her.

—*Solomon Radasky; USHMM, RG-50.030*0305*

When we got off the train at Auschwitz, my father begged forgiveness for bringing me there. He said when I was about fifteen, and wanted to go to Palestine on youth aliya, he wouldn't allow it because people's morals were not good there. They had bad reputations. He said if he had let me go, I wouldn't be here now. He promised that if ever we got out of here, he would never again interfere in my decisions. We said good-bye to the men, and the guards led us past the high voltage fences. I woke up in hell.

—*Susan Eisdorfer Beer; USHMM, RG-50.030*0326*

73

We didn't realize we were at the back gate until a little Lithuanian, not weighing 60 pounds and speaking good English, said he'd been there four years and it was called Buchenwald. Later we found out that others from our 317th regiment had come in the front gate. It took us by surprise because we had heard of concentration camps but didn't really know what they were. People were laid out in front of the barracks and we were told they had just died. Six guys came around the corner pulling a two-wheeled cart, picked up dead bodies, and loaded them on. They said they were going to the ovens to burn them. There were crematoriums with ovens working twenty-four hours a day. He said the SS had taken off, but they had locked up nineteen of them in a building. When asked what they were eating, we learned that the SS had thrown potato peelings in the dump and the inmates had found and washed them, mixed in some green grass, and that's all they'd eaten that day. Sixty-five years later, I was in the nearby town of Weimar, with invited former prisoners in Buchenwald. I spoke about what I had seen, when a man raised his hand and said he could verify everything I'd said. He told us he had been a sixteen-year-old Jewish boy stricken with typhus and brought to the death section, where he would be killed within four or five days. "You guys came along and saved my life," he said. "My name is Klein. I have been an American citizen for over forty-five years. I'm a rabbi in California, and I want to thank you and shake your hand." Then he began to cry.

—*Virgil Myers; USHMM, RG-50.030*0578*

You couldn't dwell too much on a combination of what we saw in the concentration camps and our own experiences. You couldn't afford to. You'd go crazy. I saw men in my outfit whom I considered to be the roughest and toughest, who were literally carried away, who just broke from sights like this and our missions. I saw three or four who would laugh when shells came in. Suddenly, they just broke completely and were carried away. They should have been put in straitjackets. They had to be held down, led off, and evacuated. So there was a toll on us.

—Philip Solomon; USHMM/Gratz College Hebrew Education Society, RG-50.462*0021

On a farm in Kaiserwald, Latvia, my girlfriend asked me to go out and get scallions, but I brought her grass. She got muscular dystrophy at the camp and always reminded me when I visited her, "You dummy, do you remember when you brought me the grass?" She had a boyfriend who worked with cows and he brought her milk in the evening. As there were lots of cows, we always had milk that we could steal.

—Vera Oppenheim; USHMM/Rosalyn Manowitz on survivors' experiences for Hebrew Tabernacle Congregation, RG-50.150*0029

At liberation by the Russians, my sister, her boyfriend, and I ran out of Częstochowa camp, where we produced bullets for the German Army. We slept on Polish farms. One night, my sister got a terrible fright. We were still afraid, and were very careful not to tell them we were Jewish. I have a tendency to talk a lot in my sleep. Sure enough, one night I spoke Yiddish in my sleep. Evidently they heard me speaking a foreign language. In the morning, a gentile woman asked my sister what language I had spoken. She had heard me, but it wasn't Polish. My sister told her it was German, which I had learned in a German concentration camp. They served breakfast and then we continued on our way.

—Mark Mandel; USHMM, RG-50.156*0035

Before the war, my mother would buy dairy products from the farmer's place, so it was logical for him to agree to hide us. In August 1942, my sister packed her little bundle and made plans how to meet when these terrible times were over. We said our good-byes and I never saw her again. We thought everything went well because we didn't hear from her for several days. A lot more Germans came into the ghetto, so after our meager dinner my mother told me to put on two of everything of my best clothes. She kept repeating to me how to get to the farmer's place on the other side of the river. In the chaos, we got out of the ghetto and into the river. Sporadic shots rang out throughout the night. Other people had the same idea as we did. We hid in the bulrushes and thick undergrowth of the shallow river. By morning the machine guns were firing full blast and there were screams and shouts as others made it to the river. We stayed hidden as Ukrainian militiamen yelled, "Crawl out Jew! I can see you!" My mother made me eat the awful, soggy bread to strengthen myself. The screams continued [the] next morning and I heard babies cry. I think they were liquidating the ghetto. The water should have turned red because the machine guns chattered all the time. I kept dozing off, and when I opened my eyes, my mother was gone. I was panic-stricken. Then everything was quiet. At nighttime, I walked a long way to the farmer's place. I was wet and dirty when the dogs barked and the farmer came out in his coveralls, with my father's gold pocket watch, probably given as payment by my mother. He said I couldn't stay because he'd changed his mind and it was too dangerous. He said I could stay until it got dark; otherwise, he would report me to the authorities. His wife gave me some food and I stayed in the barn. At night, they gave me an apple and some bread and told me to leave. I walked to a village and then to an open field with lush wheat. It was the breadbasket of the Ukraine. God was with me, if there is a God. I was lucky.

—*Charlene Perlmutter Schiff, USHMM, RG-50.233*0120*

People spat at us when we marched through Wittenberg to the aircraft factory. Children were taught that we were goddamn Jews, no good, and dirty. We didn't look appealing, that's for sure. But did they ever think why we looked like that? Retreating German soldiers in Russia didn't look any better than us because they had been reduced to a subhuman state. Other people had made us look like that. Other people had beaten us, tortured us, spat on us, killed us, and then had gone home to their wives, children, and dogs and played with them, and then had eaten dinner and never gave a thought to what they did, which they considered work. They did not consider us as human beings who could think, feel, love, teach, and share good things with other people. The man who was in charge of our camp lived across from the camp, which was surrounded by barbed wire and watchtowers with manned machine guns. When he left the camp, he had his god, whom he loved. He had children running around his home. I could never reconcile the fact that he was called a man. And I couldn't say he was an animal, because I liked animals.

*—Blanka Rothschild; USHMM, RG-50.030*0281*

The Hungarian Jews were driven into the gas chambers at night and it sounded like a jungle. It was a horrible noise. I can still hear it today. They were screaming like lions. But it didn't help them. They had to go in. That was the night they gassed and burned fourteen thousand people. We went on top of a building and could see the chimneys with fire coming out. It looked like a building was on fire. And it stank too. Flesh smelled like burnt steak. Ash settled on our shaven heads. We came back at night with ash on our heads and we couldn't take showers because we were allowed only one a week. So most of the ash stayed, even though we tried to get rid of it.

*—Jack Bass; USHMM, RG-50.562*0001*

During the Berlin Olympics in 1936, there were many foreigners in the streets. I would love to have gone up to someone in the street who looked like a foreigner and said, "Do you know what's happening to we Jews here? Do you care? Does anyone out there know about it? What does the outside world know about us?" But I didn't dare to, of course. You had no way of knowing who the person was that you were speaking to. It was much too frightening and much too dangerous. We did hear about one incident where a rather dark-looking man had been riding in a limousine at night, when he was dragged out by a mob under the impression that he was a rich Jew. They beat him up. But it turned out that he was an attaché at the Italian Embassy, and the Germans had a hard time apologizing.

—Susan Faulkner; USHMM/Gratz College Hebrew Education Society, RG-50.462*0005

Jews from Poland in striped clothing came aboard our cattle car at Birkenau concentration camp. They emptied all the luggage we were not allowed to take with us. One of them said to tell them my brother and I were eighteen, when I was only fourteen and he was eleven. We didn't know what the inmate meant. Germans screamed "Raus! Raus!" The German asked how old we were and we said eighteen. So we went with my father in one line and my mother with two more sisters and another younger brother in the other direction. They were sent immediately to the crematorium. There was no time to say anything to my mother. Nothing, nothing, nothing, nothing. We were just like animals driven into the slaughterhouse. We were in hell.

—Mark Moskovitch; USHMM, made possible by a grant from Jeff and Toby Herr, RG-50.562*0005

I was carrying large rocks when my good shoe fell apart on the sole. Just then a young girl next to me asked where I was from. I told her I had come from another group and should be able to find someone from my hometown in Romania. She said she was from Kraków, Poland. "You know what?" I said. "My sister-in-law is from Kraków." Astonished, she said, "I don't believe it! I know her very well, and the family." She told me she worked in a shoe department and she would fix it. She told me to wear another pair and bring her the broken one. My sister found me a replacement and I brought the woman the other one. She promised to return it the following night. The next day was Yom Kippur. We didn't eat, even though we almost fasted every day. A friend from my hometown, allowed off work with an injured knee, agreed to look after my soup until I came back in the evening. I picked up the untouched soup and the other woman gave me my repaired shoe, saying, "I'm glad you have them. You must go home with shoes every day." It made me cry.

—*Chana Mehler; USHMM, RG-50.030*0275*

Internees at Mauthausen could not practice their religion, and were absolutely forbidden even to live. There was no difference between ourselves and monks, priests, or pastors. They died in the same way we did. Sometimes they were sent to the gas chamber; at times they were shot or plunged in freezing water. Any way was good enough. The SS had a particularly harsh method of handling these people because they knew that they were not able to work as normal laborers. They treated all intellectuals of all countries in this manner. Instead of being consoled by anyone of their faith, they received, just before being shot, twenty-five or seventy-five lashes with a leather thong.

—*Francisco Boix, Nuremberg trials, vol. 6, 1/29/46; The Avalon Project, Yale University*

The only time I saw my father cry was when the Germans told the Judenrat that they wanted one thousand boys aged twelve to sixteen taken from their homes. I said he had to give them up. He said I was his daughter—how could I say that? How could he go to one mother and say her son must go, and tell the other one that her son would stay? "Am I God?" I said he had to; otherwise, the Nazis would take the one thousand boys and shoot another one thousand along the way. He agreed I was right. That night they let them have one thousand boys. Nobody slept. Of course the boys were never seen again. I went out at six o'clock in the morning. There wasn't a living soul. There wasn't a bird or a breeze. Nothing. Total stillness. I went into a rage. I cursed, "Damn you, God, wherever you are! This is not the god I want! I don't want any part of you! What's more, I don't want you to save me!" As you can see, it didn't happen.

—Lena Jurand; USHMM, RG-50.106*0109

We had to clear marshland outside of Auschwitz so they could get a clearer view from the watchtowers. I was up to my ankles in water and I came out only with the tops of the shoes, because the bottoms were already so worn that they stuck in the mud. It was October and very cold when I got back. Somebody gave me wooden clogs, but they rubbed against my feet and I couldn't walk in them. I walked barefoot, but it was horrible. Then someone gave me a good boot with laces, but it was probably made for a man as it was too big, yet it was her only spare. Another person gave me a high heeled lady's shoe. This was ridiculous. However, it was very cold and I would have come down with pneumonia if barefooted. So I had one leg up and one leg down. It was funny, and we laughed. But I wasn't cold.

—Rosalie Laks Lerman; USHMM, RG-50.030*0396

When we arrived at Auschwitz, there was a lady with polio whose father was a shoemaker in our Czechoslovakian town. She was about twenty-five years old and couldn't walk. A German pushed her out. She was crying, but they didn't care. I was a kid, about thirteen. For me to jump down from that wagon was nothing, but sick or elderly people could not make it. There were dogs and they hit us with truncheons. Everybody was running in different directions. I ran this way, while my mother, father, and brothers somehow wound up the other way. An inmate came over to me and in Yiddish said to tell them I was older, and an electrician. He said Mengele was standing in the corner. He was called the Angel of Death because if he sent you this way it was to live, but the other direction was to die. He used his finger to indicate which way. Mengele asked how old I was and I replied fifteen. When he asked what I did, I told him I was an assistant to an electrician. I was OK and he sent me that way. But any pregnant woman was sent to the crematoriums. I didn't know where my father or mother was, nor my two brothers. I was all by myself.

—*Sholom Rosencheck; USHMM, RG-50.030*0529*

In Auschwitz, we had septic tanks for the big latrines. While I was there, they put a fellow in it whom I knew very well. He was a cantor. They put him sitting up to here in the septic tank. Catholic priests, ministers, they put all of them in. Respect was tremendous for these people, and here you see them sitting in the septic tanks, forgive me for the expression, with all this crap up to their necks, and we had to walk by everyday to see them. They made a point of doing this to break our spirits. After six or seven days in there, they died.

—*Sam Bankhalter in an interview with Sandra Bradley for the USHMM film* Testimony, *RG-50.042*0005*

I was eighteen when the train braked hard and our cattle cars stopped as bombs fell on the tracks. While we waited for repairs, an SS man said we should be happy because it was April 20, Hitler's birthday. We thought, why in the hell should this make us happy? But he said we would each get an extra piece of bread to celebrate. No sooner had he spoken than the sky blackened and bombs fell near the train. We were approximately three thousand women, of whom about a third were killed in the raid. The train split open and those who were able escaped to the woods. We hid out, but couldn't stay too long as we had not received the extra bread. Two days later, we came out of hiding and saw a Russian officer. We ran toward him and he said, "Don't be afraid. You are free!"

—*Regina Spiegel; USHMM, RG-50.106*0116*

When it was cold in the camp, we made human ovens. People would make a group and create a human oven, huddled in a circle. The people from inside eventually went outside. Being very small, I managed to get back inside. We could stand for hours like that. We couldn't fall because we were all squashed together.

—*Zygmund Shipper; USHMM, funded by a grant from the Lerner Family Foundation, RG-50.030*0526*

Viktor Frankl was a psychoanalyst, a Jew from Vienna, and a great man who wrote the international bestseller *Man's Search For Meaning* [first published in 1946]. When he came to Mauthausen, he was on his last legs. He had lost his dish and spoon, without which you were dead. He plopped down next to me, and I told him he would die because he would not have anything to eat with. Some servers would pour it into his cap, but most of them would not. I found him replacements. He said, "Nu, who are you?" I told him I was Polish. He asked what I did. I said nothing. I was a student. I did a bit of work. He told me he was a doctor of philosophy. We became friends. People were being taken to the gas chambers and we both felt bad, but he said, "Sit down and talk," and we cheered up. Later I phoned him in the United States. We were not able to get together, but we talked on the phone for about three hours. I never thought he would survive, but he did. He died in 1997.

—Stefan Czyzewski; USHMM, RG-50.030*0387

I was in the infirmary with scarlet fever that made you so weak you couldn't even hold a spoon. I asked a woman why she was crying, and she said she'd just been separated from her mother and knew she wouldn't see her again. Then everyone became agitated and said pretend you're not sick. Some of the people had typhus with boils. They were tied down and screamed in pain as Mengele operated on them, without any anesthetics, to remove boils. It was horrible and they all died. A French woman, who was a Christian married to a Jew, had given birth with the aid of a Jewish doctor. The naked baby screamed from hunger, but the mother had no milk in her swollen breasts. She killed the baby, covered it up, and cried. During my stay there, Mengele had seven selections, but I was never sent to the crematorium. I was still alive. After my release, it was raining and I was wet and shivering. I couldn't take it anymore. I determined to kill myself. Suddenly a truck pulled up and I heard them yell, "Schnell! Schnell!" I asked myself where they were taking me. Probably to the crematorium. I wanted to kill myself and end it. I would have been happy to die, but they dropped me off at a barrack with a cement floor. I was soaked and crying, and all I wore was the long top of a blue dress. I don't know why I complained. My father didn't teach me that. He had always said, "You should be strong. Always stand up for yourself."

—Sylvia Ebner; USHMM/Gratz College Hebrew Education Society,
RG-50.462*0104

We were not allowed to talk to Germans and I was afraid of them, but one night a female Nazi asked me how many people I had killed. I said, "Why do you think I killed people?" She replied, "Because they told us all Jews are murderers." I said, "Do you think the women, whom you are very nasty to, are murderers?" I explained that we both spoke German, and the only difference between her and me was that she was born on the first floor and I was born on the second floor. We were not murderers. Neither were the women. I asked her please to be nice to them. She began to cry and I was afraid that the SS would come and think I had said something to her that made her cry and then send me to Dachau. That was how cruel the women were. They had been told that we were all murderers, and they believed it.

—*Oscar Baron; USHMM/National Council of Jewish Women, Sarasota-Manatee section, RG-50.154*0004*

We lost so many [members] of our families—sisters, brothers, children, mothers—how could we cope for the rest of our lives, no matter what we did. The void could never be filled. Our pain could never be healed. On happy occasions, when I invited many people, the ones I wanted most never arrived. When we went to parties, I always felt alone, no matter how many people were there, because I really could not relate completely to anybody, except to other survivors. Even if I reached out, I couldn't get that close because it reminded me too much of what I could have been, and what I will never be. When I went on vacation, I took my whole family, but I felt guilty enjoying it because I always asked myself, "How could I do this? How could I still do that? How could I enjoy myself when they suffered such a terrible death?" We even envied them their graves because mourners had somewhere to go and bow their heads, but what did we have?

—*Cecilie Klein-Pollack in an interview with Sandra Bradley for the USHMM film* Testimony, *RG-50.042*-0018*

The collaborators were often more cruel than the Nazis. Czech women and Ukrainians were sometimes more brutal in their disregard for people. We had a big, hefty, strong Czech woman, an animal type, in charge of our barrack at Auschwitz. She always called us Polish pigs. She kicked me, even when I was down. When I went to the latrine, she would raise her leg and order me to polish her leather boots. She told me to spit on them and shine them. It was so humiliating. It was a terrible, personal insult. I had already been beaten by an SS man who punched me on my mouth with the ring on his fist, and I bled. I cried over that but not about other things, like hunger. We lived at the lowest level of human existence. The latrines were behind the barrack, but you had to wait your turn and then sit on boards over holes with at least twenty people. There was no privacy. It was below what the mind considers human. It was an insult for my father to be called a Jew, and not a gentleman, when they forced him to clean the railroad station. We had been dehumanized. When we marched to the marshes, we passed private homes with geraniums in boxes and pillows airing in the windows. It broke my heart to see people living a life from which we had come. They got up in the morning, opened the windows, and occupied themselves in doing what others did in Poland. We didn't react to these awful things as we should have. We were preoccupied with survival.

—*Regina Gelb; USHMM, made possible by a grant from Jeff and Toby Herr, RG-50.549.02*0013*

People who don't believe the Holocaust ever happened should have been there, seen the real thing. They would find out it happened.

—*John Dolibois; USHMM, RG-50.030*0408*

In the afternoon of August 5, they took us in trucks to the outside of a movie theater, where I saw a woman cradling a tiny baby. One of the commandos grabbed the baby by a leg and smashed his head against a wall. There were dogs, and the Germans and Ukrainian police were using the butts of their guns to hit us and chase us into a corner. There were no toilet facilities and we had to do it on the floor. A young girl went berserk, screamed, and they shot her through the head. I volunteered to take her body outside, thinking I might be able to escape. But she was still alive, with blood oozing out of her head and spilling over me. Then they shot her again and she died. I had no chance of escaping, and they took me inside again where I met a relative who was my mother's best friend. She had sent her son away to Australia before the war. They had dragged her from an office in an oil company and she was hungry. I gave her a piece of bread and some cucumber. She directed me, "When you survive the war, please tell my son to take revenge for me." I said she was crazy, that we would all die there, and this was the end. She said, "No. You will survive the war. Remember to tell my son to take revenge for me."

—*Raoul Harmelin; USHMM/Gratz College Hebrew Education Society, RG-50.462*0084*

I think it was a Soviet small plane that came over Mauthausen and shot up the watchtowers and bombed circus tents overflowing with inmates near the SS barracks. Pieces of flesh were scattered every-where. Human tissues hung on the wired fence. When the bombing stopped, we could see living people with their buttocks missing, and their mouths still moving. The next day, while survivors were eating, an officer went around, kicking over any suspicious pot and shooting at people. It was extraordinary. It wasn't as if they were scurrying out of his way.

—*Edward Klein; USHMM, RG-50.030*0580*

I went back to Germany last summer and visited the munitions factory at Chemnitz. I stood where the camp was and recognized the railroad tracks. When I asked the German woman in town whether she had seen the camp, she said, "Yeah." I said, "Well, I was there." She remarked, "That's impossible. There were no children in there." And I said, "Madam, there were many children there." She replied, "That's impossible, we would have known." I said, "When you saw people in there, behind the wire, didn't you wonder?" "Oh no," she said, "You were not allowed to ask questions. You never knew who you were talking to. They might have reported you, and you would have gone to a concentration camp, so you did not ask anything."

—Bozenna Gilbride; USHMM, RG-50.233*0032

I was a captain in a twelve-unit dispensary assigned to special troops of the Seventy-Ninth Infantry Division when we entered Ohrdruf, a subcamp of Buchenwald, in 1945. It may have been the first camp liberated. There were piles of bodies, most of them naked and practically skeletons. At the railroad, they had just piled up the bodies, coated them with creosote, and burned them. It was still smoking. Some bodies were burned completely, some were not. I don't know if they were burned while still alive. Bodies were littered all over, including the barracks. The day before we got there, the SS had marched all the survivors out of the camp to escape detection. It was such a shock that General Eisenhower ordered everyone in our division to go through it.

—Julius Eingorn; USHMM/Gratz College Hebrew Education Society,
RG-50.462*0077

Buchenwald was hell. There were piles of dead people everywhere and I saw cannibalism for the first time. Some people were still dying. Then I went on a death march to Theresienstadt, where I was liberated. My health wasn't bad because I had always tried to keep clean. I didn't get beaten for reaching for a cigarette butt or running after food. I wanted to live and that's how I survived. My sister's husband took me away in May 1945 and I stayed a day in a hotel for the first time. We had a tablecloth and a real fork and spoon as we ate soup and potatoes. It was the first time I had eaten like a person, and I cried. When we got to the room, the bed was prepared with nice white linen. I couldn't believe it. I took a shower and went to bed. The next morning, we rose early. There was no room in the train, so we joined a lot of people on the roof, clinging to one another. We got off at Prague, where there were kiosks on many corners with donuts, sandwiches, milk, coffee, and red hearts at noon for hungry people from the camps. It was unbelievable. I didn't think anyone would be so nice, especially as they knew we were Jewish. At the station, a lot of Jews alighted. They said I was crazy to want to stay in Poland. They had just bribed Russians with vodka to leave. They said nobody was safe in Poland, where they killed people. My brother-in-law didn't like Russians, especially communists, so we crossed the border and told the American guards we were returning to Germany.

—*Morris Rosen; USHMM, RG-50.106*0119*

In the train going to Buchenwald near the end of the war, somebody told the German kapo, a criminal, that I could tell fortunes, which I had learned using primitive cards. The kapo gave me a piece of bread and told me to go ahead.

—*Antoni Golba; USHMM, RG-50.030*0081*

It is difficult to remove from memory what they did to a young man caught smuggling bread into the Kovno ghetto in Lithuania. They wanted to make an example of him, so they built the gallows in the main square. Everybody had to come and see him hanged. It didn't matter whether you were sick or healthy, young or old. I, myself, was born in 1935. They put the noose under his chin, so that he wouldn't die immediately. The young man was thrashing around just like a fish when hauled in and still attached to the line. It went on agonizingly for minutes while everyone was forced to watch. They wouldn't cut him down until every single person had seen him, even those going out on work details, or those returning from labor. Only then did they cut him down.

—Jay Ipson; USHMM, RG-50.030*0359

I have read from reliable studies that up to 20 percent of Americans still do not believe that the Holocaust ever occurred. That the murder of six million Jews was a myth. Well, the record at the Nuremberg trials stands forever. The record is bold and clear for all to see, of what the Nazis did. Had there been no trial, that figure of 20 percent might well be higher. The Nuremberg trials were a triumph of good over evil. They brought to justice the worst criminals in history. They showed that the rule of law could be applied to punish, if not prevent, war crimes. And the trial showed how low a rich and highly civilized nation can sink under ruthless leadership. They prevented those war criminals from becoming martyrs, which they would have done had there been no trial.

—Lou Dunst; USHMM, RG-50.544*0001

My friend Eva and I fantasized a lot in Theresienstadt. We dreamed that we would get out, and that kept us going. We always dreamed we would survive everything. We hoped we wouldn't be transported out because that would be the end. The big question was if one of us was transported, would the other one go voluntarily? We didn't decide that, and thank God it never came up. We dreamed we would get out, fall in love, and get married. We would have husbands and children, and lead normal lives. We were then twenty-two, twenty-three, and not familiar with love, apart from flirtations. Somebody once brought me a bunch of flowers and that was the height of courtship. It was fabulous. I still remember their fragrance and what they looked like. We promised that our children would marry each other. It actually came true. My daughter married her son, and not because we wanted it to happen. I was so surprised when my daughter phoned and said, "Joe and I are engaged!" I was the most surprised person in the world. Thirty years earlier, Eva and I had dreamed of it. That was one of the miracles of my life.

—Gerda Schild; USHMM, RG-50.030*0334

The doors were opened at Birkenau and people literally fell out. The Germans came with their barking dogs and shouted, "Raus! Raus!" There were some dead, so we had to take them out. Everybody had to give up their meager belongings. Some had prayer books. We stood in line and saw the chimneys burning and that very thick dust landing on us and on the guards. We were lined up and went through a gate where high-ranking officers in white gloves, truncheons, and shiny boots ordered us to go left or right—to death or to work. Nobody really knew up to that point that they were going to kill people. No one had any idea. Somebody said we should not say ridiculous things, and we would be given a shower. But then we saw naked women standing in line, and a nude man in another group on the other side. It was extremely demoralizing and not normal. There was nothing we could do because we were surrounded.

—Bart Stern in an interview with Sandra Bradley for the USHMM film Testimony, *RG-50.042*0025*

There was a pail we women used during the night for our needs because there was a curfew after a certain hour in the camp, and [after it] we could not even go to the latrine. Whoever's turn it was, emptied the pail, swished it out with cold water, and then put coffee in it, which was slop. We didn't have any utensils, so that's what we drank from. It didn't matter where it came from as long as you could fill your stomach. You can imagine how dehumanized we had become. Every day another woman went out and brought back bread. By some miracle we found string, and broke the bread so that each person got the same amount. We were very lucky it was a really small barrack, with about fifteen women, which was unusual, so we took turns doing things.

—Fela Warschau; USHMM, RG-50.030*0303

One could see the way the kapos behaved. Like the SS, they had full rights over us. They had the right to treat us like beasts. The SS gave them carte blanche to do with us what they wished. That is why, at the liberation, the prisoners and deportees executed all the kapos on whom they could lay their hands. It was better to die like a man than to live like a beast. But they preferred to live like beasts, like savages, like criminals. They were known as such. I lived there four and a half years and I know very well what they did.

—Francois Boix, Nuremberg trials, vol. 6, 1/29/1946; The Avalon Project, Yale University

I was in communications driving our truck when I asked the corporal, "Do they have monkeys over here? Look up in those trees." They were inmates of Buchenwald, who had spotted us and climbed the trees to hide. When we asked what they were doing there, they told us about the camp. We didn't believe them. We took them to the abandoned front gate, which the guards had deserted when they heard six American tanks approaching. We saw the piles of bodies and it made us mad. I'm going to speak a little roughly now. At a place close to nearby Weimar, a woman came out of a house with a busted jaw, a broken nose, and covered in blood from an assault. I asked her what happened. She said an SS man had tried to rape her. I asked if she meant that SS private and she said he was a captain, who had beaten the hell out of her, there and then. Well, four of them shot him. He got bullets from four MIs very quickly because he had no right to live. Decades later, I visited and got mad when the residents said they didn't know the camp was there. I told them they were full of shit. Their kids were up there, and you could smell it from miles away.

—*Clarence Brockman; USHMM, RG-50.030*0579*

The extent of the robbery may be learned from the fact that, within the Auschwitz camp area, there were thirty-five warehouses for sorting and packing the personal effects. Before the evacuation, the Germans burned down twenty-nine warehouses, together with the personal effects stored in them. In the six remaining warehouses, there were found 348,820 sets of men's suits, 836,255 sets of women's wear, 5,525 pairs of women's shoes, 38,000 pairs of men's shoes, 13,964 rugs, and so forth.

—*Israeli Attorney General Gideon Hausner, Eichmann trial, session 72, 6/9/1961, Nizkor Project, League for Human Rights of B'nai Brith Canada*

I think I was born somewhere in East Prussia, but I'm not sure because there was nobody close enough to me to corroborate it. I was an only child and I have a memory of my mother dying and my father bringing me over to my aunt's place in the same building. One day we were having dinner when I heard an enormous explosion. They said a bomb dropped close by. That's how it started. That's how I remember the war. We prepared a hiding place in the cellar. Sometimes I would dress quickly and quietly and everyone went down. Once we walked outside and I saw a pile of rubble. Our building was gone, and my friend was gone. I felt very threatened. There were a whole series of bombings and I was afraid to go to bed. We ran out of food and water in the cellar. One little boy next to me kept screaming for water. His father clamped his hand over the boy's mouth. He kicked and struggled and then he just lay very still. My father said I had to be very quiet and not do what the boy did. I knew that something terrible and final had happened to that little boy. I had to do as my father instructed. One night the Germans banged in the door and took us out with barking dogs. I fainted. When I woke up, I was in a barrack with my stepmother, aunt, two girls, and one or two old men. All the other men must have been taken away. That was the last time I saw my father.

—*Esthy Adler, USHMM, RG-50.030*0004*

I saw courageous girls in concentration camps. In one, a girl escaped but was caught. They were about to hang her in front of the entire camp when the commandant asked, "If I were to forgive you and let you go, what would you do?" She spat in his face and said, "I would run away again." He hanged her, and left her dangling for three days.

—*Eugenia Boroff, USHMM/Generations After, Inc.,*
RG-50.243*0005

I thought I could kill any SS in cold blood, but in 1945, when they were force-marched, they were torn and dirty, not spick-and-span with high boots. Suddenly I didn't hate them so much. I couldn't. They looked so vulnerable. In some way they looked worse than we did. I don't think I could have killed anybody, even though I thought I could. In 1947 on the way back from England, I went through Nuremberg, which was destroyed. I enjoyed that very much. I stopped at the station and I had oranges and chocolate in my trunk. Children were begging for food. I said to myself, "No way do I give German children anything," as if those kids had murdered all the victims. I didn't feel guilty at all. I know I was awful, but I just couldn't get rid of that feeling at that time. Now I am different.

—*Hana Fuchs Krasa; USHMM, RG-50.030*0479*

I grew up in Lithuania with a silver spoon in my mouth. My father was very prosperous, owning various businesses and importing oil tankers. He had a soap factory and owned a lot of property. On the Jewish holidays, we would go to the tailor, select fabrics, get measured, and have our clothes custom-made. We always had a maid in the house, and in the summer we would go to a cottage by the lake and play baseball or ride our bikes. In 1933, Hitler came to power and things started getting a little bit hairy. The seas were mined, there were restrictions on taking money out, and Jews couldn't go to medical school. We had about thirty thousand people in our town, of whom some eight thousand were Jewish, with eight synagogues. Lithuanians are very anti-Semitic and at Easter, we would stay inside because the priest told his flock we killed Jesus. And if our Maccabee soccer team won, we would try and leave hurriedly to avoid the fights. When the Germans invaded, they captured prominent Jewish males, made them dig their own graves and then shot them. We were put in a ghetto surrounded by barbed wire. My father lost his businesses and property. In 1944, they sent us to Stutthof in cattle cars. I didn't see my mother or sister. That was it. In the Dachau subcamp of Mühldorf, we helped build an underground airport. My father said, "Let's commit suicide." I was young and it didn't bother me, but he was dispirited and miserable. They left him there, and sent my brother and I to another camp. He was beaten to death there.

—*Leonard Gordon; USHMM, RG-50.106*0135*

A poor Jewish, handicapped woman said she learned that the Germans had demanded twenty thousand children, and the sick and elderly, be sent out of the ghetto. The essence of the speech was "Mothers and fathers, give me your children so the rest of you may live and survive." There were outcries, but the police were present. They wouldn't take children over eleven, but had to take the sick. Those who heard the speech or learned of it, were appalled. The concept was unthinkable. We were not allowed to be on the streets for seven days and nights. The Germans came into the ghetto with trucks, dogs, and guns, going house to house. They ordered everyone on our street into a courtyard and then went looking for those who were hiding. They found them, beat them up, and shoved them onto trucks. Within five minutes, they separated the old and young from healthier people. The guns stopped and the trucks drove off. We never found out where they were taken, nor what became of them. A few packages of clothing arrived in the ghetto. Some of the clothes were bloodstained. Nobody gave us an explanation. It was almost as if we had been hypnotized. We collected the soup and the food rations, but we had been robbed of our feelings and compassion. How could the speaker have asked to hand over the children? I was sixteen and did not understand.

—*Lucille Eichengreen; USHMM, RG-50.030*0417*

We marched for two nights and a day from Jawischowitz, a subcamp of Auschwitz, where I shoveled coal into carts in the mines. The snow was coming down like the dickens and we had only skimpy clothes. I had wooden-soled shoes, without socks, and no underwear. I also had on a camp cap. At nighttime we had to stop and I lay down, burying myself in the snow. I was smart enough to know that snow is an insulator, so I slept inside, burrowing myself in it. The others slept on top of it and a lot of them froze to death. It was really hard walking because the snow was deep. If you fell down, they shot you and let you lie there. Then we got on a train with an open roof with snow falling in. It was bitterly cold. We got water from the snow. Early in the morning, we arrived at Buchenwald.

—*Alan Kalish; USHMM/Jeff and Toby Initiative for Rescuing the Evidence, RG-50.562*0002*

I was a warrant officer controlling parts and repairs for vehicles in combat when we drove a jeep into Mauthausen a day after liberation by Americans. We saw emaciated people, and the farther into the camp we got, it was pretty gruesome. They were crawling around like a bunch of animals. A Polish inmate found SS people who worked in the camp and shot them. The commanding officer of our unit ordered town civilians, in vests and fedora hats, to dispose of the bodies in a mass grave. A room near the crematorium was completely full of corpses three feet deep. The ovens were still warm. The stench was terrible. I used to love the odor from a Turkish cigarette, and I can't smoke one now. Somehow I connected the odor of a Turkish cigarette to that camp. When we got back to our quarters in Linz, we bathed and then burned our clothes, but we still had the odor.

—*Donald Dean; USHMM/Jewish Community Relations Council, Anti-Defamation League of Minnesota and the Dakotas, RG-50.156*0009*

It was a question of survival when we killed a German before escaping from Sobibór. I used a bread knife, and another fellow and I killed him. I don't know how I did it because I'm not that type at all. With every stab I yelled, "This is for my father! This is for my brother! And this is for all the Jews you killed!" If you have to survive in a desperate situation, you can probably do anything. When a knife is on the throat, you will do anything. There was no choice.

—*Chaim Engel in an interview with Sandra Bradley for the USHMM film* Testimony, *RG-50.042*0009*

My friend had her menstrual period a few times, but she had nothing to use. She used paper, or whatever she found, even flax. I had maybe three or four menstruations before we were deported, because I was about fourteen. I had my period once in Theresienstadt and that was it. I had none at all. But one month after liberation, I had it again, and regularly, until it stopped at age fifty-two.

—*Gisela Zamora; USHMM, RG-50.030*0476*

They checked us out medically at Ravensbrück, where we had an obstetrician. But they knew very little. They injected me with something unknown and I overheard one woman tell another, "Oh, she's a virgin." I was already married, so you could see how little they knew. After the war, I had problems conceiving. My brother told me that his friend, the obstetrician who examined me, had said it would take a miracle to conceive because of the experiments at Ravensbrück. It took a long time, and I ran from one doctor to another, but I conceived. The miracle took place.

—*Irene Salomonawicz Fleming; USHMM, RG-50.030*0366*

Stutthof was probably the worst concentration camp ever. If you weren't killed beforehand, then you would get a thin slice of bread and dirty water. Hunger is a terrible, terrible thing. I mean hunger. I don't mean just being hungry, but hunger. It can change you no matter what your principles or morality. It means I don't care about you. If I want to go to the bathroom and you're in front of me, I don't care. If you wanted to move, then four other people had to move. You could hear screams in the night. Somebody attacked you and you didn't even know her. And they stank. They were full of lice. So was I.

—*Bella Mischkinsky; USHMM, RG-50.030*0340*

It will take another fifty years for me to trust non-Jewish people. I know that there are good people and bad people, but I will never forgive them. Do you know how many times in the Warsaw ghetto I was spat on because I had the yellow star? I'll never forgive them for not doing anything. I don't know why there is this hatred against Jews. I have never done anything wrong in my life. Not before, and not now. I feel the same as them. In Israel we have a Righteous Avenue for Christians who saved Jews, that is why it is not good to generalize. But I suffered so much. I stood in front of the gas chamber with my sister nearby. Two Germans looked at me and one said, "Look at this rotten Jewish child. She has such beautiful eyes. She shouldn't die. Get her out." My sister gestured not to follow her. She knew where she was going. She was killed. How can someone have the right to save me because of my beautiful eyes? I was a human being, a child, who hadn't done anything wrong. If a child was hungry, I wouldn't ask if [the child] was Jewish or non-Jewish. My brother will not talk about the Holocaust. I don't know what happened to him. It is a taboo subject in his home. He doesn't even ask me how my mother died. Although I was shot in my back by a

German at Stutthof on the final day of the war, the Russians saved me. But I was operated on four times.

—Dora Goldstein Roth; USHMM, RG-50.030*0197

We were the first American soldiers in Buchenwald, twenty-four infantrymen and four medical personnel, when they opened a door at the side of a hospital and I got sick. On a desk I saw a lampshade made from human skin, with a tattoo on it that appeared to be some kind of an angel. On the wall behind the desk were rows and rows and rows of bottles with human parts in them—fingers, ears, noses, hands, feet, genital organs. These were the souvenirs and toys of Ilse Koch, wife of the camp commandant [who later committed suicide, having been sentenced to life imprisonment after the war]. The ovens were still hot and we saw the gassing area. I was so sick from what I had seen that my stomach went into knots, and I wound up with dry heaves. None of us were novices to battle, and death and destruction were not strangers to us, but what we saw was indescribable. I was nineteen years old and for days I felt like somebody had kicked me in the stomach. That's how sore my stomach was. My outrage was something else. But being a civilized person, even though I was a soldier, when I saw German prisoners the feeling was that I'd like to go over and slit their throats or shoot them. But while I was trained that way, I wasn't raised that way. There are tears in my eyes, as you can see. General [George] Patton came to tour the camp a few days later and was so overwhelmed with what he saw that he couldn't finish the tour. He left, totally aghast and shaken.

—Milton Harrison; USHMM/Gratz College Hebrew Education Society, RG-50.462*0085

The Germans were basically good people. How the Nazis managed successfully to poison people with hatred would take maybe years and years from now to explain. It was not easy to take good people and transform them into wild animals, able to kill people, and especially children. I had a chance after the war to take revenge and maybe kill some Nazis, but I couldn't do it for two reasons. First of all, I'm not a killer. If I would have killed somebody, I would have had sleepless nights. And then, I never had evidence that the prisoners of war I met were the ones who committed crimes against innocent people. So I'm glad I never did it. I can leave this planet with a clean conscience.

—*Henry Kellen in an interview with Sandra Bradley for the USHMM exhibition "Hidden History of the Kovno Ghetto," RG-50.471*0006*

I asked my father many times, "Why don't we leave Germany?" I recall in 1936, when I was fifteen and shortly after the Nuremberg Laws were proclaimed, pleading with my father to leave Germany. He had already had an offer to go to England to join a film company. "Why don't you leave?" I asked. He replied, "Look, the Germans are not going to do anything to me. I'm a war veteran. I have the Iron Cross..."

—*Susan Faulkner; USHMM/Gratz College Hebrew Education Society, RG-50.462*0005*

In the winter of 1944–1945, the Germans rounded up thousands of us from the transit camp of Gross-Rosen because conditions were getting harder for them. They took us out in the snow and counted all of us several times, while we stood miserably in the cold. We had shoes with wooden soles and the snow underneath froze, giving us crooked feet. It was difficult to walk. Everybody had a blanket and for days we walked and sheltered from the snow. I can't remember how long it took, or whether we walked the whole way or were taken by transport. I think we walked. I cannot remember. Some couldn't make it and fell down. They were picked up and thrown away as if they were not human. Finally we arrived at Buchenwald.

—*David Davis; USHMM, RG-50.030*0347*

They told us we would be going to a wonderful place where there would be clean beds and plenty of food. "You're going to work hard, but you're going to have it good." My aunt said, "Wow, it sounds like paradise." Then we were crammed into a cattle car. They gave us some bread and that was all. There was a container with water, and one container for the bathroom. It took such a long time because the train stopped every few feet, while planes dropped bombs. We were praying. But we laughed as the Germans jumped out of the train and hid in ditches. We were really laughing. There was a little window on top of those old cattle cars, and we got up on each other's shoulders to see. We laughed at them because they were so scared. We yelled, "Bomb us! Bomb us! Come on!" We didn't care. We really didn't care, as long as they were killed. It seemed like we traveled a whole week, but we didn't. Time didn't seem important at all. Then the cattle cars stopped. They opened the doors and were yelling, "Out! Out! Out! Out! Out!" They kicked, and there were dogs as we ran. We knew where we were because we saw the chimneys burning. Everybody had heard about Auschwitz. We could smell it. The smell of human flesh.

—*Sylvia Green; USHMM, RG-50.030*0466*

We were marching in Poland when the senior officer in a dark green uniform approached one of the boys. He threw a piece of bread in his direction, and the boy, possibly fifteen years old, bent down to pick it up. The officer shot him, but didn't kill him. He ordered someone else to finish the job. He, as it were, justified himself and said he wasn't responsible, for the youth had jumped out of line. "If he hadn't jumped out of line, I wouldn't have shot him," he said. Then we went on.

—Zvi Pachter, Eichmann Trial, session 25, 5/3/1961, Nizkor Project, League for Human Rights of B'nai Brith Canada

I was very young and in a train that stalled because partisans attacked it while passengers escaped. Then I blacked out. Afterward, I remember a tall man telling me to wait behind a tree, not to move, and wait for him. He didn't come back, so I went to look for him and found him lying on the ground with blood in his mouth and his eyes wide open. I asked him to take me with him, and couldn't understand why he looked at me and wouldn't say anything. Suddenly a woman stepped out of the woods and told me he was dead. I asked what that meant and she explained that it was a person who couldn't breathe or speak or do anything. Years later I found out my parents were both dead, and that she had been a partisan shot by the Germans. I also recall being in a children's home, where I was beaten with a bamboo stick for urinating in bed. The children also whacked me on Christmas, when all the Christians got presents but I, a Jewess, got none. They made fun of me saying they had got something, but what had I been given? They said they would only stop hitting me with sticks if I didn't scream, so I stopped shouting and they ceased. Sometimes my backside was so painful, I couldn't even sit on it. One nun wearing white used to assault me so ferociously that I grew to hate all nuns. I had an uncle who was fighting the Germans on the Russian front, and he didn't even know I existed. By chance, a woman searching for any of my family found this brother of my father in the market place and told him about me. He went to the children's home, told them he was my father, and took me away. We stayed in Warsaw until the Jewish Agency intervened and sent me to Palestine, which had not yet become Israel.

—Esther Fol; USHMM, RG-50.030*0550

A sixteen-year-old girl didn't tell anyone she was pregnant when she arrived at Stutthof concentration camp because they would have killed her immediately. She gave birth on Christmas night in a tent shared by ten of us, and we washed the baby with drink and wrapped it in towels. But the baby froze to death and we buried it the following day. The teenager used to curse, "Jesus Christ, why did I come here!" I told her Jesus Christ would not help her at this location. I told her unfortunately she had lost the baby, but she could save herself. She had reported sick, but was only away from work one day. They wouldn't know it was to give birth. The next day she went to work like everybody else.

—Bella Simon Pasternak; USHMM, RG-50.030*0176

A Hungarian woman with a little girl came into my block. I don't know how. It was forbidden. I kept her in the block for several weeks. One day SS men came and took the child. Subsequently, we learned from men who worked in the Sonderkommando that the little girl had been thrown in the fire. That night, the mother went to the electrified fence.

—Vera Alexander, Eichmann trial, session 71, 6/8/1961, Nizkor Project, League for Human Rights of B'nai Brith Canada

103

Suddenly, toward the end of the war, they evacuated some of us from Stutthof concentration camp, where crematoriums burned and thousands of prisoners died from typhus. They put us on boats and barges and we set out for days on the Baltic Sea with nothing to eat. I knew I wasn't going to make it. We saw shooting, bombardments, and planes falling into the sea. I saw a boat with a lot of Polish prisoners. They had striped uniforms, but they were not emaciated like us. They were waiting to be liberated. A day later, we came back and their bow was up. It was a living grave for them. They were bombed. All of a sudden our boat stopped and the SS went away on a small launch. We were abandoned and didn't understand anything. Norwegian prisoners with us said an explosive charge was fixed to our boat. They tried to dismantle it and somehow we waded ashore. The Germans saw us and started to shoot, but we ran as fast as we could. Some of us fell during the shooting. We wound up in a forest. The British were there. It was May 3, 1945.

—*Beba Leventhal; USHMM/University of California, Los Angeles,*
RG-50.005*0037

From Gleiwitz we marched through the streets into a huge camp. All the inmates were working in a railroad repair shop, fixing train cars that had been damaged by the Royal Air Force on the way to the front. I used a cutting torch on damaged parts; then the cars went on to be refitted with good parts. There was a good side and a bad side. The good side was when a wagon came in with garbage I had the first pick. The bad part was that it was out in the open and we had no underwear or socks, just cotton pants and a jacket. It was very cold.

—*Edgar Krasa; USHMM, RG-50.030*0478*

It was 1939 when the Germans came to our small Ukrainian town and an officer raped me in front of my uncle and aunt, whom they had tied up. Even today I don't know how old I am, but I must have been ten, eleven, or twelve because I hadn't had my period yet. My uncle untied himself and stabbed the Nazi in the back, but only injured him. There was blood all over when they shot my uncle and aunt in front of me. I was living with them because my parents were already dead. The Germans debated whether to kill me. If only I could have killed myself. But they took me and a few teenagers on a cattle car, with straw, manure, and nothing to eat. We arrived at Regensburg labor camp in Germany.

—Ilona Stein; USHMM/National Council of Jewish Women, Sarasota-Manatee section, RG-50.154*0026

They didn't expect so many of us to arrive at Buchenwald and they hadn't finished building our barracks, so we had to sit outside on the ground and wait. In the evening we went inside and people went crazy. There were watchtowers and an electrified fence. The first three nights were the worst because we were not allowed out. People lost their minds. There were five buildings and they ran around them while guards opened fire from the watchtowers. I heard shots and the cries of victims all night long. Then we were allowed out, but many stayed inside. Buchenwald was built high in the mountains and it was terribly cold. People ran to the fence and as soon as they touched it, they were electrocuted. And anyone who touched the dead person was also electrocuted. It was a terrible sight to see them lying dead on the ground. They were left to lie there.

—Walter Schnell; USHMM, RG-50.030*0206

105

I hate to tell my story because there are so many scenes and situations in it that if I tell the whole story, no one would believe it. I wrote it in the ghetto, in the forest, and in Sobibór concentration camp. It was lost many times and discovered again. They promised to hide pages so I could retrieve them after the war. I did. I found about 30 percent. I wrote up a lot when things were slow and I was a social director in Poland. Now I have a diary written in the most dangerous places. What should I do with it? In Israel I went to a survivor of Auschwitz. He was then secretary of an organization. I told him to read it and tell me what he thought. Three weeks later I asked his opinion. He said I had written a fantasy. He had never heard of Sobibór, let alone the uprising. I was beaten many times by the SS in Sobibór, but nothing hurt as much as what he said. He didn't believe me. Later I came to understand that Auschwitz prisoners had limited knowledge of things beyond their camp. It had such an effect on me that I didn't touch it for twenty years. Later in America, after the movie came out on Sobibór, I would not publish it because it is hard to believe.

—*Thomas Blatt; USHMM, RG-50.030*0028*

The gas was thrown onto the floor and gave off acid from underneath, so everyone tried to find some air, even if each one needed to climb on top of another until the last one died. The sight that lay before us when we opened the door was terrible; nobody can even imagine what it was like. You could find people whose eyes hung out of their sockets because of the struggles the organism had undergone. Others were bleeding from everywhere, or were soiled by their own excrement, or that of other people. Because of the effect that their fear and the gas had on them, the victims often evacuated everything they had in their bodies. Some bodies were all red, others very pale, as everyone reacted differently. But they had all suffered in death. . . . To bring the bodies out of the gas chamber, there was no need to water the ground, since it was already sufficiently moist with everything—and I mean absolutely everything: blood, excrement, urine, vomit, everything. Sometimes we slipped up in it.

—Inside the Gas Chambers: Eight Months in the Sonderkommando of Auschwitz *by Shlomo Venezia, translated by Andrew Brown and published by Polity Press in association with the USHMM*

We would have killed ourselves if we had known there was such a hell as Auschwitz. We had never heard of it until we got there from Belgium. There were 110 people in the cattle car and we were in the middle. You couldn't sit or lie down. We just stood or leaned against each other for three days. We had two buckets, one with water and the other for a latrine. I can't even describe it. The wailing and screaming. Worst of all were the cries of the babies. There were prayers in all languages. When we arrived in Auschwitz it was pitch black, but they had bright lights on. Of 110 people, forty came out of each cattle car alive. Soldiers greeted us with barking dogs. One of them told a young woman to drop her child. She said she would go wherever her child went, so he shot the baby with his revolver. The hysterical mother reached down for her baby, but he shot her too. My mother was in line with me until a soldier separated us, but while he walked away I slipped over to be with her. He hit me over my head and said if he told me to stay there, that's where I should remain. That was the last time I saw my wonderful mother alive. We had to undress completely in front of soldiers, which I had never done in front of strangers. We all came from decent homes. They even checked our private parts to see if we were hiding anything. We were given wooden shoes and uniforms, had tattoos branded on our arms, our heads shaved, and finally we went shrieking and howling into the showers as we held onto one another.

—Fanny Aizenberg; USHMM, RG-50.030*0621

My mother was in the Lvov ghetto and nobody knew what was going to happen to her. So she wrote a letter of desperation to my aunt. Shortly afterward, my aunt's friends said she committed suicide because she could not help my mother. Nobody went to my aunt's funeral because I guess my uncle thought he would be recognized. After the war I spoke to my uncle by telephone and he said the real reason she took her own life was because her papers were taken away to be verified, and she was afraid she might be tortured and reveal where we were; she would have to betray us while undergoing torture. So she overdosed on pills.

—*Janine Oberrotman; USHMM, made possible by a grant from Jeff and Toby Herr, RG-50.562*0004*

A few days after war began, the Germans arrived with tanks. I saw many people lying on the ground and couldn't understand what was happening. I had never seen things like that. I asked my mother and she said they were all killed. That's the nicest way she could put it. But you know children, they try and understand. Gradually things changed. They attacked women on the streets and ordered them to dig graves. Then they told them to undress and shot them in the breasts. Some people were still alive when buried. We had to close our shops and prepare to go to the ghetto. One young man with blond hair and blue eyes was very wealthy and extremely brave. It didn't matter who you were, Marek Lieberman was very good to all. But someone denounced him. They came to his house, took all his cash, and took him to the market to be hanged. We were told to watch and I was five feet away from him when he was killed. It's engraved on my mind. I can't forget it. It's always with me. I saw a mother walking with her dead baby and crying while singing to her. When I was fourteen, I saw another mother talking to her daughter. She held the child protectively in her arms as a German soldier came forward, took out his gun, and shot the little girl. How can you erase something like that? You don't even have to close your eyes. It's always with you.

—*Zelda Piekarska Brodecki; USHMM, RG-50.030*0041*

After an eleven-day aimless forced march near the end of the war, we got to the river Elbe. The bridge was full of German Army [members] wounded and those in flight. They threw dried biscuits down to the Jews below, apparently feeling sorry for us. German guards who had fled now returned to where we had joined the local police. It was raining at night and the Germans put us on the bridge, expecting us to be bombed, while they ran toward the Americans.

—*Cyla (Tsilah) Kinori, University of Southern California Shoah Foundation, The Institute for Visual History and Education, VHA interview code 22398*

Chaim was married with a beautiful little boy. When he came to Auschwitz he found out that his wife and child were dead. He spoke to me about it. He didn't get mad. He explained to me that I was a young man who didn't have children and that life for me could be pretty good if we were ever liberated. But he told me very calmly that even if we were liberated, and that was a big if, he didn't want to live. He suffered a lot. He worked on construction and was freezing, but he didn't fight it. You could tell that he was losing his health and his strength, and he made it very clear to me that this was what he was going to do. He jumped from a very tall building and killed himself.

—*Sam Bankhalter in an interview with Sandra Bradley for the USHMM film* Testimony, *RG-50.042*0005*

Once a day they allowed us to run to the latrine. You learn things from an older inmate, telling you to pick up a pebble on the way to the latrine so you have something to wipe yourself with. And you have to save enough on the black market to get yourself a broken-down tin cup; otherwise, the soup was poured into your hands. Amid this incredible barbarity and filth, there was the German fascination with cleanliness. There were many slogans on the walls of the barracks telling us that healthy bodies kept one alive.

—*Steven Fenves; USHMM, RG-50.030*0494*

This idea that that you go up in smoke became a reality because a transport would come in with a lot of people, who would move in a specific direction and then disappear. They would never come out. So you realized that something was happening to them. Seeing the chimneys smoking continuously, especially after a transport, even at my age [a preteen], you kind of put two and two together and realized that, yes, this is where you go, behind that fence and the trees. Something goes on behind there. You go in and you don't come out again. Exactly what was happening, I don't know. All I knew is that you come out the chimney. And as the crematoriums were working, it left such a sweet taste in the mouth that you didn't even feel like eating. During those times, I can honestly say I wasn't even hungry, because it was so sickening.

—*Ruth Webber in an interview with Sandra Bradley for the USHMM film* Testimony, *RG-50.042*0030*

My daughter is a lawyer on Wall Street in New York in the tax department of a large law firm, and she went with a partner to a client, a German firm. Afterward, she told the partner that she felt very uncomfortable in the presence of middle-aged German men. He said, "Didn't you hear the name of the individual you were talking to?" She said, no. "His name is von Ribbentrop. He is the son of the foreign minister of Hitler's Germany [Joachim von Ribbentrop], and was evidently a baby at the time, because he must be in his middle to late forties." Our daughter said all the color drained from her face. She was speechless. The only reason our children went to Germany is because my mother is buried there. Otherwise, they would not have gone there.

—David Eiger; USHMM/Jewish Community Relations Council, Anti-Defamation League of Minnesota and the Dakotas, RG-50.156*0011

I was almost nine when my friend and I looked down the hill to center-city Stuttgart and saw flames and smoke coming out of our synagogue and the adjacent Jewish school on Kristallnacht, November 9, 1938. We hopped on our bicycles and rode opposite the burning buildings. They dragged out our rabbi, set fire to the Torah, and held it up in the air. I'm having trouble saying this because I was there. They made the rabbi watch as they paraded around, desecrating our holy place and sacred scroll. It's something I will never forget. It's etched in my memory. It was not a good place to be, so we got the hell out of there. As we got to the street where I lived, open-air army trucks, loaded with Jewish men the Nazis had rounded up passed by. We saw SS men and the gestapo on the street. One of my Christian friends I played soccer with said it wasn't good for a Jewish boy to be outside, and he invited me into his home.

—Harry Gluckman; USHMM, RG-50.106*0051

111

They called every Jew to barrack A, where the camp commander sat, and we thought this was it. Somebody pushed me and ordered, "Jew! Inside!" I was asked my name. "Heinz Ludwig Rosenberg," I answered. "Idiot!" he said. "You are Heinz Ludwig *Israel* Rosenberg!" Dutifully, I said, "Yes sir!" He asked my nationality and I told him I was stateless. "You are German!" All of a sudden I was German again. You never knew where to take those people. He asked what I had studied, what I did, etc. and wrote it all down. "Out! Next one!" About three weeks later, they announced on the loudspeaker that our block should not go to work, but report to the gate. The kapos hated Jews, but this time the camp commander was there. We each got a piece of bread and some liverwurst. A little bit at a time, I ate mine. At 5:00 p.m. an SS man came with a basket to collect the bread and liverwurst because the train had failed to arrive. Someone said I didn't have any, and the SS told me to come forward. I told him I was so hungry I'd eaten mine. When he asked how I spoke such good German, I told him I was born in Hamburg. Immediately he called out, "Next one!" He didn't do anything to me, somehow. It was all a matter of luck.

—Henry Robertson; USHMM, RG-50.233*0111

I'll never forget when we saw the crematorium at Buchenwald. I still remember vividly an L-shaped building with hooks on the wall, like meat hooks where you could hang up a side of beef. People would come in that yard, who were still alive or dead bodies, and were dumped down that hole just like a carcass. They hanged bodies on the hooks in the wall until they were ready to burn them upstairs. You could still see embedded in the walls the human bloodstains of the shoulder blades, the buttocks, and the heels, dripping blood, to give you some idea of how they were dumped in there. And the sleeping quarters, many crawled under dead bodies to keep warm. The next day dead bodies were removed and others supplanted them. There were gaunt faces, sunken eye sockets, and people were emaciated. Some were too weak to move. But even so, there was a smile on their faces. They were liberated, and they had hope. Even though many couldn't speak, they might grab your hand. If there was any reason for a just war, this was one. I was born and raised in Hudson, Wisconsin, and I'm willing to offer my own personal witness. We've heard strange tales that the whole Holocaust was a fabrication. As a Scandinavian Lutheran, I can say that this is a pure hoax. I was there. I saw it with my own eyes. I can testify.

—Arthur Johnson; USHMM/Jewish Community Relations Council, Anti-Defamation League of Minnesota and the Dakotas, RG-50.156*0024

We had a very large wooden barrel in the barrack used as a latrine. Whoever was in charge at night would wake us up with truncheon whacks on the legs. Those selected would have to carry out the barrel. It was a big wine barrel, carried by two, three, or four inmates. If they spilled it, they were beaten. If nothing spilled, they were still beaten. Some people were so weak or deranged that they couldn't lift it. There were two brothers with us who spoke only Dutch and knew no German. One of the brothers wasn't able to carry the barrel, so they beat him to a pulp. His older brother had to watch it. This wasn't an isolated case. It happened hourly. It never stopped. It didn't get better. It just got worse. We were convinced we would never get out of Auschwitz. But there is something about the human being that always has hope. People who didn't have hope fell apart quickly. For some reason, I didn't. I always had hope.

—William Lowenberg; USHMM, RG-50.030*0139

We got to Dachau about thirty minutes after it was liberated and the first thing we saw was about forty coal-type cars and boxcars full of dead people. There had been a snowfall the night before and some of them were covered in snow. It was pitiful and gruesome. I had been in the US Army for three years and was used to seeing dead soldiers on the battlefield, but when you see things like that train, it kind of hits you. You know darn well they didn't have a chance. They had apparently starved to death. It looked like a little girl's head was sticking out of the pile. We ran into a cluster of dead German guards. Outside the crematorium there was a huge pile of corpses, at least twenty four feet by thirty feet, and inside there was a roomful of thin bodies already decomposing. Someone was using a pair of ice tongs to pick them up. Everyone had fled from about half a dozen ovens, but one inmate continued to cremate the dead. It was his job, and he kept right on doing it. I was the commander of a machine gun company that followed the riflemen into Dachau while many of the inmates stood near the fence and just stared. The residents of the town a few miles away claimed they had no idea what was going on in the camp. They were made to bring their horses and wagons into the camp to take away the dead for mass burial.

—*William Landgren; USHMM/Jewish Community Relations Council, Anti-Defamation League of Minnesota and Dakotas, RG-50.156*0031*

My mother was with me at the selection on arrival at Auschwitz. She was holding me tight and said the two of us should stay together. Then somebody from Greece came over and said I should let my mother go because if she came with me, they'd make her work just as hard as me. I thought it was a good idea because she wouldn't have to work and would be better off. The reason she agreed was to save me. If I had gone with my mother, they would have done the same thing to me, the gas chamber. I found out what had happened almost at the end.

—*Rachelle Perahia Margosh; USHMM, made possible by a grant from Jeff and Toby Herr, RG-50.030*0486*

I bought the movie *Schindler's List*. It was something very new to me, but I cried when I saw it. My girlfriend asked why I watched the movies. I said because I can cry out loud at what I felt when I was there. *Schindler's List* was just a country house, a country place. An enjoyment. I wasn't in a house like that. My girlfriend wasn't in a concentration camp. She went from Germany to Israel in 1938. She asked, "Why are you watching that junk?" To me, it's my life. It's not junk. Everyone had a different life. So many millions dead. I never saw my mother after she was forty-five. I don't know where she's buried. I don't know if she's cremated, or where her bones are. Also my sisters. I buried only my father in Montreal.

—*Rose Warner; USHMM, made possible by a grant from Jeff and Toby Herr, RG-50.549.02*0058*

When we saw thousands of gray-looking women at Ravensbrück, with white handkerchiefs on their heads and SS women shouting next to them, we felt we had fallen back into the Middle Ages. We felt we were in a place with neither law nor security. Fear overtook us. They took everything we had. They even took wedding bands from married women. We had to take prison clothes. I took a slip that was quite long. I was surprised because it had black stripes. Then I realized they were made from prayer shawls. It was typical of the Nazis. To them nothing was sacrilegious.

—*Anise Postel-Vinay; USHMM, RG-50.027*0007*

When I was a medical captain serving in the British Army in World War II, I met a BBC photographer in Bergen-Belsen days after it was liberated. We were both shocked by what we saw. It was impossible for a normal human being to believe it. I said to him, "I'm sure that in ten years time, nobody will believe what we have seen, and we ourselves will also not believe it." I asked him to give me photographs of what we had seen, so that I could relate ten years later that I had witnessed these scenes and would be able to utilize them against those responsible. [Shows photographs.] This is a collection of bodies inside a large pit, which we saw there. There were hundreds or thousands of corpses. In the background, one can see a number of people wandering around. Among them were some in a condition the like of which I had truly never seen before. They walked, but had no human gaze whatsoever. Their facial expressions did not change. I saw a few walking into each other. They walked backward and after that walked forward again, without any change of expression and without any response, as if they were incapable of understanding what they were doing. Here [points to photograph], there is a collection of bodies indicating an exceptional degree of emaciation, which I have never encountered since. I asked for this photograph for a special reason. There were many people in the hospital where I worked and also people to whom I spoke in the army who did not want to believe that victims had been starved to such an extent that they died in such great numbers, as we had heard. They expressed the opinion that, perhaps, they had died of typhus. But if one looks at this picture, one sees a condition of almost 100 percent lack of subcutaneous body fat. There are even cases where the bone had begun to cause ulceration of the skin, the laceration of the skin. It is not possible that such a condition could be the outcome of typhus, for the patient would die of poisoning from the toxic effects of typhus before he could reach such a stage. It is conceivable that a man could have died from typhus in addition. But a condition of such emaciation cannot be caused by an infectious disease. They weighed 66–75 pounds. There were some even less than that.

—*Mordechai Chen, Eichmann trial, session 71, 6/8/1961,*
Nizkor Project, League for Human Rights of B'nai Brith Canada

We had to be tattooed after the selection at Auschwitz. I was standing there waiting, but I fell asleep because I'd already been standing for two days in the train. I didn't know the line had moved. All of a sudden, somebody hit me in the face and my head turned from one side to the other. They put a tattoo on me, number 106377. It hurt, but I didn't feel it that much because I was in a state of shock. It was bleeding and the blood mixed with the ink. Some were sick and got infections from it.

—*Jack Bass; USHMM, RG-50.562*0001*

After two and a half years of internment in France, I was deported to Mauthausen in Austria. We arrived in twelve degrees below zero and were naked from the French border for three days, with little air, in a cattle car holding 104 deportees. The SS officer who received us said Germany needed the use of our arms. "You are therefore going to work. But I want to tell you that you will never see your families again. When one enters this camp, one leaves it by the crematorium's chimney."

—*Maurice Lampe, Nuremberg trials, vol. 6, 1/25/46;*
The Avalon Project, Yale University

We marched in heavy snow for three days from Auschwitz to Gliwice and it was a disaster. About half the group of several hundred sat down and the SS shoved them into ditches and slaughtered them. They told all Jews to step forward. I didn't try to hide because I had the whole city of Jerusalem written on my face, and the bloody Polacks betrayed anyone trying to hide among them by telling the SS, "Here's a Jew!" We went on a train's open cars through Czechoslovakia, where citizens threw us bread. But the Nazis wanted to see us scramble like mad dogs for food, so instead of allowing an orderly distribution, they watched people kill for a slice of bread. There was no room at Mauthausen, so we went on through Berlin, which was a heap of ash like we saw when people landed on the moon. It was our only consolation. When we got to Sachsenhausen, where they made Heinkel and Messerschmitt planes, there were only thirty people left from our original of at least two hundred inmates. None of us would have survived if it had not been for the snow that fell in our open cars. Then I worked in the stone quarries at Flossenbürg, where the former French Jewish prime minister Léon Blum was an inmate in a neighboring barrack. I was so weak I couldn't even lift a shovel. Every morning several died, or were killed by the SS who got mad at them. Frequently, American bombers dropped their loads and we had to clean up the damage. Again we marched, but it was spring, with bright yellow wild flowers. Suddenly the SS vanished and we were free.

—*Edward Grossman; USHMM/Jewish Community Relations Council, Anti-Defamation League of Minnesota and the Dakotas, RG-50.156*0019*

I had never seen a train in my life and thought cattle cars were the only way to travel. I was only eight years old. What did I know? They rounded up people and very quickly pushed us into the wagons.

118

There were too many people, so we ended up standing shoulder to shoulder. In a cattle car there are no windows, just elongated slits on top. You could barely breathe with so many people. And there were no facilities. I don't remember food or water being given to us. I know that mothers were crying because they had no room. They wanted to nurse their babies, but they couldn't because there was no room. When we arrived in Freiburg, Germany, and the doors slid open, I knew we had left people behind, but I didn't know that they were dead. They were babies and old people. They just fell down when we started to file out from the wagons. They probably died standing up because there wasn't enough room to lie down. They put us in an abandoned building, where my mother and father worked in a factory making leather goods for Nazi troops.

—*Bozenna Gilbride; USHMM, RG-50.233*0032*

Auschwitz was surrounded by an electric fence. You got a sense of others because you heard how they talked to you and other women. They had no respect for life. Nothing. It was only survival of the fittest. They were not the fittest, and we couldn't survive there. Some people went so mad that they ran to the fence. They wanted to run away and they got electrocuted. A lot of people died this way.

—*Frances Davis; USHMM, RG-50.030*348*

In my delirium in the basement of an Austrian hospital, I must have mentioned that [the] thirtieth of May was my birthday. There were two nurses, one Ukrainian, one Austrian. They brought me a birthday card. That's the first time during the war that I cried. Then the war ended.

—*Edward Klein; USHMM, RG-50.030*0580*

My sister had been given Aryan papers, a birth certificate, and the name of a deceased Christian child. A guide took her to another part of Poland and gave her to a gentile family, who were told she was the daughter of Polish officers executed by the Russians. The guide had surreptitiously christened her, and they didn't tell my aunt, who had previously shielded her. My aunt was a dentist and I suppose she had paid the guide in dental gold. But on the way a German had called out "Jude!" because my sister looked very Jewish. My sister was terrified, but the guide extricated her by denying the charge and showing the German her papers. It was a tough time, with my sister locking herself in the bathroom and refusing to leave. When she got out, she later explained to me that she wanted nothing more to do with her Jewishness. She sat in front of Mary's picture and addressed it, "I don't know if you're really there, or if you were, but I promise that if you save me, I'll stick by you." And she did. She felt she was saved because she was a Christian. After the war, I went back to Poland. She came out and said, "Where's my mother?" That's how she greeted me. The next day, she went to mass to atone for the sins of our parents, who killed Christ. That's when I said to myself, "I lived as a Jew, although not very Jewish, I suffered as a Jew like the rest of them, and I'm going to die like one." Then I left.

—*Irene Shapiro; USHMM, RG-50.233*0125*

I was with my father at Mühldorf, a camp near Dachau, when he said to me, "Let's commit suicide." He was miserable. He had lost all his possessions. He had been very prosperous, importing oil tankers, having a soap factory, and a lot of property. I grew up with a silver spoon in my mouth, and we had observed all the holidays and kept kosher. But I was young, fifteen, and it didn't register. It didn't bother me. My older brother and I were separated from our father, at that time probably in his forties, yet knew his whereabouts. We would send him food with other people, and I don't know how he got it. But I knew he was beaten to death. When we got word, I cried, but the kapo kicked me and told me to get a move on, because I could not bring him back. My sister never spoke about my mother. I learned through friends that my mother felt she couldn't make a forced march, but she had a sweater which she gave to my sister for protection. She probably fell back and froze to death.

—*Leonard Gordon; USHMM, RG-50.106*0135*

They told me to go to the crematorium to get liquid gas. I don't recall whether they needed it for clothes or delousing prisoners. An armed SS woman went with me. I asked the Sonderkommando to get it for me. He must have opened the wrong door. I just stood there. I saw people piled into the gas chamber. They were adults with children. They couldn't even fall down because they had been squeezed in. I said, "This is impossible!" I had known all along what was happening, but to see is to believe. Quickly, he closed the door. The SS woman escorted me back. I never told anybody. I was too horrified. I didn't want other females to feel bad and have nightmares, although I had them. It took me a long time to talk about it.

—*Carola Steinhardt; USHMM, RG-50.030*0368*

They shot many people in Auschwitz. They used to count to ten. They took the tenth person with no questions asked. I saw them shoot that person in front of us, so we would see it.

—*Bella Simon Pasternak; USHMM, RG-50.030*0176*

German prisoners in charge of us at Płaszów were convicted murderers and completely out of control as we opened graves to pull out gold teeth. I saw Amon Goëth, the camp commandant, many times, but as soon as I heard he was walking through the camp, I ran away. We knew he shot at human targets and didn't care what you looked like. He just took pot shots. He wanted to see how close, or how far he could shoot.

—*Sylvia Green; USHMM, RG-50.030*0466*

Only the strongest tried to keep a semblance of being human beings because the Germans did everything possible to destroy it. Some tried to keep clean no matter what. Others did not. Some tried to walk with their heads held high. It was not easy to keep your dignity. To me, every survivor is a hero if they could withstand all that and then join the world and become useful citizens. Heroism isn't necessarily groups of soldiers attacking. You had to separate from your loved ones. If you came together, the men went one way, women another way, and children a third way.

—*Bella Mischkinsky; USHMM, RG-50.030*0340*

While I was working as a distributor of edicts in the carpentry workshops, an order arrived for gas-proof doors, "For Special Treatment Of Jews." They never talked about [the] "Final Solution," but we knew it was the same thing. Drawings showed how they should look. They were about three to three and a half inches thick and insulated with gas-proof material. The edges were padded. A visor in the middle of the door had glass on both sides. There were at least five, with the first one being for the gas chamber in Auschwitz and the others for Birkenau. If I had a drawing board or something, I could draw exactly what the door looked like, because I remember it so well. If anybody today tries to say that the Holocaust didn't exist, then why did they need gas-proof doors?

—*Leonard Zawacki; USHMM, RG-50.030*0271*

I knew of the existence of the different concentration camps from notices in the *Stars and Stripes* and listening to the armed forces radio network. But we didn't attach much importance to it, never realizing that one day we would come upon one of these camps. We liberated a camp called Buchenwald. The moment I walked in, it was very difficult to hold back the tears because of what I saw. Stacks of bodies lying off to the left and the right. One man, with mangled fingers that appeared to be broken, had almost no teeth. I was told he was a former professor at a university in Hungary, a Jewish man. His English was rather broken, but he said to me, "When you go back to your country, please tell them what you have seen. Never forget what your eyes have seen. Let them know what went on in Germany. Let them know how we were treated, and what they have done to extinguish our hopes and dreams for the future." Being of Jewish birth [I felt] the war was just. You had a feeling of unbelievable triumph among these ragged and starving people. We were liberating this country from the scourge of Nazism. People came up in their concentration camp garb and said shalom or welcome, or whatever language they used. The sight before my eyes will never go away as long as I live. I don't think I'll ever forget it, because of man's inhumanity to man. It's an experience that will stay with me forever.

—*Fred Walters; USHMM/Gratz College Hebrew Education Society,*
RG-50.462*0100

123

When the block leader at Mauthausen told us we were going to be gassed, I wanted to commit suicide. But if I committed suicide, I would violate the commandment "Thou shall not kill," so I couldn't come to a real decision. We were taken into the gas chamber and the doors were locked from the outside. There were maybe one hundred at a time or one hundred fifty. Maybe two hundred. It was crowded. We had no strength to fight or anything. Nothing happened. Five, ten, fifteen, twenty minutes later, I cannot judge, the door opened up. Everybody ran out in a hurry to the appellplatz. The commander of the camp said that the fuel to burn our bodies was too expensive, that he would send us to a place where we would vanish without any cost to the Third Reich. We were taken to the railroad. The last stop was at a new place where a camp was being built, Ebensee, a branch of Mauthausen.

—*Lou Dunst; USHMM, RG-50.544*0001*

At Dachau I slept with my shoes on. They were very good and I was afraid that, being in a place with all kinds of people, I would be exposed to theft and assault. I had photographs of my family in the shoes and had wrapped them in cloth. They were a bit damaged, but I saved them. People thought I was crazy. One night I put my shoes under my head, like a pillow. Lo and behold, somebody was watching me. The lights went out and everyone was sleeping when all of a sudden I felt somebody trying to pull them out from under my head. I screamed, they turned on the light, and we caught a Ukrainian. He didn't get the shoes, but I didn't get the photographs either. They apparently fell out of the shoes and somebody grabbed them. I was beside myself. I would have given the shoes and ten years of my life to get the photographs because those were the only ones I had of my family, my parents, and my wife. I was sick because of it. I walked back and forth, but had given up. What could I do? I couldn't get over it. Suddenly, someone in the barrack parallel to ours looked through the iron bars. He never showed his face, but yelled out, "Hey, did you lose something?" I didn't know whether he was yelling at me, or whatever. I said, "Yes, I lost something." All of a sudden, a package with the photographs flew out. God is my witness. The person was apparently afraid. I don't know how he recognized me because one of the photographs was of me in 1938, so he must have known me. I never found out who he was, but I got my photographs back. I considered it a miracle.

—*Jules Zaidenweber; USHMM/Jewish Community Relations Council, Anti-Defamation League of Minnesota and Dakotas, RG-50.156*0059*

Warsaw was in flames and the Germans had left when I entered with Rabbi Kahane. The first place we went to was an old synagogue which was empty and burning. The ark was still there, but the Torahs were gone and it was empty. The rabbi stood silently. Then several dozen Jews came out of hiding and entered. They joined us and the crying and lamentations were indescribable. The rabbi climbed three steps up to the ark. He put on his prayer shawl and said, "God, all the years of my life I have asked you to forgive the sins of my community. Today, I stand in front of You and say, I don't know if we will forgive You Your sins."

—*Ari Falik; USHMM/Manuscript Archives and Rare Book Library, Emory University, RG-50.010*0032*

Chief among the methods utilized for the annihilation of the Jewish people was starvation.

—*Major William Walsh, assistant trial counsel for the US, Nuremberg trials, vol. 1, chapter 12; The Avalon Project, Yale University*

Before my deportation to Theresienstadt, I was a hospital nurse in Berlin where we had many visits from the SS, including Adolf Eichmann. He was young, good-looking, sleek, spotless, arrogant, and a smoker. While he was in the room, we had to stand up. He thought it was great merely to harass the Jews. We didn't know at that stage that he was in charge of the entire Jewish section. He was constantly around our necks. That was his job. Then an SS man arrived from Vienna and told the Jews to select fellow Jews for transports out. He said if they didn't show up, twenty hostages would be killed. Some of those chosen killed themselves, went underground, or ran away. He killed those twenty and sent the ashes to their parents, so we knew he meant business. He summoned the head of the Jewish community, but the man had a heart attack in front of him and dropped dead. The SS man responded by saying, "Take away this dead person. He's just another dead Jew." Finally, I was told to leave. I was completely alone, but was relieved, thinking I would see my family again. I boarded the transport without looking back.

—*Gerda Schild Haas; USHMM, RG-50.030*0334*

The first thing I remember seeing in Bergen-Belsen when they marched us in were mountains of bodies. I couldn't take my eyes off them. Ravensbrück was bad, but Bergen-Belsen was horrible. There was another little girl, a little older than me. Her mother kind of adopted me. But sometimes the mother took some of my rations and gave them to her daughter. The potato peels were at the back of the kitchen. Women pushed me through because I was so small. People told me I had saved their lives. It made me feel good, but there was nothing left for me. Thereafter I ate inside and then brought out their potato peels.

—*Eva Brettler; USHMM, RG-50.030*0546*

A train arrived at night with Hungarians when the flames from the crematorium were ten feet high. They already knew their fate and put on their prayer shawls to chant their last prayer. Others were screaming and crying. I told them just to go. It would be OK. A young woman told her mother she would have a shower and a nice, clean bed. "Don't worry," she said. "Just move ahead. Just go." She stayed close to her mother. I walked over and took her by the hand. She looked at me and said in Yiddish, "I'm only eighteen and haven't even made love yet. Why are you leading me to my death already?" I said, "No, no. What are you talking about? Come with me. You'll be fine. You'll see. I will put you among all these young people." I was able to save her. But she went crazy and destroyed herself. I was able to go into the women's camp by changing places with someone bringing in food. I wanted to see if she survived. She lived only a few days but said to me, "Why do you hate me? Why do you want me to die? I'm only eighteen." It was terrible. The scene will remain with me for as long as I live.

—*Froim (Erwin) Baum; USHMM, RG-50.030*0016*

My tattoo number was A7268. I told very young children that when I was a little girl my mother didn't want me to get lost, so that was my telephone number. As they got older, they never questioned why I said that. When they learned and heard about the Holocaust, they were old enough to know that I didn't want to scare them or burden them. When they were already older, they might not talk about it, but they apparently knew. Whenever they asked a question, I would answer them. But I would never elaborate, because whatever they wanted to know they were told.

—*Ann Green; USHMM, RG-50.030*0509*

I saw the first homicide in Auschwitz within twenty-four hours of arrival. One fellow tried to throw himself in front of a German truck, but it hit him and [only] broke his arm. He was taken to the infirmary where doctors, mostly inmates, set his arm, put a big cast on it, and a sling. Then the SS made him carry huge boulders from one end of the yard to the other, with his broken arm. In the evening, some other SS guards put him on trial and sentenced him to many lashes. He was beaten to a *pulp*. Whenever he fainted, he was revived with cold water. Then he was put in a barrel of cold water. They placed a board in front of his neck and one behind to keep him upright, so he wouldn't slip under the water. He was then shoved under a dripping downspout or something. It also rained on him. Of course, in the morning he was dead. That was the first death in the new camp.

—*Fred Baron; USHMM/Jewish Community Relations Council, Anti-Defamation League of Minnesota and Dakotas, RG-50.156*0005*

I was an obstetrician/gynecologist in an infirmary at a camp near Riga [Latvia] in 1943 when three fellow Jews asked me to get permission for them to pray after work on Rosh Hashana. I told them I would try. I went to see Inge, the German-Jewish woman who took care of the room of the camp kommandant, Gustav Sorge, nicknamed Iron Gustav. I asked Inge what kind of mood he was in. "Bad mood," she replied. I didn't want to see him, but on the third or fourth day, she said he was in a good mood. He liked people talking to him in a military manner, so I stood at attention and spoke like that. "Herr Kommandant, our most sacred holiday, the Jewish New Year, is in a couple of days. Will you permit the prisoners to pray after work? The work will not be interrupted. But for one or two hours will you allow them to pray?" He was dressed like a soldier, but in reality was a mass murderer. "Why not," he replied. So I got permission to have the prayers. All my life I had been basically an atheist, not interested in these things, but when I heard them praying and crying, I could not forget that evening. They were fathers without children, children without fathers, husbands without wives, wives without children— all of them with torn families. There were hundreds of them. The commandant was standing outside. I think this was hard—I don't know how to say it—for a murderer. He didn't say a word. I have the impression he understood. It was not the regular Jewish prayer, but you knew they were praying. You could feel they were praying, "Save us. Help us."

—*David Klebanow; USHMM, RG-50.030*0104*

After the Nazis murdered thousands of people in the Sarny ghetto in Poland, we wound up with thousands of others at Ufa labor camp in the Ural Mountains. I was six, but my mother worked at least ten hours a day making ammunition and came back exhausted with icicles on her eyebrows. She was shivering, with her hands so frozen that one of her frostbitten fingers had to be amputated. My major memories are of cold and hunger. My mother searched for roots and leaves and made pancakes out of them. The poor woman had to keep herself alive. This went on for the last three years of the war. When the kids first discovered I was Jewish they teased me, called me zhid, poked me, and beat me up, but it didn't last long. I was friends with a boy my age, but we had chores, such as alternating the days when we had to carry waste buckets from living quarters, and empty them in pits. After the war, we returned to Sarny. The kids picked on me because I was Jewish. The first few days were bad, but it dissipated as time went on.

—*Ira Segalewitz; USHMM, RG-50.030*0557*

They [the Americans] had no idea where I came from. I was a skinny, skeletal runt. First of all, they cleaned me up from head to toe. They had these traveling army showers, wide open with a little shower head, and they gave us soap and DDT powder. They gave me a clean uniform, clean fatigues, and a clean pair of boots. It was the first time I had underwear, socks, and a pair of army boots in almost three years. They knew nothing until they hit the first concentration camp and even then they didn't understand. They saw this mass of bodies coming out of cattle cars, walking over dead people. They couldn't understand how anybody could do this to anybody. And then I began to tell them. See, this is what happened in Auschwitz. This is what happened in the camps, in the Nazi death camps. Then, of course, they were angry on the streets. Every time they saw a German on a bicycle, they kicked him off. They wanted to beat up every German they saw. Their officers stopped them because you don't do these things in America. They didn't know how to treat us. Every good-hearted American Joe would give you his rations and feed the heck out of you and then top it off with a Camel cigarette. Meanwhile, they were killing us because our bodies couldn't take the food. As good as they were, thousands and thousands of survivors died after liberation because they didn't know what to do with us. So they opened up the displaced persons camps. I go to bed at night and have nightmares. Not a day goes by that Auschwitz doesn't come into my head. In Auschwitz, I was this close from running into the electric fence.

—*Michael Vogel; USHMM, made possible by a grant from Jeff and Toby Herr, RG-50.549.02*0007*

We were all asleep in Magdeburg, Germany when the Nazis broke into our apartment on Kristallnacht. They took everyone to the courtyard, where they burned the synagogue's religious scrolls and books. I remember it vividly. The upper part, where the women sat in the synagogue, had caved in. It had detached from the walls. They didn't totally destroy the synagogue, but it was a mess. About two or three in the morning, they ordered us back into the house. Things were pretty much upside-down. They had smashed a lot of stuff, and I slept on a mattress on the floor because the beds had been torn up. Early the next morning, they came for my father and arrested him. The soldier had already gone out the door when my mother asked if she could make a sandwich for dad. He agreed, so she made it and told me to run after them. They were already down the street, with my father in the middle, when I gave him the sandwich. My father was in Buchenwald about eleven days. It was dramatic to see him again. He had a lot of hair at that time, but now he was totally bald. They had shaved it off. He had been ordered to get out of the country within thirty days. We made our way to Rotterdam, Holland, at a sort of internment camp.

—*John Rosenberg; USHMM/Holocaust Survivors in Kentucky, made possible by a grant from Jeff and Toby Herr, RG-50.549.05*0007*

Two weeks after the war ended, we saw the horror of Buchenwald. I was a private first class with the 76th Infantry Division, an assistant gunner with a light machine gun. There were long lines of bodies, 100 yards long, stacked as high as your head and slicked down with lime. There were special little stacks of babies' bodies. Stacks of eyeglasses. It was just a horror sight, and by that time, there were Allied Military Government people and correspondents there. Of course, the Germans all denied that they even knew this thing had existed. You could have smelled it from Weimar. They cremated the bodies there. [Showing photographs] You can see one of them sitting in an oven. He's still in human form. Your top picture, that's an incinerated body, but not quite gone, that's in an oven. It was so terrible, it was almost beyond belief.

—*Frank Nathanson; USHMM/National Council of Jewish Women, Sarasota-Manatee section, RG-50.154*0021*

Fritz Schäffer had suffered a lot. He was a wonderful man. He loved music, had a beautiful tenor voice, and as a hobby was a cantor in his community. He looked terrible and said he had enough and was giving up. I tried to convince him that he couldn't commit suicide because he was a traditional Jew. I told him he had no right to kill himself. He knew the teachings of the Bible. He pointed out our suffering and said he simply could not go on. He was sick, probably with pneumonia, and needed a hospital, but it was feared because patients were usually selected for death. They refused to admit him, so at dawn he ran toward the electrified fence. The guards would open fire on anyone running toward it. When we went to work, a friend asked if I had heard the shooting that morning. I had. He said Fritz had run against the barbed wire to be shot. He said he had enough. Death was cheap in Auschwitz, and could be attained immediately if desired.

—*Norbert Wollheim; USHMM, RG-50.030*0267*

This story came to me from a friend who worked in the Sonderkommando and who was later killed. He told me that before people went into the gas chambers, an SS man marked their foreheads or hands. Nobody understood its significance, and it was not possible to erase the mark. Later, when the Sonderkommando removed the bodies from the other side, out of the crematorium, and I saw the gate with my own eyes, those people with chalk marks were moved to a special place. It was a sort of abattoir built like a butcher's shop, with all the knives. They were used to carve up the victims and search their stomachs for hidden valuables, mainly diamonds, which were easy to swallow.

—*Gedalia Ben-Zvi, Eichmann trial, Session 71, 8/6/1961, Nizkor*
Project, League for Human Rights of B'nai Brith Canada

In the dead of night, we heard a lot of noise and shattering glass. We looked out the window that ninth of November 1938, and saw storm troopers all over the place, knocking out store windows. Our synagogue was burning. They came upstairs and arrested every Jew and then took us to a large square in the middle of Fürth, where men, women, and children were forced to stand for five hours. Then they let the women and children leave. They took all the males into a large hall, and throughout the day they took us onto the stage and beat us up. Those below waiting their turn had to watch everything. In the evening we had to go up to a table where they decided what to do with each person. They sent the majority to concentration camps and prisons. When my turn came, they saw that my papers were ready for emigration and let me go. I was very lucky because I was allowed to go home. I was twenty-two. One or two days later, we had to go to city hall and sign away ownership of our houses, property, and businesses. We had almost nothing to live on. While leaving, we saw Jews bloodied all over. We asked what happened and they said they fell down the stairs. But we knew they had initially refused to sign and then were beaten up and forced to add their signatures. Only one of us was allowed to emigrate, and being a male I was more vulnerable, so my family agreed to let me go. But I was missing a document to say I didn't owe any taxes or money to others. I wrote three times to Berlin but never got an answer. I went to gestapo headquarters in Berlin, where everyone dreaded to go, and an official yelled at me, saying I must be crazy and what was the matter with me writing him three letters. Did I think he had nothing better to do? He said he felt like sending me to a concentration camp, but he let me go. Five days later, the document arrived in the mail, and I left in January 1939 for Holland and then America. My entire family died in concentration camps. I am the only survivor.

—*Fred Goldman; USHMM, RG-50.106*0146*

The Germans held a Hanukkah celebration. On the outside poles of the barracks at Birkenau they hung up prisoners by their feet, head down. We had to pour oil on them and make a bonfire. And we had to sing Christmas songs while our brothers, fathers, or cousins were burning. What do I accomplish by hate? I am more rational about it. I will not buy German goods. I will not go on vacation to Germany. I will not sponsor their events. But that is as far it goes. The only thing I can say for the deceased is what I do every day. I say a memorial prayer for them. Just like they would for my father, brother, sister, or mother. Yet we have to watch out. We cannot let these things occur again. Unless we know about it and tell it to others, it's bound to happen again.

—*Bart Stern in an interview with Sandra Bradley for the USHMM film* Testimony, *RG-50.042*0025*

The Germans ran away when I came through Dachau with an armored division. There were five packed freight cars outside the camp. I went to one and shot off the lock. A live individual fell out into my arms. The car was packed with dead bodies, but some were still alive. At the crematoriums, there were four ovens, and shovels and wheelbarrows for bones to be taken out and dropped in the cemetery. In a basement, corpses were stacked at least eight feet high.

—*Ralph Miles; USHMM/University of California, Los Angeles, RG-50.005*0043*

I had a rather interesting experience on the train to Berlin in 1936. I got into a conversation with a man who was a postal clerk, and he started talking to me saying what a nice girl I was, and I seemed so bright and everything. Somehow he managed to say he always knew what Jews were like. They smelled terrible and looked so awful, but he could always tell a Jew. I said nothing and we just kept on talking about all kinds of interesting things. It was not a question of him making a pass at me, or anything of that sort. I think he probably was old enough to be my father. He just seemed interested in talking to me. When he had his foot on the lower step to get off the train I said to him, "Didn't you say that you could always tell a Jew when you met one?" He said, "Oh yes, I certainly can." Then I said, "Well, you missed one." He almost fell off the train. That was one of the very few satisfactions I had in those years.

—*Susan Faulkner; USHMM/Gratz College Hebrew Education Society, RG-50.462*0005*

I was in Stutthof concentration camp when three women escaped. I don't know how, because there were electrified wires, but they did. We were punished as a group by having to stand naked for twelve hours in cold weather. Then the Germans took four or five women and raped them in front of everybody. My mother was next to me and shielded my eyes with her hands so I shouldn't see sexual intercourse for the first time. Probably she thought if I saw it, I would be forever difficult with men. But the Germans saw what she did with her hands and beat her so much that all her front teeth were knocked out. Later, my husband-to-be was my first date. I felt loved and he loved. When I married him and had sexual intercourse, it never took me back to that scene. It is probably due to my strong nature. I know how to disconnect myself. I wish my mother could have known that I became a normal person.

—*Dora Goldstein Roth; USHMM, RG-50.030*0197*

My tattoo number at Auschwitz from 1942 was 3931. I was in the second Jewish transport to get there. The first were only German prostitutes who were our kapos. We had to shovel sand into lorries and push them up a high hill. It was very hard work. I am alive now because a female head supervisor summoned me and twenty other girls to the office. I told the truth and said I was in a lawyer's office for three years. We had to type. First they gave us a shower and clean, striped dresses to get rid of lice. Our hair had to be shaven because the SS females didn't want us to look like women. My luck was that my penmanship was very good and the SS man liked it. I filled in death certificates. We lived in a room in the cellar of the general staff building and were kept clean because the SS didn't want to get lice or fall sick. The prisoners didn't steal our tiny pieces of bread because they were afraid we would tell the SS. One day I had a very bad experience. I filled out some forms and ink spilled on them. An SS male asked who did it and the kapo said I did. He hit me on the face about twenty times. I was sure he would send me to Birkenau, which meant death, but he didn't, so I survived.

—Else Turteltaub; USHMM/Gratz College Hebrew Education
Society, RG-50.462*0072

We had passed the selection by an elegant SS officer in leather gloves and shiny boots, pointing to the left or right, when a woman recognized someone in our transport. No one was allowed out of the barracks when a train arrived. She screamed out a name. The SS man, who was next to me, and maybe eighteen, pointed his rifle and shouted, "Get in or I'll shoot you!" Then he shot her. She screamed but lay in a pool of mud, colored red by her blood. That was the first time I had ever seen a person shot at point blank range. It is something I will never forget.

—Ursula Pawel; USHMM, made possible by a grant from Jeff and
Toby Herr, RG-50.030*0488

We didn't think anything [as Sonderkommano]. On the contrary, it was even a liberation for us. Some people asked me if it wouldn't be better to get it over with. Perhaps—or even certainly. But I didn't think of it; we had to keep on going, day by day, without asking ourselves any questions. Keep on living, even if it was terrible. To my knowledge, nobody in the Sonderkommando committed suicide. I know that some of them said they wanted to live at any price. Personally, I think I'd rather have died. But each time, some words of my mother's used to come to my mind: "While there's life, there's hope." We were too close to death, but we carried on, day by day. . . . We kept conversation to a minimum. Nobody felt much like talking. We'd come back to the barrack after a day's exhausting work; our brains were empty, and we had nothing to say to each other. There were a few intellectuals among us. But we were the force and we'd long since lost our dignity.

—Inside the Gas Chambers: Eight Months in the Sonderkommando of Auschwitz *by Shlomo Venezia, translated by Andrew Brown and published by Polity Press in association with the USHMM*

We were often deloused. Our hair was checked for lice. We tried to keep our heads clean to keep the lice away from us. First they checked my sister's hair and they found it clean. When the kapo came to check my hair, I said to her, "I keep my hair clean." She looked at me sadistically and without even checking, just to spite me, she went quickly and shaved my whole head and called me, "You Polska swinia!" I was hysterical. Since my hair grew back a little, I had looked more human. To comfort me, my sister said, "Don't cry. If your head will survive, your hair will grow back." She was so right. I will forever remember her remarks.

—*Joyce Wagner, author of* A Promise Kept: To Bear Witness

Three people were doing the tattooing. I was at the edge of my life, or edge of death, or whatever they called it in Auschwitz. In the nicest way, I went to see who did it. That was because I had seen inmates with irregular tattoo numbers. Some numbers were big, others small, some sideways. I wanted to have it done neatly. Then I lined up. You see [showing arm], it's very regular and neat. But I don't know why they didn't do it here [indicating another position]. My number was 11636.

—*Edgar Krasa; USHMM, RG-50.030*0478*

Soon after the war, I visited my hometown of Starachowice for a day, with about twenty-five Jews including five children, who had survived Auschwitz. In the middle of the night, Polish fascists attacked the community elsewhere, and two children and a few adults were killed. Then, at about 2:00 a.m., the murderers knocked on the door of the house we were in, demanding the door be opened. "We know that the Laks sisters are here and we want them!" The widow of this highly respected family said, "How dare you disturb my sleep! Yes, they are with me, but as long as they are under my roof, you are not going to lay your hands on them. Please leave us alone." It became quiet, but we didn't know what had happened. The following morning, one of the young women went to find out what it was all about and ran back as white as a ghost. She begged us not to leave the house. We should stay there. The people looking for us had earlier attacked that small group of Jews, killing some. That night she went to the train station to buy us tickets, and when its whistle sounded, she took us there by horse and buggy, waiting until it left to see us off safely. I made a promise never to return to Starachowice.

—*Rosalie Laks Lerman; USHMM, RG-50.030*0396*

138

You heard everybody say, "Oh, we've got to survive and tell the world what is going on."

—*Ruth Webber in an interview with Sandra Bradley for the USHMM film* Testimony, *RG-50.042*0030*

I had a friend whose daughter's child was taken to a monastery. After the war she knew where she was and came to take her back. The child said, "You are not going to take me. I'm not Jewish. I hate Jews. They told me to hate Jews. I'm not going to go out." She had a very hard time getting her out.

—*Sally Abrams; USHMM/Gratz College Hebrew Education Society, RG-50.462*0026*

Ammunition fired by the Germans took off half the head of the fellow next to me, by a window in the Warsaw ghetto uprising of April 1943, leaving him dead. I thought I'd also taken a bullet as I looked at him. It was scary and I never was a hero. I looked at my hand and saw blood, before passing out. Germans had been mined and killed, but other Nazis pulled me and others to that spot, dumped us around the crater, and shot many. I was waiting with others for a train when they yanked off my ring and stole my watch. I was bleeding from an open wound in the train and threw up. When the bleeding stopped I had difficulty closing an eye. The car normally ferried only animals and we were packed so tight you couldn't fall down. I only lived due to a physician friend of mine who treated my wounded eye with his pocket knife. Then we arrived at Budzyń labor camp.

—*Joseph Koplewicz; USHMM, RG-50.106*0121*

On a Friday night, the rabbi came to our house in Copenhagen and said he'd heard the Germans would be rounding up all Jews, and none of us should go home. The maid agreed to stay and look after the apartment, and with toothbrushes in our pockets we fled—my parents, sister, myself, and an uncle (who was married to a non-Jew who stayed behind). The next day my parents took a cab to the bank and withdrew enough money to pay the fisherman who would take us to Sweden. At that time, my father had a men's clothing store on the main street of Copenhagen. He also bought a bracelet for my mother. Nobody stopped us at the train station, not even the Germans. We took the train as far as Snekkersten, closest to Sweden's seashore. I was a little scared in the train, but I didn't really know what it meant as we hadn't experienced anything bad, so it was exciting for me. Later, the maid told us that they came looking for us and she told them, "They wouldn't be so stupid to stay home," and they left. When we returned from Sweden, Hitler's picture was all over the walls. The Danish movers were so angry that they kicked the pictures. A lot of our furniture was still there when we moved in.

—*Tove Schoenbaum Bamberger; USHMM, RG-50.030*0014*

Some children were kept alive at random in the Children's House in Auschwitz, with beautiful toys in case an inspection came from the Red Cross in Switzerland to evaluate how well these little kids were treated. My niece arrived, and her two aunts were fighting over who would go and be killed with [their sister's daughter] Rachel. The older one said her son was with her husband and they would be taken away, so her sister should step aside. She won, and the married sister went with Rachel. Both went into the gas chamber and were killed.

—*Sally Chase; USHMM, RG-50.029*0010*

Without Israel I don't think I would have wanted to have children, to marry, and to lead a normal life. That's the only thing that made me feel that life is worth living. Before the war, there was no place to go to if you were being persecuted. That was the tragedy of the 1930s. It's much easier than it was before the war. Now we have a place to go. As Jews we should know about our roots, try to defend ourselves as much as possible, and not let the world control us. My family didn't ask about the Holocaust when I came to Detroit, except to ask me if it was true my mother died in Auschwitz. I told them about my father, who had been shot to death as a hostage. But they didn't know him, so they were not that interested. They never asked me what happened in Auschwitz. Never. I remember a cousin, within a year or two of my age, who wanted desperately to know what happened, and to be my friend, but they wouldn't let her. They told her, "Don't ask her; it might make her sad, or you may not want to know." Absolutely unbelievable. To this day I find this appalling. I can't forgive the Germans, ever. I know it's unfair, but that's the way it is. I know they were not all like Mengele, but for me they were the perpetrators of a horrible nightmare that devastated my family and those of others. I can't forgive them for that. Ever.

—*Simone Horowitz; USHMM/Gratz College Hebrew Education Society, RG-50.462*0087*

Any one of my troops who went into Dachau with us would not become the parent of a skinhead, or a neo-Nazi, or any one of those things, because what they saw could never be duplicated in history and hopefully never will be. The things we saw at Dachau were horrible. It didn't matter what you were or what your religious background; this thing was so horrendous that no matter who you were, or what you were, it was going to plague you forever.

—*Henry Plitt; USHMM, RG-50.030*0181*

When the Nazis came to my hometown of Krzepice in occupied Poland, the first thing they did was grab religious Jews with beards and cut the beards off with a knife. You've seen the picture of my father with a beard. Either they beat you to death or took a knife and cut off the beard. They did anything they wanted with Jews. At night the soldiers broke into the homes and raped the women. If there was any little incident against them, they would take out a bunch of people, put them up against a wall, and shoot them down like dogs. It was nothing to them. It was like killing a fly today. My two brothers were very religious. One had a nervous breakdown and could barely walk on the outbreak of war, so they took him and my mother in the backyard and shot them. They took the other brother away. He wouldn't touch the soup. The only thing he ate was a piece of bread. He didn't last long. People told me my father died in a concentration camp.

—Solomon Klug; USHMM, RG-50.030*0109

Our kapo was six feet, six inches tall, weighed over 300 pounds, and you couldn't tell by looking into his eyes that he was a murderer. When he saw someone, he didn't [look] like he would kill him. One time I saw him pick up a shovel and kill someone by slamming him over the head. He reported that the victim had tried to run away, and no one accused him of lying. I was scared of him. My colleagues suggested I make him a cap, but I had nothing with which to measure him. I needed material, a needle, thread, and scissors. They took care of it and instead of a tape measure, I said I would take the size by wrapping a piece of paper around him. I was scared of approaching the kapo to talk to him, but while I was in the latrine in the morning he saw me. I asked him to take off his cap to be measured and told him I could make another in two or three hours. But I worked for two days in the same latrine. He brought me a piece of bread while I worked, and he

142

was happy with the result. For eighteen months after that, I continued to work under him, but he never laid a finger on me. He never beat me.

—*Solomon Radasky; USHMM, RG-50.030*0305*

My brother-in-law was terribly hungry, and he saw that the dog had a lot of food, which it ate and then walked away. He stole what the dog had left. The SS came back with the dog, who had been trained to tear people apart. Some would do it as a sport. The SS told my brother-in-law to kneel in front of the dog and ask its forgiveness. He had to call the dog, Herr, while the SS called him "You dirty swine!" The SS told him he was going to let the dog tear him to pieces. While one whipped him, the SS were laughing because they liked to see a Jew calling a dog Herr. He was told to beg for his life. My brother-in-law was terribly scared and wished he could die a different death, but luckily, for some reason, he was only beaten senseless. Then some friends of his were allowed to take him away.

—*Cecilie Klein-Pollack in an interview with Sandra Bradley for the USHMM film* Testimony, *RG-50.042*-0018*

I know my mother and four siblings were killed in Auschwitz. Then a man from my hometown in Romania told me he was with my father and brother two days before liberation when the Germans moved them from one camp to another, and they had to walk and walk. He said my brother skipped out of line, to a store, and the SS ran after him. But my father also ran after my brother to bring him back. Then my friend heard two shots. They must have shot both of them because only the SS came back, and my father and brother didn't come out of the store.

—*Ernie Pollak; USHMM, RG-50.030*0582*

Two of my brothers were married in the Latvian ghetto and their wives gave birth almost a week apart. When the Germans came, the first thing they did was go to the hospital. The fathers were imprisoned, but they had to throw the babies out the window onto a pile of bodies. Then they threw out the women who had given birth. Some were still alive. They gave us shovels, and we had to dump the bodies in an excavated grave. One of my brothers recognized his wife and baby on that pile, and he had to help bury them. It was incredulous. You cannot believe it. I cannot forget it. I still have nightmares. I have been depressed ever since. I take medication to be happy. You just cannot erase those things. In a death camp, the SS chased women into a room. We were shaven and totally naked on a table, like a fashion show, while they looked at our bodies, considering whether we were worthwhile saving or should be gassed. I had a horrible rash from dirt and malnutrition and knew I would be gassed, but I walked close to my girlfriend so the front of my body wouldn't show how bad it was. As we dressed again, we heard the other women screaming because they were being killed by gas coming out of showerheads. I had been saved again. It was another miracle.

—Sonja Gottlieb Ludsin; USHMM, RG-50.030*0262

Mauthausen was completely choked, so when seventeen hundred survivors arrived from Sachsenhausen, the commandant encouraged the sick, old, and weak to come forward. These four hundred men, who had either come forward of their own free will or been arbitrarily selected, were stripped naked and left for eighteen hours in weather eighteen degrees below zero, between the laundry building and the camp wall. I witnessed this. Several rapidly got congestion of the lungs, but that did not seem fast enough for the SS. Three times during the night, these men were drenched for half an hour in freezing water and forced to come out of the showers without being dried. When gangs went to work in the morning, the corpses were strewn on the ground. The last of them were finished off with blows from an ax.

—*Maurice Lampe, Nuremberg trials, vol. 6, 1/25/46;*
The Avalon Project, Yale University

During air raids at Buna, the young man sharing a bunk with me would run to the Germans' trash to look for anything they'd thrown away from their kitchen. Sometimes he would come back with food, like old sour soup. I told him not to do it; otherwise, he'd get hurt, but he said he was hungry. I told him I was also hungry, but I wouldn't do it. Well, he went, and finally he was caught. His punishment was hanging. I had tried to warn him, but he wouldn't listen. We were forced to watch him hang with three others. A German got up and read something, but I didn't understand a word of it. They had ropes around their necks and I never found out what the other three had done. After they were hanged, the Germans brought in the regular orchestra. They started banging the drums and clashing the cymbals, just like they do at a high school football team. That's what the Nazis thought of Jews or anyone else. They were inhumane. That's the only way I can describe them.

—*Henry Greenbaum; USHMM, RG-50.106*0128*

The food in Buchenwald was terrible and we drank soup from the same bowl. Conditions got worse and worse. Many people wouldn't eat because the food was not kosher, but the rabbis went around telling people they had to; however, some still refused to. We arranged to have secret prayer services every morning. Somebody was appointed lookout to see that no Nazis approached. On the first night of Hanukkah, a wonderful thing happened in the barrack: we sang Hanukkah songs.

—*Walter Schnell; USHMM, RG-50.030*0206*

There was sheer terror when the first German planes came over Warsaw. The government building next to us was bombed and flames licked our windows. After Warsaw surrendered, my father and brother trudged east with all exiled males, and German planes strafed the refugees. They took my father's firm and my mother's shop. Jews had to obey everything and were shot if outside after the 7:00 p.m. curfew. For a young girl, it was like being in a cage. Poles pointed out Jews to the Germans, and men were afraid to go outdoors because they might not come back. The Germans grabbed young girls, made them wash floors with their underwear and then raped them. Hunger began immediately. A doctor in our home said, "They'll kill all of us!" My mother got very upset at this, but he knew what he was talking about. That's when the Resistance started. The ghetto burned and we fled across the rooftops. That's where I lost my father. Suddenly, we saw uniformed Germans, but they were members of the Resistance in disguise and took us to safety in a cellar. But the Germans found us, shot all the men, and squeezed us into cattle cars to a concentration camp. When I crawled over corpses, I had arrived at the first of six concentration camps. Those who couldn't keep up with the rest were finished off by German dogs. My mother died on the cattle car to Majdanek, and my brother perished during the uprising at Treblinka. When I was freed, I thought I had won the war. I wanted to see them lose, to suffer, and be paid back. At least there was a sense that "You couldn't kill me!" American kids ask how we could go like sheep to our deaths. They can't understand how helpless we were, empty-handed against men with guns. I hope nobody is in that situation again.

—*Eugenia Boroff, USHMM/Generations After, Inc.,*
RG-50.243*0005

There was no water to wash ourselves in Bergen-Belsen. When I got up in the barrack in the morning, I was always covered in lice. I would shake out my uniform, which had gray and blue stripes, but you wouldn't know it was blue because it was covered with lice. Our barrack was like a big barn with nothing on the floor except straw. We were cold and crowded and couldn't stretch our legs; we sat with our knees close to our chins. But it didn't stay crowded for long. Women died almost immediately and we carried them outside to where there were big piles of dead bodies. I never looked at their faces. It was rough.

—Bella Tovey in an interview with Sandra Bradley for the USHMM film Testimony, *RG-50.042*0028*

I remember in Belgium about two hundred Jews were marching down the street. I was in a streetcar when a young girl said, "Look at those Jews." The conductor interjected, "How can you say that? If today it's the Jews, then tomorrow it's you." She looked at him as if he didn't know what he was talking about. I had non-Jewish friends who were good friends. People are good, but they are still influenced and ignorant. The moment they hear you say you are Jewish they say, "You killed my God." And I answer, "How could I kill your God?" Education is very important. You cannot educate hate out of people, but you can get rid of superstitions. After the so-called Anschluss, a young lady down the street embraced my mother and said, "Hitler is here." I asked what she was talking about. Didn't she know we were Jewish? She answered, "I know, but they don't mean you." She was ignorant. These are the people who have to be educated.

—Henry Sontag; USHMM/Phoenix Holocaust Survivors Association in affiliation with Cline Library of Northern Arizona University, RG-50.060*0050

We were liberated on the last day of the war in Europe, May 8, 1945. A lot of the Germans had run away. They threw away their uniforms and put on civilian clothes to make believe. Some escaped. A young girl was so excited that the Russians were coming that she wanted to greet a soldier, but was run over and killed by the same tank. When the Russians came they said, "We liberated you, but now you don't want to love us?" So we knew what was in store for us. At nighttime we barricaded all the doors and windows with heavy oak furniture, benches, and chairs. We didn't sleep until the barricades were up to the ceiling so they couldn't open the door. We were afraid of being raped. They hadn't seen a woman for I don't know how long. They were women crazy.

—*Frances Davis; USHMM, RG-50.030*348*

The commandant of Płaszów concentration camp, Amon Goëth, was walking toward my cousin, Jankek, when the teenager whistled, which he always did when upset, even though he was unaware of it. They arrested him, built the gallows overnight, and brought him out to hang. They made his father, Uncle Henek, watch from the front row. The rope broke and they sent for another. My poor little cousin, then fourteen or fifteen, was scared to death. He crawled up to Goëth and kissed his boot, but the commandant just hissed. My uncle had to watch; then he had a stroke. He was a vegetable.

—*Sylvia Green; USHMM, RG-50.030*0466*

I questioned God because I was very religious when I came into the camp. My grandmother had raised me, and she was an orthodox lady and made me say prayers every morning. When I saw I was living in hell, I asked, "Where is God? How can He see what goes on here, in this terrible hell, and let it happen?" I would sneak out of the barracks in Auschwitz at night, risking my life by doing so because we had watchtowers, and if they saw something in a shadow, they would shoot. But there were times when I had to be all by myself, with my own thoughts. When I thought everybody was sleeping, I would go all the way to the back of the camp and talk to the stars. I would say, "Where is God? Why is he punishing us like this? How long will it go on?" And I would talk to the stars and say, "The stars are looking down at us in the camp and they see what is happening, and the same stars are shining to the outside world, where people are free, and they can do what they want to do, and be happy, and live a wonderful life, and we live here in a hell and don't know from moment to moment if we're going to live or die. How come the free world allows this and does not stop this terrible thing?" After I cried myself out, I would sneak back into the barracks.

—Lilly Appelbaum Malnik in an interview with Sandra Bradley for the USHMM film Testimony, *RG-50.042*0020*

When I got to Auschwitz, I still believed in religion, a belief in God, but I soon lost that. If God wanted to punish us Jews, if we did something that terribly wrong, punish us for a day, a week, whatever. But why let us suffer from 1939 until 1945, being systematically murdered and thrown into the ovens. And seeing with my own eyes, and knowing that this mass of thousands upon thousands of people were being herded like sheep, not knowing where they were going. I am angry with God. I have a problem with God.

*—Michael Vogel; USHMM, made possible by a grant from Jeff and Toby Herr, RG-50.549.02*0007*

The worst guards at Treblinka were Ukrainians, not Germans. I did not know if I would survive, so while in the ruins of wartime Warsaw, I described my sufferings at Treblinka in a notebook. One sadist, taking pleasure in what he did, was a man we called Ivan the Terrible. I didn't know then that he was John Demjanjuk. He dropped gas into the gas chamber. Once he whacked people with an iron pole. Their screams were unbearable, but he enjoyed it and continued. I was close to Ivan's workshop and saw him often while I had to remove teeth from gassed victims. I was washing bloodied teeth with my friend Finkelstein, when Ivan took a drill and ran it into Finkelstein's backside. Finkelstein was screaming and crying while Ivan carried on laughing. Ivan used to grab people and cut off an ear, and while they bled he ordered them to undress. His sadism was so great that it is difficult to speak about.

—*Chil Rajchman; USHMM, RG-50.030*0185*

At the beginning of 1942, a Jew escaped from Chelmno. On the way to Warsaw, he went into a town and told the rabbi that in Chelmno, Jews were being driven out of the city in trucks and put to death by gas. The rabbi was convinced that the Jew had gone crazy and didn't believe him. The Jew came to Warsaw and told us the story. In previous years, even we could not picture to ourselves that a nation in the twentieth century would indeed execute a death sentence on an entire people. We asked ourselves more than once: they are degrading us, they are suppressing us, but are they truly thinking of destroying all of us? We did not believe it.

—*Zivia Lubetkin-Zuckerman, Eichmann trial, session 25, 5/3/1961,*
Nizkor Project, League for Human Rights of B'nai Brith Canada

Jacques, a Jewish waiter at one of the biggest kosher restaurants in Antwerp, went around with Germans pointing out Jews. My father was walking in the neighborhood when Jacques told him, "Drop your pants!" Then Jacques told the Germans he was circumcised. They took my father to a cellar at gestapo headquarters where a young SS officer asked, "You're circumcised?" My father said, "No, I'm not. It was part of a kidney operation." The officer called in an old German Army doctor and yelled at him, saying, "Tell me! Tell me!" The doctor was angry with the young officer for yelling at him, and my father saw the physician grind his teeth. So the doctor said, "Yes, this man was operated on his kidneys, and that was part of the operation." That saved my father. The doctor didn't believe my father. He knew he was circumcised, but he was angry at the officer. My father took eight different trams home so he could not be followed.

—*Freddy Schumer; USHMM, RG-50.030*0668*

When I had the lowest bunk, women above could throw their lice on me and vice versa. Prisoners were dirty and starving. When we woke up, more people were dead than alive. [One day] I had to go to the bathroom as I had terrible diarrhea. The door was closed and there were German guards, so I sneaked out the window. Coming back was another matter. I had to come through the door. They were waiting for me with a welcoming committee. A guard knocked out a few of my teeth and kicked me. My friends came and scooped me up from the snow. I thought that was the end, but it wasn't.

—*Beba Leventhal; USHMM/University of California, Los Angeles,*
*RG-50.005*0037*

They put us in a Berlin synagogue for two days and as we were more than one thousand people, we slept on the floor. There were a few young people, but most were middle-aged and elderly. All they would say was that we were going east. The Jewish community made sandwiches for our trip and we boarded an old, unheated train. It was so cold that the drinking water froze. My father was unable to take the medication that had kept him free from asthma for several years, and he suffered his first attack on the train. We were on it for four days before arriving at the freight station outside of Riga. The SS told us trucks would transport us to the ghetto several miles away, but there were only enough for the elderly and infirm. The others would have to walk. My father boarded a truck when my mother said, "Your father might have difficulty understanding orders," because he was hard of hearing. So she left me and got up on the truck to be with my father. That was the last time I saw my parents. I was only nineteen years old.

—*Ilse Sauer; USHMM, RG-50.030*0273*

The Germans searched house to house, and being organized, they always came with a list. Mostly they took away the elderly, undesirables, and people who couldn't work, like those with a limp or eye problems. My parents, sister, and I went up to the attic of our house on the outskirts of the city, with a roof overlooking the cemetery. At nighttime we heard the columns of Jews under German escort passing by to the woods behind the cemetery. Later we found out that's where they were shot. During the day, I looked through the shingles, even though my father told me not to, because I was a curious kid. Dead bodies were brought in on wagons; then groups of Jews would dig ditches, into which they dumped the dead. Then those who had dug the ditches were shot and also thrown in. Lime was thrown over the corpses and the next group covered the ditches and dug new ones. They also brought in pregnant women, using bayonets. I can still hear the screams of children, held in their mothers' arms. The Germans took pleasure in taking little infants and smashing their heads against the cemetery wall. They played games with babies. One grabbed a leg and another took the other, and they tore them apart. My father said I should never talk about it. Nobody would believe me. They would say I made it up. He was partially right. Even the Jews questioned it. I don't understand. How can anyone make up a story like that?

—*Martin Spett; USHMM, RG-50.030*0218*

A youngster who spent his youth at Auschwitz came to the dispensary in Poland and asked for a doctor because he felt he was losing his mind. He spoke in a loud voice and cried. He trembled. His hands shook like an old man, and his face was bruised with wrinkles. The doctor himself was a victim of the war, having been taken away to Siberia during the Russian occupation. After returning to Poland, he went to Auschwitz to witness the horrors. He told us about piles of human hair, eyeglasses, gloves, and shoes. When I came with this boy, the doctor's face turned ash gray. His eyes filled with tears on seeing the victim. He greeted the boy warmly, but he kept on crying. We were witnessing a child trying to free himself from tragedy. Every time he came, he told of the atrocities, of being humiliated and beaten, experiments, having cold water thrown over him, forced to throw himself on his own father, marches to faraway places in winter without shoes, and constant hunger. Those who lost their strength were left to freeze to death. He was in need of a warm home where he could become normal again. Who knows if he ever recovered from the horrors of the Holocaust? He stopped coming.

—*Sophie Roth; USHMM/Gratz College Hebrew Education Society, RG-50.462*0096*

When we left Berlin for the East we had about sixty to seventy people in the boxcar and a bucket for sanitary purposes. No water, and hardly any air. But we were in such a good mood that we even started to sing a Hebrew song from the youth movement which went, "*How nice it is when friends sit together in friendship.*" I vividly remember it was a Friday night and there was an elderly lady who had taken some candles along. She lit them to celebrate the Jewish Sabbath and prayers were said. Probably 95 percent of the people did not live to see the next evening. However, on that Friday night, they said their prayers and prayed to God, giving Him credit for I don't know what.

—*Norbert Wollheim; USHMM, RG-50.030*0267*

We were the only light tank on reconnaissance, looking for the enemy for the fourth and sixth Army Divisions, when we neared Ebensee concentration camp in Austria. We smelled dead bodies. It's an odor that you won't forget. There were no guards in the watchtowers. It looked like everyone had run off. The inmates looked terrible. They were happy to see us, but it was hard. You can't understand what these people went through. Their eyes were sunk in. They were wasted to nothing. They would put these men into salt mines and whittle them down to nothing. We tried to feed them, but they were just bones. They didn't have anything to digest. They could only digest soup. They had tattoos on their chests, not on their arms. Four or five inmates would jump on a cigarette butt if we threw it away. I saw at least five hundred dead bodies stacked in one room at the crematorium. I am not exaggerating. There was a sign there that read, "MY BODY WOULD RATHER BE BURNED THAN GO INTO THE GROUND." They pushed them into the crematorium to burn them. Hitler wanted to exterminate the Jews and this was terrible. I was in Ebensee about a month and took photographs for the Judge

Advocate General. My photos were also used in the Nuremberg trials. I wanted to leave a little legacy of this to remind the youngest Jewish children that it did happen, because I witnessed it. I was there. They should never forget. Those dead people stacked in that room. You don't forget those things. You cannot.

—*Thomas Ward; USHMM, RG-50.030*0244*

During our evacuation from Dachau, it was cold and snowing, and those who couldn't make it froze to death. We went by train to the border of Germany and Austria and were unloaded in front of a stream and rocky mountain. An SS captain told us to walk toward the stream; then he opened fire with a machine gun. Suddenly, a very elegantly dressed woman in a fur coat distracted him and enticed him over. Other SS men told us to sit or lie down. I have no idea who she was. When we woke up, the guards had vanished. I was with about fifty people who walked toward Munich. Three or four miles later, a sentry stopped us. We told him the SS had abandoned us. A drunk German captain ordered us taken out and shot, but a major reprimanded him and then told us to climb the mountain and stay there for a few days until the situation changed in our favor. That's what we did, climbing inside a hut of hay we found in a plateau. We ate snow and kept silent because Germans were passing by. All they had to do was toss a hand grenade inside our hut. That night artillery shells whistled overhead. Two days later another fellow and I peered over the edge and heard another language, either English or American. We went down and were told to get away from the front line. The military policeman gave me a Hershey bar and I was as sick as a dog.

—*David Eiger; USHMM/Jewish Community Relations Council,*
Anti-Defamation League of Minnesota and the Dakotas,
RG-50.156*0011

It was so depressing; I can't describe it. Everybody was out of his mind. We saw death before our eyes. Whether it was going to be today, tomorrow, or the next day, everybody knew that when people got sick, they took them away and they never came back. We knew they'd been killed. We knew there were crematoriums in Auschwitz. We were there. We smelled the smoke and everything, and waited for the day they would come and take us away.

—*Berek Latarus; USHMM/Jewish Community Relations Council, Anti-Defamation League of Minnesota and the Dakotas, RG-50.156*0032*

There were three thousand people in the room: men, women, and children. Within five minutes, everybody was dead. The bodies of the women, the children, and the aged were at the bottom of the pile. At the top, the strongest. Blood oozed from their noses and mouths. Their faces, bloated and blue, were so deformed as to be almost unrecognizable. The Sonderkommando squad, outfitted with large rubber boots, lined up around the hill of bodies and flooded it with powerful jets of water. This was necessary because the final act of those who die by drowning or by gas is an involuntary defecation. Each body was defiled and had to be washed. The separation of the welter of bodies began. They knotted thongs around the wrists, which were clenched in a viselike grip, and with these thongs, they dragged the slippery bodies to the elevators in the next room. The elevators stopped at the crematorium's incineration room. Human hair was often used in delayed-action bombs . . . so they shaved the dead. The dead were next sent to the "tooth-pulling" commando. Gold teeth were collected in buckets filled with an acid which burned off all pieces of bone and flesh. Other valuables worn by the dead, such as necklaces, pearls, wedding bands, and [other] rings were taken and dropped through a slot in the lid of a strongbox. The bodies were cremated in twenty minutes. Each crematorium worked with fifteen ovens, and there were four crematoriums. This meant that several thousand people could be cremated in a single day.

—Auschwitz: A Doctor's Eyewitness Account *by Dr. Miklos Nyiszli,*
translated by Tibere Kremer and Richard Seaver

I will never go to hell because I'm living it already.

—*Lilly Appelbaum Malnik in an interview with Sandra Bradley for*
the USHMM film Testimony, *RG-50.042*0020*

Every ten days in Mauthausen, a different barrack was gassed. The whole barrack of four to six hundred people would go on tiptoe in deathly silence. Everybody was given a piece of soap and stared at the showerheads, because sometimes, instead of water, little granules of hydrogen cyanide came out and your goose was cooked. When water came out it was bedlam, with people jumping, yelling, shouting, laughing, and hugging one another. We never knew which barrack was going to be chosen, which made us apprehensive. But if you got out, you exclaimed, "Yay, I'm going to live another ten days!" They chose up to fifty prisoners to take the bodies to the cool chamber, a kind of underground tunnel. With a little flatcar, we pushed to the cool chamber, next to the crematorium. Sometimes burning the dead took too long, but the cool chamber could hold about two thousand bodies. We did this willingly because we got an extra bowl of SS soup or peas, perhaps beans mixed with pork. Oh my God, that was heaven! We abhorred it, but we went along. Whatever took place was normal for that time and place.

—*Stefan Czyzewski; USHMM, RG-50.030*0387*

My wife and I had contact with some Resistance people, so we left Belgium for France, where there was an underground. I hung a crucifix on my wife. We came to a little town and a woman who gave us food warned, "I can see you are Catholics. Be careful, there are many Jews out there." We went to the house of the commander, where kids ran around. When he came in, I told him that someone had told me who he was, and he blew up. But then he calmed down and said I could stay there and go out with him. "But first I have to ask you something. Are you Jewish?" I said, "No." I had false papers. The next day we went into the forest where there were maybe twenty people. He asked again if I was Jewish. I said, "No. But what is the difference?" He said he wouldn't waste one of his men for a Jew. We left and never stayed two nights in one spot. We went to the other side of France. In 1943 we tried to go to Switzerland, but they wanted to keep my wife and my son and send me back. My wife screamed and grabbed my legs. They said, "OK, you can stay for a while, but you cannot contact anybody here." Then I got a letter that the war was over.

—*Henry Sontag; USHMM/Phoenix Holocaust Survivors Association in affiliation with Cline Library of Northern Arizona University, R-50.060*0050*

I was working in the kitchen when a girl brought in potatoes and one fell on the floor. I picked it up, looked around, and decided to eat it raw. The SS woman saw me and inflicted the punishment of twenty-five lashes on my rear and three days in a tank filled with water. I climbed up a ladder into the tank, which kept filling with water. They removed the ladder and the water rose higher and higher until it was up to my hips. I got thirsty and drank some. I had to go to the bathroom, so I did it on the spot. Getting no food was part of the punishment. I went to sleep and almost drowned. After three days, I was back in the kitchen and hungry, but the SS woman was staring at me. If I made a wrong move, I was in for it. I knew that.

—Ilona Stein; USHMM/National Council of Jewish Women, Sarasota-Manatee section, RG-50.154*0026

Instead of three hours, it took three days for us to go by train from Kraków to Auschwitz in the hottest recorded summer. There were about 130 of us in one cattle car, and I must have dozed off. I woke up when the train stopped, and I thought I was losing my mind. Rain was falling on my head, but I knew we had started out with a covered roof. How could rain come in? Then I discovered that the humidity was so great that drops were falling from the ceiling. We had absolutely no food or water. Finally they opened the doors and I thought, *thank God we are in Auschwitz, and perhaps going to the gas chamber*. That would be the end of our journey. But we weren't gassed. They were so rushed that we only got shaved later, though we were full of lice, and then tattooed. By that time, we didn't care. We had ceased to be human beings. We were just numbers. It was already beyond us.

—Kate Bernath; USHMM, RG-50.030*0023

We got the tattoo three days after we arrived at Auschwitz. It was done with a little pen and ink and some tried to take it off, but it remained. They were surprised to get it because they were told it was only for prisoners. They said they were lucky because at least they did it on the arm. They could have done it on a cheek or on the forehead, and nobody would have stopped them.

—Lucia Franco; USHMM, RG-50.030*0452

When I told our new camp commandant, Gustav Sorge, nicknamed Iron Gustav, that I needed medication, he stared at me. "Medication?" he repeated. Then he booted me down the stairs. But his attitude changed because I was an obstetrician/gynecologist. He knew I was performing abortions. He even wanted to be present at one. He was a womanizer, with a female in his quarters every night. If a woman did become pregnant, he didn't have to ask around for a gynecologist. So he changed his attitude toward me. There was another physician, Dr. Kronzon, whom he beat up frequently. But he never laid a hand on me. I don't know why, but he was quite good to me after that first encounter, when he knocked me down the stairs.

—*David Klebanow; USHMM, RG-50.030*0104*

After Hitler became chancellor in 1933, I was the only Jew in my class. Every day we stood up and instead of saying, "Good morning, teacher," we had to raise our right arms and say, "Heil Hitler." But soon Jews were not allowed to say it anymore, which I didn't mind. Then I was told to leave the school, and I got a job in the photographic section of an art school. A very kind non-Jewish assistant had an SS boyfriend, but whenever he visited, I slipped into the darkroom, and she never said a word to him about me. But after a few months, Jews were not permitted to be there either. In 1938, on Kristallnacht in Berlin, I heard a woman walk past one of the stores that had been broken into, telling a non-Jewish little boy, "Go ahead, child. Why don't you take something." I also saw the fashionable synagogue, where I had my bar mitzvah in 1934, burn down. Then we got word that the gestapo was in the neighborhood, and it would be better if we didn't stay there for a couple of nights. So my mother, brother, and I stayed with other women, who were considered alright by the Nazis. All the Jews wanted to leave, but it was impossible. Somehow I got permission to go to London, where I got a job in the Photostat division of Kodak.

—Roger Bryan; USHMM, Gratz College Hebrew Education Society, RG-50.462*0076

We had a very good orchestra, with Jewish musicians and a Polish conductor. They played on Sundays when we weren't working. We also had a wonderful tenor from Italy who sang arias. It was an unbelievable contrast to what was happening there. The orchestra played in front of the horseshoe-shaped kitchen, where there was a big open space. It was the same place where the next day, they would hang inmates or beat them up. The orchestra played marches when we went to work. During summer they played outside. In the winter or when it rained, they played inside, next to the open windows. They usually played waltzes, but it was ridiculous. The orchestra used to play *The Merry Widow* and *Land of Smiles*.

—Jack Bass; USHMM, RG-50.562*0001

I never got my period in Theresienstadt. Many women will tell you that when they went to a concentration camp, it stopped. But they forget that they may not have gotten it in the ghetto. The first three or four weeks nothing happened and that was it. This was lucky, because we had no way of getting anything. You didn't worry about health in those days. We were young and thought nothing could touch us. It was fortunate that it stopped. We just forgot about it. It started again after we returned to Prague.

—Hana Fuchs Krasa; USHMM, RG-50.030*0479

161

At 6:00 a.m. I heard explosions and looked out the window to see smoke rising from [the] airport at Kaunas, Lithuania. I switched on the radio, found Berlin, and heard Dr. Joseph Goebbels, Minister of Propaganda, announcing war with Russia, which he said they would destroy, along with the Jews. A few days later, four German officers stepped out of their car and asked permission to have breakfast in our garden. They never asked about our religion, but I noticed the belt buckle on one of them said, "God Is With Us." I thought nothing would happen to us if that was their slogan. Slaughter of the Jews did not start immediately. The terror came instead from the Lithuanian people, which was surprising because Jews had lived there for eleven centuries and I had never experienced hatred toward Jews when I was in the Lithuanian Army. You cannot accuse the entire population, but bloodshed against Jews, especially in small towns and villages, could not be understood because we were part of the country. We were ordered to wear the star, and locked up behind a fence. The next day the Germans demanded five hundred professionals and college graduates to meet at city hall for paper work, with a promise they would return that night. On June 18, 1941, my brother went as directed. He never came back. After the war, I discovered that they had all been shot dead.

—Henry Kellen in an interview with Sandra Bradley for the USHMM exhibition "Hidden History of the Kovno Ghetto," RG-50.471*0006

We already knew that if they told us to have a shower, we would be gassed. I said, "Thank God, everything will end." We were naked. I expected gas to come out, but it was water. Could you believe it? "We're wet!" We waited for gas, but it was water. After a while, the Germans struck us with rubber whips. Ten of us were left nude. Others probably grabbed two dresses. I was shivering. The block leader gave us a quilt to cover ourselves. We didn't know whether to lie down in the mud, cover ourselves, or lie naked on the blanket. We put the quilt on the mud and it felt nice on top, but on the other side felt mud. We stayed five days like that, completely naked. Then they brought us rags. I don't know how I survived. It's really unbelievable.

—*Sally Abrams; USHMM/Gratz College Hebrew Education Society,*
RG-50.462*0026

My father was in the wholesale textile business and we were upper-middle class in Budapest. But Hungarian Nazis discontinued all Jewish schools, so I was raised and educated by private tutors, except for a half-year in a Swiss finishing school. I was finished with God. I went down the street and headed straight to the Basilica, where I was never allowed to go, and went into that Catholic church. Then I ate non-kosher meat on purpose. I was not hungry anymore, but I went to my girlfriend's house, who was married to a non-Jew, and I ate pork for the first time in my life. I threw up, but ate it. Then I had another portion. That was the end of my religion. I haven't been to a synagogue since, except when my two children had their bar mitzvahs. I got married to a very good Jew who went to the synagogue. I had such a strange experience when I made my peace with God. I said, "I forgive You, God. I wonder if You forgive me?" But I really didn't, because I saw people interned in Budapest before they were put in cattle cars. I saw people killed, many with side curls and beards, and little children with side locks and hats. Why? I don't think that any superbeing would let that happen.

—*Pearl Herling; USHMM/Gratz College Hebrew Education Society,*
RG-50.462*0109

We were about one thousand yards from the Landsberg camp, unaware that a massacre was taking place. Had we known, we could have saved many who were slaughtered at the last minute. We got to a railroad trestle bridge at 4:00 a.m., but the Germans had been shelling it to try and knock it out. About five hours later, we crossed over. We smelled smoke and saw prisoners, some alive, who had been locked in barracks, which had then been set on fire. We rushed in and saved about twenty. A lot of the bodies were nude and charred. Some were still glowing from the fires. We came upon hundreds of bodies scattered over the area. They had been dumped there. They were piled in some places six, seven, eight deep. It was just grotesque. And the stench, their appearance. Horrible, horrible atrocities were before us. We were in a state of shock. Maybe forty dead people were just hanging there, swaying in the breeze. It was hard to distinguish between the dead and the living. Their skulls looked so big for their scalps. Bones protruded from the sackcloth they were wearing. Pitifully, we couldn't do anything for them because we had nothing to give them. We were on a mission to seize and hold a causeway between Landsberg and Munich for six US divisions about forty miles in back of us. All we could do was radio back to the nearest units in our rear. Later, we found out that it was the prison where Hitler was confined and where he wrote *Mein Kampf.*

—*Philip Solomon; USHMM/Gratz College Hebrew Education Society, RG-50.462*0021*

The orchestra played especially when the Red Cross came for an inspection. They came over and asked a question, and you couldn't say anything bad because the German was standing right there. You were so afraid that you shivered when you saw those gestapos. That's how bad they were. The Red Cross used to give packages to Russian, Polish, Lithuanian, and Romanian inmates. Only Jews did not get packages.

Would you believe that? What was a Red Cross package? There was a piece of chocolate, maybe a couple of cigarettes, some fruit, or cake, or cookies. Whatever it was, it was a package. If you would ask me what I wanted, the Red Cross package or a million dollars, I wouldn't take the million dollars. You couldn't do anything with a million dollars there.

—Sholom Rosenheck; USHMM, RG-50.030*0529

The cruelty of the German women soldiers surpassed that of the men. For them to kick and beat was not unusual. We were constantly reminded that Jews should not exist and that we should be terminated. We were not worthwhile to live. We were taken to Birkenau, where it was subhuman. It was degrading when men came by the latrines to look at us. We slept on the floor, and very often when it rained, we had four to five inches of water on the ground and nowhere to lie down. The food was so bad, I vomited all the time, and it was hard to swallow. There was very little to drink and we suffered from thirst more than from hunger. There were rumors that we were going to Buchenwald to be exterminated. One girl had a nervous breakdown and was locked in a basement and then sprayed with ice cold water. We were marched out of the camp in March 1945, our faces green from working with chemicals and our hair orange-red. During the night, we sneaked away from the group. One side was forest; the other part open field. We walked to the field. In the morning, the English or American planes bombed us, but we lay in a ditch till they left. Some of the girls who went to the forest were killed. Later we heard noises and the first jeep arrived with American soldiers.

—Agnes Tennenbaum; USHMM/Phoenix Holocaust Survivors'
Association in affiliation with Cline Library of Northern Arizona
University, RG-50.060*0055

I saw it. I was passing by and witnessed them burning bodies. They didn't want to have a grave with bodies, so they burned them. They excavated all the bodies from the mass grave and set fire to them. There was a pile of dead people when I got there. A member of the gestapo and a Ukrainian had whipped entire families and pushed them to the gas chamber. On the other side, they dragged the corpses to the grave, where they burned victims. It was a hard job because everyone was entangled with others, and they had to be pulled apart. While I was there, big cranes, like those used to shovel earth, were used to lift the dead out of the grave, swivel around, and drop them in the fire. Then they filled it up with a lot of dirt. I can draw it with a pencil and show you exactly how it was.

—*Isadore Helfing in an interview with Sandra Bradley for the USHMM film* Testimony, *RG-50.042*0014*

There was anti-Semitism in Lithuania even before the Russians occupied it at the beginning of the war. My father bought a bicycle for my brother, who was a year older than me. One day we went cycling and I begged him to let me ride his. Suddenly, two non-Jewish boys shoved a stick in the springs and broke my brother's bicycle. We chased them and accused them of breaking the bike. They got to a church, where a policemen let them in. One of the boys put his foot in the door and said, "Go away, you zhids!" I told him he broke the bike, but he kept telling us to get out. I wasn't able to fight him, but it was an experience. We went home and my father got it repaired. But I had a feeling that I was not welcome because I was Jewish.

—*Israel Gruzin; USHMM, RG-50.030*0088*

I had some lucky breaks in Auschwitz. At roll call, the SS in charge asked if anyone knew Hebrew and German fluently. I couldn't for the life of me wonder why he asked that question. I spoke reasonably fluent Hebrew, so I raised my arm, together with one or two colleagues who were at a Jewish school with me in Berlin. The Jews of Salonika had arrived and they only spoke Greek and Hebrew. The Germans needed interpreters to find out their names, ages, place of birth, and professions. We had an opportunity to save some of their lives because if they said they were teachers or violinists, they would probably be sent to the gas chamber. But if they were carpenters, bricklayers, welders, or locksmiths, they were safe. So very often, Salonika Jews would say they were teachers or violinists and we translated it as bricklayer, welder, or laborer, without the knowledge of either them or the SS. You could almost say that my knowledge of Hebrew saved my life.

—*Gert Silberbard Silver; USHMM, RG-50.562*0010*

One evening when we came back from work, there was a roll call and one laborer was missing. Whenever someone was absent, there was a circus. Everybody had to remain standing, but there was still one shy. He was not in the barrack where he was supposed to be. Maybe he was hiding in the woods. So they said they would look for him, beating all over with clubs. At length they came back laughing. They had found him hanging from a tree. The SS man said the next time one of us Jews decided to hang ourselves, we should let them know in advance so they wouldn't have to go about searching. For months afterward, I always said to myself that the man who hanged himself was the only one with brains among us, because he killed himself in the first week at Ebensee, before he suffered so much.

—*George Havas; USHMM, RG-50.030*0378*

Again the cattle cars to nowhere. As the American troops came closer, they decided to evacuate us wherever there were no bombs being dropped. If they took us north and the bombs fell, we would turn east. We went in circles. The Americans bombed the train, killing people. One of them was my wife's cousin, killed by the Americans. Nobody cast blame, but he was killed by them. The only reason we knew the war was over was because Germans no longer guarded us. The first open truckloads of soldiers were black troops. We had never seen a black person before and I thought, "Here comes the Holocaust." We didn't know who they were. It was strange and scary. But they turned out to be the best-hearted and friendliest people. They threw us whatever they had—chewing gum, cigarettes, pens, pencils, whatever they had in their pockets. Some of them had tears in their eyes. What we saw in them, they had seen in us. They didn't know what to expect. We didn't look like normal people because we were hungry and either swollen or skinny. I didn't want to pick up typhus from the camp, so I escaped in the dark. Bullets whizzed by, but they were either bad shots or didn't want to hit us. I met up with a friend in Munich and we took revenge wherever we could. Without hesitation, we killed, robbed, and plundered. Whatever we did to the Germans was out of revenge. Nobody should ever say that people who did these things were cruel or bad. They should be considered heroes. The war was over and we were trying to straighten out our lives.

—*Manfred Simon; USHMM/National Council of Jewish Women,*
Sarasota-Manatee section, RG-50.154*0025

I got a call about 4:00 a.m. from the president of our congregation to say our synagogue was on fire and to go there as fast as possible. The sky looked on fire, but it took me only five minutes to get there. There was nothing I could do, but I will never forget it. The cantor, who lived next door to the synagogue, had salvaged one of the Torah scrolls. About two hundred people stood around. No one recognized me, so I ran home and woke up my wife, mother, and uncle. Shortly afterward, my mother-in-law phoned to say her physician husband had been arrested and that we should try to flee. The phone line was already bugged and was cut off, so we didn't get the full story. But I wouldn't have dared run into the streets or hide someplace or even run up the mountains, because they would have killed me. We were eating breakfast when a policeman came in and asked if we would go by ourselves to the court building, which was also the jail. My uncle and I walked out, but people knew what was happening because the synagogue was burning and the windows of all the Jewish shops had been destroyed. Glass lay all over the street. That was Kristallnacht, and the following afternoon, November 10, 1938, my wife and other women were told to clean up the mess. It was terribly degrading, but they were not molested. I spent three days in a jail cell, one of them all alone. It was terrible. Then we were shipped out with other Jews.

—Herbert Prover; USHMM/Holocaust Memorial Foundation of Illinois, RG-50.031*0057

The Germans didn't have boxcars anymore so they put us on flat cars, but we never really moved because by that time, April 1945, the railroads were bombed out. We had no food at all once we got on the train at Allach, a satellite camp of Dachau. But we were allowed off the idling train and ate grass for the last few days. We really feared the end because we always thought they would kill everybody. Overnight, at the end of April, the guards disappeared without explanation. Around noon, the first American tanks approached. It was Patton's Third Army.

—Herbert Finder; USHMM/Gratz College Hebrew Education Society, RG-50.462*0035

We knew what the Nazis were capable of because of what they had done to Polish Jews living in Germany, the concentration camps and the euthanasia program. The socialists and communists were persecuted and then came Kristallnacht. But within days, the Germans packed up everything, even taking telephone wires, and left us as the Soviets arrived. On one street, I saw Jews waving a red flag and throwing eggs and other things at the departing Germans. You could only do that if you knew they wouldn't respond. It wasn't that the Russians loved the Jews, but they had freed them from the Germans. Everybody knew about the purges in the Soviet Union, but they were glad to see the Russians. Yet I'm sure the Germans remembered Białystok, and that the missiles came from the Jewish sector.

—*Irene Shapiro; USHMM, RG-50.233*0125*

In 1943 our ghetto was liquidated and my younger sister and I were sent to Dunawerke labor camp and my pharmacist father to Kaiserwald concentration camp. My late mother was a dentist. My younger sister, Raya, and I stuck together and looked after each other. There was loneliness and abandonment. My sister had gone through a very hard time in the ghetto because she was only a little girl, and she was very hungry and undernourished. She didn't have her friends and we didn't know what to do with her. She spent most of her time waiting for me, my aunt, or my father, to come back and bring her something to eat. My sister, even now, suffers very strong bouts of depression. She does not remember things. I don't know if she blocked it out or if it was intentional, but when she needs something, she has to ask me. I was four years older than her but assumed the role of mother. The whole world crumbled around her. I was never a teenager, but she was never even a child. So many lost years. She hardly had any school. There was no joy in her life. It was just misery, hunger, and cold. It was six years of indescribable suffering, moral and physical. She lost everything. She lost her mother, her father, her aunt, her house, her friends, her school, her ballet, her piano lessons—everything that was important. Even if the other horrors hadn't occurred, just the moving around, the uprooting . . . she lost everything. She was only eleven years old in the ghetto.

—Lily Margules; USHMM, RG-50.233*0084

About five or six o'clock in the morning, the train stopped and the grown-up people said it's a concentration camp. I didn't know what a concentration camp was. Immediately they [the Nazis] began shouting, "Raus! Raus! Raus!" People were wearing striped things and striped caps and we still didn't understand that. Then we saw chimneys. We had to jump down and it was pretty high. Some Jewish inmates of Auschwitz helped people jump down. We weren't allowed to take our suitcases, which they told us to leave behind. Then we had to go through a selection. Everywhere, there were German officers with dogs and truncheons. They rushed everybody, right and left, right and left. Then we realized what was happening. People going to one side were disabled people and women with babies or children. There were screams because they took a child away and ordered the mother to the other side. Can you imagine a mother giving up a child? The mother ran toward it and she was beaten, but she was left with the child. We found out soon afterward from the guards that an hour after the train arrived, those people were dead. They were gassed. Would they take us away to the gas chambers? As a child of fourteen, it never entered my mind that I would be killed. I couldn't accept that I would die, that eventually it would be the end.

—Zygmund Shipper; USHMM, funded by a grant from the Lerner Family Foundation, RG-50.030*0526

While in bed in Frankfurt, we heard the Nazis marching and singing, "When Jewish blood squirts from a knife, then all goes doubly well." I put my head under the bed covers. It was horrible, horrible. They had taken over several houses, with their guards in front. I had to pass by daily, so you can imagine my feelings. I always turned my head to the other side, so as not to look at them. It was horrible. We knew something was going on, but nobody really opened their eyes. People said, "After the storm, the sun comes out again." They said it wouldn't last long. Whenever my husband was on business in one of the smaller cities, he came home and said some people were terribly scared of the Christian people. So we left Germany in February 1937 and went to Montevideo, Uruguay.

—*Ada Speyer; USHMM, RG-50.150*0038*

I was in the kitchen during the uprising at Auschwitz. Only one crematorium was destroyed. It would have been better if uprisings were at all the crematoriums. The SS were shooting at everybody, even outside the camp. I saw two blond, blue-eyed gypsy boys whom the kapos had saved. The SS sent out dogs to hunt for them. They were caught, brought back to the gas chamber, and shot in the head. It took three minutes to kill in a dry chamber and twenty minutes when it was wet. They sprayed water in the chamber to clean up the bodies. It was the worst death because some were still alive. No one could say they did not see or smell the crematoriums. You could smell them from miles away. I left Auschwitz because I was a good worker. I worked for a week in a factory making bomber planes; then we were taken to Sachsenhausen.

—*Mark Weinberg; USHMM/Holocaust Memorial Foundation of Illinois, RG-50.031*0075*

My mother, sister, and I walked to where Mengele stood. He pulled my mother, forty-seven, to one side, and us to the other. I said, "I want to go with my mother." I followed her, but he pulled me out and sent me to the other side. She wanted me to take care of my sister, six years younger than me. In a symbolic way, my mother in Auschwitz gave me the task of taking care of my sister. That was what she meant. We knew her fate right away. We were taken to the showers at Birkenau. We were greeted by being told to take off our clothes until we were naked. Both men and women were there. First we were shaved by a man, our heads and all the hair on our bodies. My sister and I, naked and shaven, were taken to the showers. We already knew that the showers meant death, which we all expected. As it happened, we really did take showers and nobody was killed. Then we were given so-called clothing. One shoe had high heels and the other low heels. We also had a sort of shmata and were led to the barracks. I found out after the war that my father was probably killed during a forced march from Auschwitz to another camp.

—*Paula Szmajer Biren; USHMM, funded by a grant from Carole and Maurice Berk, RG-50.030*0500*

Every day, my late brother and I washed our faces with our own urine so we wouldn't get scabs from the lice. It killed them. It was common sense. Others had faces full of crust, pimples, and scabs. I kept clean, even my bed. A little water trickled out of tiny faucets in a basin in our room. Every day, as soon as I woke up at 4:00 a.m., I washed myself in this cold water. And I washed myself before going to sleep. They didn't find a single louse on me. You did a lot of things to survive. Feelings were dead. You didn't have feelings for anything.

—*Jacob Brodman; USHMM/National Council of Jewish Women, Sarasota-Manatee section, RG-50.154*0008*

"One day they selected twenty-five hundred Jews over 50 years old. They said they were going to a special camp, and the Jews believed them. They took only the best clothes they had and jewelry—only as much as they could carry. They had to assemble in the market. It was 10 am." Shmuel spoke very softly. "Over twenty-five hundred people. My mother, my sisters, and my two brothers-in-law." At about 2 pm a few hundred SS men came and surrounded the market, setting up machine guns. "You can't get through. Who tried, he was killed. And then, after that they let in about a thousand. I can't believe it, Ukrainians and Latvians. All drunk. You can't imagine how drunk. Drunk, Meshuga." Shmuel sighed but he continued with tears in his throat. They were armed with "hammers, axes, knives, anything else they could get. The gestapo ordered the old people to undress and pile up all their belongings, which were carted away. Then they loosed the drunken men into the marketplace. And they started killing. Just like in a butchery, killing, cutting to pieces. I think that half of them just died of..." Shmuel didn't finish the sentence. Then after a few seconds he continued. "My mother was sick, heart trouble...I don't know if she was alive or dead. From the shock she died, you know. Twenty-five hundred people were just cut to pieces like sausages."

—A Typical Extraordinary Jew: From Tarnow to Jerusalem
by Calvin Goldscheider and Jeffrey M. Green

Every time the sirens wailed and bombs fell, people smashed store windows and looted the insides. My sister and I were walking in an Antwerp street while my mother helped out in a bar, when we passed a shoe and clothing store. I kept looking at a pair of white boots in the window, a silly thing to do in the middle of a war. Oh, I would so love to have those white boots. A lot of windows were shattered and many people were coming out with packages. Inside was an absolute mess. Somehow we got in and I snatched them, a pair for my sister, two raincoats, and another coat. We didn't even wait to try them on; we fled. We both loved what we'd got. At the bar, my mother asked what in the world we were carrying. I told her and explained that the store was open and everyone was helping themselves. She told us we were not supposed to take things without paying for them, but she didn't take them away from us. Later, as I was walking down the street, someone grabbed me from behind. It was the owner of the store. He made me take off the boots and raincoat, which I wore whether it rained or not, and that was the end of that. I was told I had stolen things and it was a long time before I stole again. My mother was faced with a dilemma because it wasn't the time to teach children honesty. We just survived.

—*Flora Mendelowitz Singer; USHMM, RG-50.030*0356*

We lived in Antwerp, Belgium, when there was a curfew only for Jews. Then we couldn't go to school; teachers couldn't teach; doctors couldn't practice. My father, a plumber, couldn't work. We couldn't go to the theater. Our civil rights were taken away. We had to wear the yellow star. In August 1942, my father received a notice to report to the train station, to go to a labor camp in northern France. My father said the war could not last much longer and he would be back shortly. At that time, we had heard about labor camps but not concentration camps. That's why my father decided to go. My mother, father, little sister, and I went to the train station. My father said to me, "You're now the man in the house. You'll have to take care of your mother and sister until I come back." I told him I would. That was the last time I saw my father.

—*Daniel Goldsmith; USHMM/Gratz College Hebrew Education Society, RG-50.462*0106*

I lined up with my mother for the selection at Auschwitz. If you refused anything, or if they didn't like you, they would slap you across the face with gloves, or shoot you. We came to a person who differentiated between the old and the young. My mother was a heart patient and made the mistake of telling him she was very sick. Naturally, he separated us, taking her to one side and me to the other. She walked on. I stared at her, but she never turned around. She just continued walking. From that moment, I lost my emotions. I don't remember responding to anything. I did not know how to cry. I did not do anything. I did not say anything. I just tried to obey to avoid any physical abuse.

—*Friedel Treitel; USHMM/National Council of Jewish Women, Sarasota-Manatee section, RG-50.154*0027*

After the war, when my mother would fix a chicken and try to burn off the little feathers left, I couldn't stand the odor and had to get out of the house. I couldn't smell that odor, which had got into my nostrils at Ohrdruf concentration camp, where I arrived with US forces in April 1945. The odor never leaves. I've never bought a pair of striped pajamas because that's what they were wearing. I kept salivating, and I had that feeling you get before throwing up. Some of the dead were in grotesque positions, leaning against a tree with their legs covered. Some in fetal positions. Others in the barracks were so weak that if the one inmate next to him was dead, he didn't have the strength to push him off. We talked briefly, me in fractured Yiddish, and I understood a bit of German. Both of us would cry. There was a whole cacophony of languages, but we knew they were laborers and the majority were Jewish. They'd love us and kiss us and we'd hug them and give them whatever we had. My platoon was the first to take casualties to hospitals in the rear, and we did whatever we could to make them comfortable. I couldn't help but think that there, but

Jews captured during the suppression of the Warsaw Ghetto Uprising, in Poland were marched to where they gathered for deportation to concentration camps.

USHMM, courtesy of the National Archives and Records Administration, College Park, MD.

Five-year-old Avram Rosenthal and two-year-old Emanuel Rosenthal in the Kovno ghetto in Lithuania, before their deportation and murder.

USHMM, courtesy of Shraga Wainer.

A man committing suicide clung to an electric fence in Mauthausen-Gusen concentration camp in Germany.

USHMM, courtesy of the National Archives and Records Administration, College Park, MD.

SS troops arrested the Jewish department heads of the Brauer armaments factory in Poland, during the Warsaw Ghetto Uprising.

USHMM, courtesy of the National Archives and Records Administration, College Park, MD.

A corpse photographed in a crematorium oven in Dachau concentration camp, thirty minutes after liberation.

USHMM, courtesy of William Landgren.

Former Auschwitz commandant Rudolf Höss, about to be hanged outside the Auschwitz-Birkenau concentration camp, where he presided over the greatest mass murder in history.

Courtesy of the Auschwitz-Birkenau State Museum.

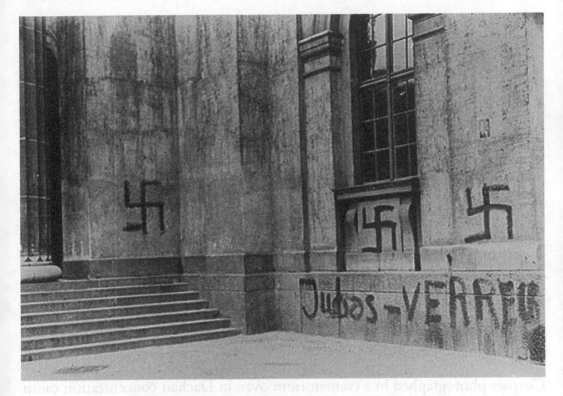

Swastikas and other graffiti painted on the Kottbusser Tor Synagogue in Kreuzberg, Berlin, Germany.

USHMM, courtesy of Abraham Pisarek.

Corpses photographed in a crematorium oven in Dachau concentration camp in Germany, just thirty minutes after liberation.

USHMM, courtesy of William Landgren.

General Dwight Eisenhower, Supreme Allied Commander (center, with hands on hips), listens to a survivor explain the use of gallows at the newly-liberated Ohrdruf concentration camp in Germany.

USHMM, courtesy of the National Archives and Records Administration, College Park, MD.

Jewish women and children forced to wear yellow Stars of David await selection, and, for many, death by gassing in Auschwitz-Birkenau.

USHMM, courtesy of Yad Vashem, Israel (public domain).

Jews lined up awaiting selection at Auschwitz-Birkenau concentration camp in Poland.

USHMM, courtesy of Yad Vashem, Israel (public domain).

German prisoners of war watched filmed newscasts of German concentration camps.

USHMM, courtesy of Joseph Eaton.

Two starved survivors stand near a barbed wire fence as American troops liberate Ebensee concentration camp in Austria.

USHMM, courtesy of the National Archives and Records Administration, College Park, MD.

Holocaust survivor Israel Gluck's charcoal drawing of a skeleton running alongside padlocked cattle cars bound for Auschwitz. The people inside the padlocked cars were unaware that they would be gassed or used for slave labor.

USHMM, courtesy of Mordecai E. Schwartz.

Holocaust survivor Israel Gluck's charcoal drawing of an SS guard forcing two emaciated prisoners to hop because they didn't remove their caps quickly enough when he passed by.

USHMM, courtesy of Mordecai E. Schwartz.

Jewish men publicly hanged by the German police in the Zduńska Wola ghetto in Poland.

USHM, courtesy of Jerzy Tomaszewski.

for the grace of God, go I. My grandparents, aunts, uncles, and cousins were wiped out. I learned later that they were stuffed in a burning barn, and those trying to escape were machine gunned to death.

—*Joe Friedman; USHMM, RG-50.030*0380*

We worked outside, carrying rocks almost bigger than myself, when we looked up at planes overhead. We hoped they would bomb our camp, Auschwitz. An SS man saw us and screamed, "Do you think help will come from those planes? No! Your help will come from that! You see the chimneys? You are going there! You won't go out from here." As punishment, we had to crawl on our knees toward the soup.

—*Chana Mehler; USHMM, RG-50.030*0275*

At camp Gross-Rosen in eastern Germany, I met a fellow from my hometown who said to me, "You see the two chimneys? They work day and night. Any time they have a transport, get out, because you won't come out of here alive." If you did something wrong they took a big stone, one hundred pounds maybe, and tied it to the back of your shoulders and then made you walk around the whole day with the stone, in the sun, without water to drink or something to eat. After you collapsed, they took you to the crematorium. That was the end. I was lucky somehow. I was there only eight days and then shipped out to Wüstegiersdorf.

—*Nathan Form; USHMM/Gratz College Hebrew Education Society, RG-50.462*0079*

177

The Germans removed skin and then tanned it. Tanned skins were given as gifts to certain guards and visitors, who used them to bind books. I witnessed SS men coming out of block 2 carrying tanned skins under their arms. When the camp [Auschwitz] was liberated by the Americans on April 11, 1945, they found tattooed and tanned skins in block 2, the pathological block.

—Alfred Balachowsky, Nuremberg trials, vol. 6, 1/29/46; The Avalon Project, Yale University

Christian was a very sweet, young, naive little girl who was picked up in the street and didn't know why she was in the camp. She came from France, so we always spoke French. Somebody gave me a little bit of soup and some coffee and I ran back to the barracks to feed her, but she could not make it and died in my arms. I pretended she was asleep and did not tell anyone for two days because I wanted to have her food. Then I was afraid they would discover that she was dead and that she would start smelling. I told the block leader that Christian died and they took her away. They just piled them up outside the barracks. The pile of corpses was six or seven feet high in front of each barrack. For days I could not look at her because I knew she was lying there. One day I decided to go and see her. When I looked up at her, something puzzled me. Somebody had stolen her skirt. She was lying down, naked as a skeleton from the waist down, which in Birkenau was a muselmann, meaning before you died you were skin and bones. She had a navy blue jacket, but it wasn't blue; it was grayish or white. Why would somebody steal a skirt and change a jacket from a blue one to a white one and just leave her there? So I leaned over closer to the pile of dead and saw that Christian's navy blue jacket was covered with lice. They were crawling all over her body and jacket and made the navy blue jacket

[look] white. I almost fell over the dead; I was in such shock. It was too much for me and I never looked at Christian again.

—Lilly Appelbaum Malnik in an interview with Sandra Bradley for the USHMM film Testimony, *RG-50.042*0020*

You must have experienced it yourself; otherwise, you cannot understand what we went through. I've run into a number of them who don't understand what Nazism meant at that time, what it did to the Jews. I had a conversation with a man I know quite well. He said he didn't understand how we German Jews didn't go to the nearest gun store, buy a rifle, and defend ourselves. This is sheer nonsense. I knew what went on and what the circumstances were like. It was absolutely impossible. If I had shot a German in those days, they would have killed one thousand Jews within ten minutes. I couldn't understand how a well-educated and informed man could think like that. It was inconceivable to me.

—Fred Goldman; USHMM, RG-50.106*0146

Well, unfortunately, the smell was the burning of those bodies. Then it was people who had dysentery. It was awful. I had to smell, and we watched a lot of those people die. Many were beaten to death just for that alone because they could not keep their bowels … and they had no way of going to a bathroom.

—Cecilie Klein-Pollack in an interview with Sandra Bradley for the USHMM film Testimony, *RG-50.042*-0018*

179

Our train went back and forth in Germany because the allies were on all sides. German kids stood on mounds near the railway tracks and yelled, "Where are you going? You're going into the fire!" Wave after wave of warplanes bombed as our train stopped in a forest to hide. The commandant didn't know what to do, so he went to the nearest village to phone Berlin. When he returned he said he was sorry, but he had orders to shoot all of us. Heavy machine guns were set up to liquidate all of us, but the German Army retreated past our train. We were really scared because they might have thought of killing us as they retreated; but by morning, it was a beautiful day and all was quiet. Children went down to a nearby stream. We saw the commandant wave to us as he rode away on a bicycle toward the village. Only seven of the seventy guards remained, and they were Ukrainians. Then we heard a rumbling sound of metal and saw a tank on a hill pointing its barrel toward the train. A soldier jumped off and ran toward us. A surge of people ran to meet him and kissed his boots. The soldier also wept and told us President Roosevelt had died on April 12, 1945. Suddenly a guard pointed his weapon at the American, but two of our people jumped on him and took his gun away. We told the soldier to kill the guard, but he said he had orders only to take prisoners. He was a young soldier called Schwarz from Brooklyn. Then we realized we were liberated.

—*Martin Spett; USHMM, RG-50.030*0218*

The kapos at Auschwitz told us to look at the smoke and smell it. They said it was from the crematoriums. We didn't know. We had never even heard of such a thing as gas chambers. As we walked on the right side into the camp, we looked back and saw my parents, my father, my mother, and my sister, with the little children. That was the last time I saw them.

—*William Klein; USHMM, RG-50.106*0123*

They put us in a barrack where twelve hundred slept in one room. A big barrel in front of the door was the sanitary facility, which we had to carry out every morning. In the beginning, we carried stones from one block, back and forth. It was tormenting, with no purpose. Our shoes were never tied. It was terrible. When we got back, everything was moist and smelled. And the mice, maybe rats, who knows? When they walked over us and woke us up we just pushed them off. We didn't care and went back to sleep.

—*Lily Blayer; USHMM/Holocaust Memorial Foundation of Illinois,*
RG-50.030*0005

In 1936, I was fifteen and going through the Tiergarten in Berlin when we were stopped because Hitler was passing by a block away. A storm trooper stood almost directly in front of me with a revolver in his holster. I wondered what would happen if I grabbed the revolver and ran toward Hitler to try and kill him. It was totally irrational. I had never had a revolver in my hand and was a terrible runner. Yet it was almost like a compulsion for me to fantasize. But even if I managed to kill him, ten others would take over. I was not worried about being killed. I guess I was going to lead my people out of bondage and be their savior. It was in keeping with my adolescent sense of needing to be a hero and feeling omnipotent. But the one thing that stopped me was a fear that they would get hold of my mother and sister, and torture them. We had heard horror stories of eggs heated to boiling point and then placed in women's vaginas. The whole thing was a daydream. It was totally pointless to try and resist the prevailing atmosphere.

—*Susan Faulkner; USHMM/Gratz College Hebrew Education*
Society, RG-50.462*0005

About mid-morning, people looked out and didn't see any Germans in uniforms. If they saw a German, he was running away. They told everybody something was wrong, something's going on. The kapo came in and said the Americans were coming. But if we went out then, we might run into a German who could do us harm. I was too weak and too young, still twenty years old. The others had opened up the stores and brought food back to the barracks. An older fellow came in with a jar of honey, which I jumped up and grabbed. He had honey all over his face and was very angry, but I ate it. Some hours later, the Americans came in jeeps. They didn't know how to feed us and gave us too much food. Hundreds of people were lying outside, hardly breathing because their stomachs were swollen. But then the Americans got somebody in who advised them what to cook and what to serve; otherwise, we would die.

—*Ernie Pollak; USHMM, RG-50.030*0582*

We reached the entrance door of the inner crematorium and found ourselves inside a large hall. They ordered us to get undressed. We did not want to, and they began shooting. Then they ordered us to hang our clothes on the nails and to remember the serial number, so that when we came out, we would know where to find our clothes. This was a deliberate fraud, which we already understood. One of the Sonderkommandos, who was working there, told us in Yiddish, "Boys, at least don't show them that you are worried. Sing!" Some of us, like me, were petrified and could not utter a sound. Others began to recite the prayer of confession, and yet others actually sang. They opened a large door and there was absolute darkness, apart from the opening by which we had come in. They closed the door and then, for the first time, I heard crying. Then the door opened again and we were told to return to the same hall where we had been before. I was terrified. The German ordered me to fall to the floor, get up, and

182

run to the wall and back. Then he sent me to the right-hand side. In this way, he chose fifty boys. The other boys saw that some kind of selection was being made and they began moving to our side, but the SS men kept us apart. The same Sonderkommando told us it was the first time he had seen anyone taken out of the gas chamber alive. We were ordered to turn around. The other boys, nine hundred to one thousand, were taken into the gas chamber. The door was closed, and we were ordered to get dressed. We understood we had been taken out because there was a shortage of manpower. I never met any of those other boys again.

—*Nachum Hoch, Eichmann trial, session 71, 6/8/1961, Nizkor Project, League for Human Rights of B'nai Brith Canada*

Walking back to the camp, I saw a large onion ahead of me on the side of the road. I looked back to see where the guard was and then told the person behind me to step a little bit out of formation and cover me. I bent down, picked it up, and put it in my jacket to take it back to the camp, because we shared whatever one of the three of us found or stole. Then we were lined up on the roll call area to be frisked, something that happened randomly as we worked with tools and could have made a weapon like a knife. What was I to do with the onion? If I threw it away and said it wasn't me, everybody would be collectively punished. If I said it was me, they would beat me to a pulp because they wouldn't believe that I found it. They would think I had stolen it. The only way out was to eat the onion quickly, together with its peel and roots. Tears flowed down my cheeks and my nose ran. My forehead was sweating even though it was a cold and wintry day. But I finished it before he came over to me. I didn't dare breathe while he frisked me.

—*Edgar Krasa; USHMM, RG-50.030*0478*

When we walked through Leipzig, American bombers flew over and I didn't flee to the bunkers, where they rushed most of us. We were not scared. We felt nothing at being bombed. If I had to die, I wanted to die then and there. At the end of the forced march, the female German guards asked what it was like to be a woman without hair. It was their worst fear. They agonized because the war was ending and if they were taken as prisoners, they would have their hair shaved off. That was their concern.

—*Cyla (Tsilah) Kinori, University of Southern California Shoah Foundation, The Institute for Visual History and Education, VHA interview code 22398*

A lady appeared in our Richmond, Virginia, store and wanted me to talk about my experiences, but I told her to give me advance notice. The next time I said I'd be delighted, but when she came, I just couldn't reminisce. Ask any American soldier what they went through and they can't talk either. A doctor came in with a lady and she noticed my accent. She told me to ask where he was in 1945. He didn't mind and said he was in Dachau, and she was his nurse. I embraced and hugged him and gave him a kiss. He was my hero. All the soldiers are heroes, every one of them. I was liberated by Russians, but that doesn't matter. Look at what the Americans did. They suffered, believe me. I wish people would give them more respect. They deserve it, and their families. A lot of soldiers were mistreated and hurt and also put in concentration camps. I tell them all; they are my heroes. The first time I went to the US Holocaust Memorial Museum, I couldn't go in. I couldn't look. A lady recognized a photo of herself when she was seventeen and started screaming. I went in a few times later and saw German soldiers beating someone. Immediately my father and those Nazis came to mind. I just couldn't look. Then I came to the cattle car, and it got to me. A lady collapsed there. I still don't understand it.

Why? What had we done? When I was growing up I thought everyone was nice, and kind, and good. Then I saw all those things happen.

*—Sonia Brodecki; USHMM, made possible by a grant from Jeff and
Toby Herr, RG-50.549.02*0071*

We were put on a train and transported to Leipzig and back to Holland, not long after the end of the war. Our train went through Berlin
and everybody cheered because all you could see were bombed out
buildings and many walls held up by poles. Along the way, the Germans looked up at our Red Cross train with their mouths open. The
Dutch people would say "Heil Hitler" at them and laugh and laugh.

—Doriane Kurz; USHMM, RG-50.030*0120

When we were leaving the Łódź ghetto for Auschwitz, they told us
to take whatever we could carry, so we took a lot of things. But when
we got to the boxcars, they didn't let us take anything. They herded
us into the boxcars while our possessions remained outside. Then
they closed the doors, and we moved out. Hunger in the camps was
so great that I saw a son steal food from his father, and the father
died a few days later. Bread was hidden under a mattress, but it was
still stolen. People don't realize what hunger means. They couldn't
control themselves. At the beginning of 1945, when they moved
inmates from one camp to another, there were a lot of sick people
included, and they died in the boxcars. Hunger was so acute that I
saw people biting and eating the flesh of the dead.

*— Berek Latarus; USHMM/Jewish Community Relations
Council, Anti-Defamation League of Minnesota and the Dakotas,
RG-50.156*0032*

185

We had to go to the latrines when ordered to go, but one night I had to go. The female kapo wouldn't let me and another girl go until we had emptied a bucket of excrement, about two and a half feet high. It was like a drum with handles and we would have to carry it to a ditch and pour it in before we could use the latrines. It was not pleasant, especially if we had an accident when there was no way of washing it off or putting on clean clothes. It was pretty full and we tried to carry it very carefully, so that it wouldn't splash over us. These were probably the worst times, probably much worse than not having enough food.

—*Anna Maxell Ware; USHMM, RG-50.030*0427*

There were selections all the time. Gongs would sound, whistles blew, and we'd have to go outside and remove our one garment and then file by the SS. Sometimes they selected people whose ribs showed, or who were pale and sickly. They would take them to the gas chambers. By then we knew. In November 1944, I was selected. We were taken to the gas chambers and I could smell the odor of burning flesh. We were told to undress. They ushered us into a room with bleachers and benches. We sat there, two thousand at a time. Half of us went through the doors into the gas chambers. We never heard from them again. The other half, where I was, waited our turn. When an air raid siren sounded, they stopped and took us back to our bunks. It was a very close call. After that, I found myself in a selection again. I was put in a cattle car and taken to the Guben labor camp near Berlin. I promised that if I survived the nightmare that was Auschwitz, I would talk about it. I have lived up to that promise.

—*Judy Freeman; USHMM/Gratz College Hebrew Education Society,*
RG-50.462*0081

We had scarcely arrived at Stutthof concentration camp when we were welcomed by blows from the same criminals, with green triangles pointing downward, that we had known at Auschwitz. Out of roughly one thousand to fifteen hundred men at registration, only five hundred were left. We were given a thin slice of bread daily, and in our threadbare clothes, during very frosty weather and amid beatings, we had to offload gravel and cement from the barges. The SS men made fires and warmed themselves not far away. Some prisoners who tried to get near them were immediately shot by the guards. The Germans used another trick. They would come over to an exhausted man, no longer able to lift his shovel, and say, "Why not sit down here, sir? Be seated and rest a little." Anyone who did not work, froze. Naturally, this man would freeze on the spot, in the midst of a pool of mud, unable to get up again. Opposite us was a women's camp. We were able to get close and saw women sitting in the snow and frost, covered only in blankets. The block did not have a roof, so they sat there, froze, and died where they were.

—*Gedalia Ben-Zvi, Eichmann trial, session 71, 8/6/61, Nizkor Project, League for Human Rights of B'nai Brith Canada*

On Christmas day, 1944, we were working at the IG Farben factory at Buna, when two laborers ran for cover in a shed, because Jews were prohibited from sheltering in cement bunkers. Pressure from a bomb dropped close by killed them. I was standing in a doorway about fifty yards away when the blast from another bomb flung me into a cabin. The windows shattered, the door broke, and timber fell down, shielding me from further harm. That's why my spine hurts. But it saved me. The odds are one in a million that you survive such a bomb.

—*Jacob Brodman; USHMM/National Council of Jewish Women, Sarasota-Manatee section, RG-50.154*0008*

A Ukrainian took a liking to me and ran through the barrack screaming, "Where's the beast?" We all knew he had immoral intentions. He threatened to shoot everyone unless I came forward. He must have been drunk because his behavior was totally out of place, even for a German. While everyone hid, he tried to kiss me, but I minimized what he had done and managed to stop him. A week or two later, they took about three hundred of us to Majówka concentration camp. Two very large graves had been dug and the same Ukrainian was in charge of us. He stood at the edge of the grave, saw me, and said, "You have one minute to say your prayers, then you'll all be shot." I knew that animal was capable of doing anything. My mother looked like a ghost. I had to do something, so I jumped on his back and started to choke him. I put my legs tightly around him so he couldn't walk. We both fell and Germans ran up and pulled us apart. A girl cried out for help, saying I may have fainted. I played dead. He shot me, but didn't know that it only grazed my skin and bone, leaving a lot of blood. I didn't move. It was getting dark, the searchlight was on, and Russian planes flew over and bombed. They turned off the searchlight and chased everyone to the barracks. I thought all was lost and everyone had been taken to the crematorium. When the searchlight came on again, the Ukrainian came to check on me. He raised my arm, but I let it drop like a piece of wood. Then he searched me for money and valuables and left. I dragged myself under the barrack. In the morning I heard them, squeezed myself out, and I saw my father turn white and my mother and brother were crying. Everybody was agitated and excited. They hid me, but the Ukrainian found out what had happened, charged in, and said he would shoot everyone unless I came out. I was ready to die and wasn't even scared. He pulled me out and locked me in a storage room. About an hour later, the head of the camp, who wanted to send everyone to Auschwitz, asked what had happened. I told him I had wanted to plead for everyone's life when the Ukrainian shot me and I fell and blacked out. My husband was listening with others and surreptitiously gave the camp commander a diamond ring. The official then accompanied me to the infirmary.

—Guta Blass Weintraub; USHMM, RG-50.030*0250

In January 1945, I had survived the forced death march out of Auschwitz when our train slowed down near Munich. You could see the havoc wrought by planes bombing the area. We were in a wooded place and guards had fled their posts on top of the railroad cars. It was chancy, but now or never. Thank God, we were successful. We were in water when French prisoners of war helped us change out of our prison clothes. We hid in the woods. Two or three days later, when the fighting finally stopped, we went onto the streets and were stopped by an American patrol.

—Fred Bachner; USHMM, made possible by a grant from Jeff and
Toby Herr, RG-50.549.02*0032

You wouldn't believe the amount of lice and fleas in Auschwitz. You lay down and it was like an entire army creeping over your body. You could feel them. It was like a never-ending army of lice and fleas. You couldn't get rid of them. We had only one shirt and wore it throughout the day and night. If the fleas were in the shirt in the morning, then we had to go to work in that shirt. It was terrible. It was also painful because they bit. I don't know what they ate because we certainly carried nothing they could eat. The water was red, probably because it contained the typhus bacteria or because the Germans had bombed the water mains and rust had set in. Some inmates drank it and nothing happened to them. Others died of dysentery.

—Jack Bass; USHMM, RG-50.562*0001

I met one man in Dachau who had a very, very low number tattooed on his arm. This man was not a Jewish man, but he was most articulate in his speech and was a political prisoner. He told me something that I have never forgotten. He told me that when you entered the camp, you knew your fate was sealed. You just didn't know what it was going to be other than death and how you were going to meet it. That was the thing that he didn't know.

—*Jerome Goldman; USHMM/National Council of Jewish Women, Sarasota-Manatee section, RG-50.154*0013*

The concentration camps were utilized to dispose of literally millions of Jews, who died by mass shooting, gas, poison, starvation, and other means. The part which the concentration camps played in the annihilation of the Jewish people is indicated in an official Polish report on Auschwitz concentration camp. In Auschwitz, during July 1944, Jews were killed at the rate of twelve thousand daily. As the crematorium could not deal with such numbers, many bodies were thrown into large pits and covered with quicklime. The official Polish Government Commissioner Report on the Investigation of German Crimes in Poland describes the concentration camp at Treblinka in these terms, "All victims had to strip off their clothes and shoes, which were collected afterward, whereupon all victims, women and children first, were driven into the death chambers. Those too slow or too weak to move quickly were driven on by rifle butts, by whipping and kicking. Many slipped and fell, the next victims pressed forward and stumbled over them. Small children were simply thrown inside. After being filled up to capacity, the chambers were hermetically closed and steam was let in. In a few minutes all was over. The Jewish menial workers had to remove the bodies from the platform and bury them in mass graves. As new transports arrived, the cemetery grew. From reports received, it may be assumed that several hundred thousand Jews were exterminated in Treblinka." The total number of Jews who died by Nazi hands can never be definitely ascertained. It is known, however, that four million Jews died in concentration camps, and that two million Jews were killed by the state police in the East, making a total of six million murdered Jews. The source of these figures is Adolf Eichmann, Chief of the Jewish Office of the Gestapo. The figures are contained in an affidavit made by Dr. Wilhelm Hoettl, Deputy Group Leader of the Foreign Section of the Security Section, AMT VI, of the RSHA. Hoettl, in his affidavit, states as follows, "Approximately four million Jews had been killed in the various concentration camps, while an additional two million met death in other ways, the major part of which were shot by operational squads of the security police during the campaign against Russia." Hoettl describes the source of his information as follows, "According to my knowledge, Eichmann was at that time, the leader of the Jewish Section of the gestapo, and in addition to that, he had been ordered by [Heinrich] Himmler to get hold of the Jews in all the European countries and to transport them to Germany."

—*Major William Walsh, assistant trial counsel for the US, Nuremberg trials, vol. 1, chapter XII; The Avalon Project, Yale University*

One morning we were marched out to work and the orchestra was playing. A truck full of naked young men drove by, with their strong voices singing Hatikvah, a Zionist anthem, on their way to the crematorium. It was an expression of their defiance in the face of death. Every time I hear Hatikvah, I remember them. This image comes to my memory very often. I will never be able to forget them, and I wonder, "Was my brother Shymek one of them?"

—*Joyce Wagner, author of* A Promise Kept: To Bear Witness

I was a captain, twenty-six, with the first war crimes investigative unit, commanded by a major who was an attorney. There was a photographer, a forensics expert, interpreters, and regular service personnel. We went to the secret camp of Nordhausen, Germany, as it was captured by the Sixty-Ninth Division. They had dug tunnels into the mountains to produce V-bombs. And they had a crematorium. There were about three thousand dead concentration camp victims when we came in. The volume of people they destroyed can be judged by the fact that the crematorium was working constantly. There were bodies in the crematorium at the time we got there. They did not have time to burn them. They could cremate fifteen people at a time. The general put the three thousand bodies in a field and made his soldiers march through them. Most of the twenty-five to thirty thousand prisoners were Jewish, and they ran all over the place, into the town, the hills, the woods. Those that couldn't run were the only ones who remained. When they saw us, they were overjoyed, but they were incapable of movement. The reaction was a strong one. Some got angry. Some got sick. They wanted to defeat the people who had done this. We were at Buchenwald a couple of times. Remains were still in the oven. Around the crematorium, there was a terrible odor. When you see a great deal of death, you are shocked; then you get accustomed to it. You can't be in a perpetual state of shock.

—*Herschel Auerbach; USHMM/Holocaust Memorial Foundation of Illinois, RG-50.031*0002*

On the third day, I said wherever we are going I won't make it because I am totally exhausted. That night we slept on a farm. The village houses looked empty, the conclusion being that they [their occupants] had fled. We thought it would be easy to reach a house if we picked a time when the guards were not nearby. We jumped into a stack of hay and stayed quiet. It was dark when we heard people speaking. We opened a door and there were some men and women sitting around. They knew who we were by our shaven heads. "You are Jews! Get out of here!" So we left. We saw many dead Germans on the road, their guts spilling out. Then we entered a well-stocked house with nobody inside. We made ourselves at home and got sick overeating. One night we heard marchers on the road. We didn't dare move, but they were Russians. We threw ourselves in their arms and said thank God they had saved us. But they were on their way to Berlin. Later we saw a bunch of young women approaching our house. We recognized them from Auschwitz, but they didn't look the same. We asked what happened. They said they had been raped by the Russians.

—*Paula Szmajer Biren; USHMM, funded by a grant from Carole and Maurice Berk, RG-50.030*0500*

I was a bazooka man carrying ammunition and ended up with the Ninetieth Infantry Division in Flossenbürg concentration camp, Germany, on the edge of Czechoslovakia. We were so flabbergasted and angry that anything like this could have happened. When we saw the crematoriums still smoldering and the shoes piled up, we just could not believe it. Ashes and human bones were thrown into gravesites almost six square feet. About seventy people were just wandering around. They were emaciated, just bones. You wondered how they had survived. We had to guard against any escapes, so with fixed bayonets, we marched the German SS from the railroad station. They didn't think anything they had done was wrong. The American soldiers were so upset because of what they had seen at the camp that if we had not been told not to harm them, I don't know what the guys would have done. I think this should be a lesson to all of us. It happened once, and it could happen again if we're not careful.

—*Charles Press; USHMM, RG-50.029*0027*

We prisoners were treated very badly. Burning into ashes. If the SS saw someone was missing, we stood outside for three or four days in the cold. My hands and feet were frozen. All frozen. Fingers, ears, and noses of some people, frozen. They fell down. In another barrack, I found my father dying. His feet and legs were swollen from the cold. My father died there and I brought his body to the Sachsenhausen crematorium like a piece of fruit on my shoulder. We didn't have any hope of getting out alive. There was no hope anymore. Every morning, there was a heap of dead bodies. The living ones, the ones that couldn't work, were all exterminated.

—*Max Liebster; USHMM/Watchtower Bible and Tract Society,*
RG-50.028*0034

We found a dead American soldier by the side of a road with a German luger in his mouth. The Germans had apparently shot him and left the weapon sticking out of his mouth, as if to tell us, "Enough!" It didn't stop us, and we were out for revenge. After we crossed the Ruhr River, our trophy catch would be to get an SS trooper. They were the ones with tattoos under their arms. They were the ones we really wanted to torture. Even when we captured German soldiers, they would say to watch out for the SS. When we did get one, we really worked him over with any torture we could think of, and we could think of quite a few. But I wasn't involved in much of that. My first experience of the SS was after we crossed the Ruhr River. German soldiers walking toward us told others to get rid of their uniforms and wear civilian clothing. An SS man had made the switch but was doing anything to save his skin. However, we were well aware that we had to look for the tattoo under the arm. Then we treated him accordingly.

—*Edmund Motzko; USHMM/Jewish Community Relations*
Council, Anti-Defamation League of Minnesota and the Dakotas,
RG-50.156*0042

The Germans thought my mother was part of the Polish underground working inside the camp. She was beaten terribly to reveal the names of other suspects, but there were no more to disclose. The more she denied, the more she was beaten. Toward the end of 1944, she was sent to Ravensbrück concentration camp where she was sterilized so she would never again have children. They put it to her this way, "So there won't be any more Polish bastards born in the world."

—*Bozenna Gilbride; USHMM, RG-50.233*0032*

We had a German supervisor in the ammunition factory at the Częstochowa ghetto in Poland who was easy to get along with. As long as we didn't bother him, he didn't interfere with us. He was foolish but didn't do anything wrong. I even did some tailoring for him. Then they replaced him with someone who lashed out for no reason. We called him the crazy one. Whenever he passed by my wife, working at a machine, he hit her, and she cried. I asked her what was the matter and she said everything was going well until he hit her with a screwdriver. So I went over to a Jewish worker and said that as he was trying to bribe the supervisor, he should at least be decent to us. He replied, "If not today, then tomorrow," meaning, if we won't be finished today, then we'll be finished tomorrow. Weak as I was, I said I didn't buy it and it was enough. I went over to the supervisor, a short man no taller than me, and yelled at him for hitting my wife. "If you are going to hit her for nothing, then hit me! I can take it, but leave her alone!" He lashed out at me, even as I screamed out the same reprimand. He didn't even have to take me outside. He could have killed me on the spot. But he didn't touch her again.

—*Morris Steiman; USHMM, RG-50.233*0131*

I saw Buchenwald's torturous devices when I was assigned to go into the field and entertain with a piano and microphone on a two-ton truck, where USO [United Service Organization] troops could not go. There was a contraption where prisoners' hands were tied behind their backs and then ropes pulled them upward and backward as they hung from posts. A prisoner did not have to hang for long before the arms were detached from their sockets. It was here that the wife of the commander, known as "The Bitch of Buchenwald," displayed her lampshades made from human skin. For anyone who doubted that they were human skins, she had left the tattooed concentration camp numbers on the lampshades. The ovens were still smoking. In their frantic efforts to destroy evidence, the Germans had kept the ovens going for twenty-four hours a day, nonstop. Half-burned bodies were still in the ovens where they had been left as the Germans fled. Beside the ovens were the emaciated bodies of prisoners they had no time to burn. They were naked, stacked like firewood. A cement chamber was where they punished inmates. The walls were three feet thick to muffle screams. Hoses washed away blood from the beatings and it drained down the middle of the floor. Prisoners were hanged like chunks of meat from huge hooks fastened to the walls and left to die. I thought, "No one will believe this. I must take pictures." But my hands and whole body were shaking, so that I dropped the camera and jammed the shutter, and I was unable to take any photographs. But the picture of the reality will remain in my mind forever.

—*Kay Bonner Nee; USHMM/Jewish Community Relations Council, Anti-Defamation League of Minnesota and Dakotas, RG-50.156*0043*

My best friend was a Czech called Freda Ringler and we shared everything. When Freda got an extra bowl of soup for more work, she would save me half of it. When she got an extra piece of bread, she would leave me some. When I had her soup, I would always make a line on the bowl to mark her half. I never cheated on Freda and I don't think she cheated on me. Shortly after we got to Bergen-Belsen, a Jewish woman came into the barrack dressed better than us and probably got better food. She had gone through Auschwitz and was now part of the camp management. She called for Tila Ringler. Freda had an older sister called Tila who ended up in Auschwitz. Freda stepped out and said Tila was her sister. Freda looked like Tila and the woman said because she had saved her life in Auschwitz, she would take her away from the barrack. "If you stay here you will die." But Freda insisted I go with her. The woman said if she didn't want to go without me she could stay put. I told Freda that was stupid. We would both die. But if she saved herself, maybe she could help me. So she left and became a runner in the infirmary and visited sometimes. It wasn't easy because she wasn't allowed in our part of the camp. She would bring me a potato or some bread. By that time, I was skin and bones, a dangerous way to look because it meant I was going. I was dead. Freda managed to get me into another part of the camp, where I worked and shared a bunk. But I have something on my conscience that I am not proud of. I had another friend called Hella, a lovely, gentle, sweet girl I was very fond of. I had just survived typhus. Hella had a fever when she came over and looked sick. She asked to sleep in my bunk that night. I had room because the girls I shared with were out working. I was scared because I feared I would catch it again. I told her she couldn't sleep with me because she was sick. She looked at me and said, "It's OK, Bella, I understand," and walked away. I found out she died that night. Maybe she wanted to die with a little dignity, on a bunk, and I didn't let her. I don't think I'll ever forgive myself.

—*Bella Tovey in an interview with Sandra Bradley for the USHMM film* Testimony, *RG-50.042*0028*

I actually saw people eat human flesh when we walked into Bergen-Belsen. It was unreal. There were skeletons, dead people left and right. Typhus was raging. Lice were as big as roaches. I can't find words for it. There was chaos. I'll never forget. I was lying in the barrack without furniture or beds. Nothing. The Germans knew the British were coming. They made me tie two skeletons together and drag them half a mile along a road to large graves. I had five sisters and a brother. None of them survived Auschwitz.

—*Jack Fuchs; USHMM/National Council of Jewish Women,*
Sarasota-Manatee section, RG-50.154*0011

We were pushed around in the latrines because there were more people than holes. It was ugly, sitting there, doing your business. I had diarrhea. Bloody diarrhea. It's horrible. No medication. You couldn't even clean yourself. You had to wait until the morning and then take some tea to clean your posterior. The water they gave us was infected and that's why we got diarrhea. Some women used the bowls to eat from and also to do their business; otherwise, they thought they wouldn't survive. But that's how they reinfected themselves, and no matter how much we tried to dissuade them, it didn't help. I never did that. I got myself a can and used it whenever I had the urge to do something during the night. I would urinate in it and keep it in front of my legs until morning, when I would empty it into a bucket three bunks below. I left the empty can on my bed, and it was never thrown away by block personnel who came in to check the bunks. Most people had no energy to climb up to the top bunk where I liked to live.

—*Helen Spitzer Tichauer; USHMM, RG-50.030*0462*

After we were shaved, we stood naked. We climbed steps into a large sink. I had a decorated handkerchief in my hand that belonged to my neighbor. The German female kapo told me to give it to her. I said it didn't belong to me. As revenge she disinfected me so severely with a hard brush that I bled. Later we had to register. What did we do? Did we kill someone? Did we steal something? Are we different from others? I was in the first transport to Auschwitz, so my number was low, 1287. They used a needle. I took things as they came. But in Slovakia afterward, I joked that my parents didn't want me to get lost so they wrote our phone number on my arm. But I couldn't joke in Montreal, so I had it taken off. You see the scar? I tried to survive day by day and not think of tomorrow because who knew if I would survive today? But logically, no one would survive. They would kill all of us.

—*Alice Jakubovic; USHMM, RG-50.030*0469*

When they closed the synagogue in Volosyanka, Czechoslovakia, my grandfather rescued a Torah scroll. He was clutching it when he came out of the train with us at Auschwitz. They ordered him to throw the Torah into a ditch, but he refused. Then they assaulted him. We pleaded with him to put it down, but he would not agree on any account, and they continued to batter him. Again we tried to get him to put it down, but he steadfastly refused. They continued to maul him and he collapsed, still embracing the Torah scroll. The beating never stopped until he was dead. Then they threw his corpse in a truck. We had watched the entire activity unfold in front of us. I had to survive to talk about it; otherwise, no one would believe that it happened.

—*Helen Lebowitz Goldkind; USHMM, RG-50.106*0139*

In the summer of 1942, I took a bus from Montauban, an old southern French town about twenty-five to thirty miles from the Swiss border. The bus was filled mostly with Jews from Poland who had lived in France or Belgium for years and were trying, like me, to escape from the Nazis and their death camps. They didn't speak; they only whispered. After a while, the bus was stopped by the French police. One of them came aboard the bus, saluted, and asked for our papers. Then he went from one to the other of these terrified people, who didn't look like Frenchmen, who couldn't speak French, therefore didn't speak at all and who didn't dare breathe. He took their brand-new, forged identification papers, looked at them, and gave them back, saying each time, merci, and saluting. When he was finally finished with the last passenger, he turned around, saluted all of us again, left the bus, and waved the driver on. Everybody was crying, even the driver. This unknown policeman, who had orders to check the bus for Jews and to arrest them, but who let them go free in plain view of his colleagues, who risked not only his job but his liberty and his life, who rather was human than an ally of Hitler Germany, was the greatest hero I have ever known.

—*Letter by James Loewenson published in the* Star Tribune *(MN, 11/6/1982); USHMM/Jewish Community Relations Council, Anti-Defamation League of Minnesota and Dakotas, RG-50.156*0033*

When my divorced father remarried, he became a Lutheran, and I was baptized and also became Lutheran—going to church and having nothing to do with being Jewish from age eleven. But I was born Jewish, in Vienna, with parents and grandparents on both sides being Jewish. Nobody knew I had a Jewish background because I went to church and everything. Then in 1939, officials told a man where I lived, "You have a Jew up there." The man, an engineer, said, "What are you talking about? You must be crazy. Mr. Weihs?

No way! Let's go up and find out." I had to say yes. Even though I had been Lutheran for so many years, it didn't help. As long as you were Jewish and your parents were Jewish, that's it. We thought they would leave us alone. The Viennese, of course, were on Hitler's side. They had hated the Jews for centuries and were glad they had a chance to get rid of them. So they said I could not stay in that house. The fellow who owned the plant nursery where I worked as a gardener couldn't believe it, but I told him I had to quit. My father had already passed away, so I lived with my stepmother in the suburbs for some time. But whoever was Jewish had to wear the star. Me too. People didn't like some Jews living there. I got engaged to a woman whose mother was Catholic and her father Jewish. One day the Germans told me I had to be at a certain place at a specific time. It was an ultimatum: do it, or else! I was put on a train and taken to Theresienstadt. Later I went to Auschwitz, Kaufering, and was walking to Dachau when liberated. After the war, we figured we were Lutheran again and married in Vienna, in church.

—*Ernst Weihs; USHMM, RG-50.030*0248*

The only Jewish children in Auschwitz were a few that Mengele wanted. If they had a mother with them, they were all killed. A very beautiful young woman was in the barrack with me and she was very depressed. I hardly had any contact with her, but suddenly she said to me, "You know what I did? I knew they would kill the children, but I let them go. I couldn't help them because I would also be killed." I don't know what happened to her. I don't know how she lived through it. I hope she is alive and can have children again.

—*Helen Waterford; USHMM, RG-50.030*0246*

My commanding officer said I was going as an interrogator to Mondorf, Luxembourg, to the central prisoner of war enclosure coded as Ashcan. The palace hotel with a casino now had a fence around it, lights overhead, camouflage material, machine gun towers, and military police riding around. A sergeant said to get inside, you had to have a pass signed by God and then verified. An officer assigned me to my room and said I would live there and interrogate prisoners of war. I heard a knock on the door. Before me stood none other than Hermann Göering, the Reichsmarschall of the Third Reich. I was the most surprised person in the world. He clicked his heels and said, "Göering, Reichsmarschall." It was his business to find out who the newcomers were. I was twenty-six at the time and a lieutenant. Before I could answer him, he asked if I was the welfare officer to see that they were treated properly in accordance with the Geneva Convention. I was about to say no, but agreed, and he was satisfied. So he then started a list of complaints. He had brought with him eleven suitcases with all of his uniforms and decorations and his Reichsmarschall's baton. He was the head of the German state, successor to Hitler, and he thought he was going into exile, like Napoleon. Instead they had brought him to this meager hotel, with a folding army cot, straw mattress, GI blankets, a stool, bucket of water, and Lifebuoy soap. He was very unhappy. He clicked his heels, bowed, and left. From then, my cover was welfare officer and my name was John Gellen. I was told to listen to the prisoners for interrogation reports. They went to each other's rooms and got into arguments and were mad at each other. That was part of our technique for gathering information. Each one was out to save his own neck. We couldn't treat these people like convicted criminals serving their sentences. We had to interrogate them for the prosecution and then try them.

—*John Dolibois; USHMM, RG-50.030*0408*

Out of five hundred inmates selected for the crematorium, only thirty were sent to peel potatoes in the Germans' kitchen, just for a visit by the Red Cross, and I was one of them. I remember it as if it happened today because it was my birthday, February 21. I was tall and clean, and I looked healthy. I saw bread, salami, and butter! I couldn't believe it! It was like a palace. The leader told us if we wanted to live, we couldn't touch any of those items because our stomachs were not used to food. We would get diarrhea and die the next day. I listened to him. He put a potato on a small fire, cut it in four, and said that's what we would eat every four hours with black coffee. He gave me a piece of bread and I toasted it. I said I would never survive outside and asked him to let me stay because every four weeks they exchanged only one person, while the others were permanent. The leader begged the SS man in charge, saying I was a fine man with good hands. He got permission for me to be a steady worker. It was heaven and hell. Outside was hell, and this was heaven. I just couldn't believe that something like this existed in Auschwitz.

—*Nathan Krieger; USHMM/William B. Helmreich's book* Against All Odds: Holocaust Survivors and the Successful Lives They Made in America, *RG-50.165*0058*

My mother said to take my religious articles such as the phylacteries, the tallit, and the prayer shawl. They got damaged when I swam through a river, but she wanted me to take them because they would remind me of who I was. She told me never to forget who I was because if I forgot, there would come a time when somebody would remind me of it. If the Nazis could remind us, at the end of a gun, who we are, surely we owe it to ourselves to know who we are without the gun.

—*Leo Bretholz; USHMM, made possible by a grant from Jeff and Toby Herr, RG-50.549.02*0016*

We crossed the Rhine and came to a small German town. My troops were going to sleep there, so I told the people in a house to get out. They could come out once in the morning to get pots, pans, clothes, and whatever they needed and again just before sundown. If they were seen in the streets, they would be shot. From the interior of the house, it was evident this was the home of a Catholic family. There were crucifixes, icons, and pictures of Mary. In the morning two men came back to the town and seemed on edge. They stared at me and asked my name. When I gave it to them, they must have been pretty sure I was Jewish. They didn't ask, but I told them, "I am a Jew." They got very excited and told me to come with them. We walked to the house and they jabbered eagerly to the women inside. In the attic they moved furniture, rolled back a rug, pulled up the floor boards, reached down, and brought out a Torah, prayer shawls, and religious paraphernalia of their religion. They were talking so fast I couldn't follow anything. But it was obvious what had happened. Two Jewish couples had been hidden throughout the war by the town's Catholics. They had gone out of their way to protect the couples, giving them all the artifacts to make it look like another Catholic home. By sheer accident, I had picked that house for us to stay in.

—*Frank Nathanson; USHMM/National Council of Jewish Women, Sarasota-Manatee section, RG-50.154*0021*

On the first day in Flossenbürg, I went to the latrine and saw a mountain of dead people on the side. Then we were marched off without food or water. At a grassy field, we stopped to rest and I ate flowers. Whoever was unable to march was shot to death. As I pulled a two-wheeler, the wheel went over my foot and I couldn't walk with shoes. Minutes later, a poor fellow couldn't walk anymore and a German soldier shot him in the head. He was wearing sandals, so my friend ran over, took the sandals, and gave them to me. I felt fine with them. Then it was so dark you couldn't see. I told my friend we could run away, and he was gone. I went after him. We found potatoes cooked for cows and pigs and filled ourselves. We hid for three days. Then my friend heard foreign languages and went to see what was going on. Someone said, "You don't know? We've been liberated." Of the two thousand that began the march, about five hundred survived. We got food at a refugee camp and then went to concentration camps to look for relatives. At Bergen-Belsen, I found my cousin.

—Anthony Lazar; USHMM, RG-50.233*0066

When I was an adolescent in Poland, I came down with scarlet fever. It was terrible and I almost died. My mother looked at me and was scared because I was as skinny as they come. It was 1941, and even though my mother thought she would lose me, the illness served us well when the Nazis came. They had carte blanche to go into Jewish homes and do whatever they wanted and remove anything they liked. My mother put a sign on the bedroom door that read SCARLET FEVER. If the soldiers came in and saw that sign, they would run away. Germans were pretty careful about health and didn't want to take chances. But sometimes it didn't work. A drunk German came in and wanted to sit down and have a cup of tea, which he did. We couldn't object, except once when my father was absolutely heroic. I still had scarlet fever and had lost most of my straight hair, which had grown back curly, so I was pretty cute and young. The intruder finished his tea and then asked for soap, which my mother gave him. I don't know what he had in mind, but before leaving, he told her she could be proud of me. It didn't pay to be ill because sick Jews were sooner or later dead Jews. After that incident, we never used the sign again.

—Janine Oberrotman; USHMM, made possible by a grant from Jeff and Toby Herr, RG-50.562*0004

This exhibit, which is on the table, is a human head with the skull bone removed, shrunken, stuffed, and preserved. The Nazis had one of their many victims decapitated after having had him hanged, apparently for fraternizing with a German woman and fashioned this terrible ornament from his head. "There I also saw the shrunken heads of two young Poles who had been hanged for having relations with German girls. The heads were the size of a fist, and the hair and the marks of the rope were still there."

—US executive trial counsel Thomas Dodd, Nuremberg trials, vol. 3, 12/13/45; The Avalon Project, Yale University/US Army report, including affidavit of Lt. George Demas associated with US chief counsel for prosecution of axis criminality, Buchenwald

There was no time for childhood. I was safe in Holland from Germany. My parents and brother left for America but left me because they wanted me to finish school, and my uncle Wilhelm, an international grain merchant, was convinced that Holland would remain neutral. They left in 1940, and a week later Germany invaded Norway and overran Denmark. My mother was in a panic. We woke up to hear planes. I told my uncle they were Junkers transports used by parachutists. He said I was crazy, but he was wrong and I was right. The Germans bombed Rotterdam and I was interned by the Dutch. My uncle was not touched because he was a Dutch citizen. But the Dutch guards knew it was over and there was no sense in holding us, so they told me to go home. My uncle was out, so at fifteen, I collected a few things for my rucksack and rode out of the city on my bike. He was glad to see me when I caught up with him, but I saw Germans everywhere. We were occupied. My passport was at the American consulate, which went up in flames, so I waited about three months to get a new German one with a big J stamped inside. I was not afraid because I was prepared, ready for anything.

We rented a farmhouse and my aunt kept house while I went to a trade school. A lady in Holland organized a children's transport to reunite children with parents already in America. I got my American visa in 1941. In America my mother waved and cried, but she wore lipstick, which only hussies used in Europe. But my visa had expired from movements in so many countries, and I waited four weeks for Washington to relent and let me stay. I thought it symbolic that I saw only the back of the Statue of Liberty. She had turned her back on me, but I see humor in almost anything.

—*Kurt Roberg; USHMM, RG-50.106*0141*

My commanding officer agreed with my idea that I should go to Theresienstadt in the Russian zone and get the names of German Jews who had survived liberation, so my driver and I stocked up with gas and food to the hilt, and off we went. I was taken by a Russian soldier to meet Leo Baeck, the famous German rabbi who was in charge of Theresienstadt's Jewish community. We sat on his bed as he told me the Germans had apparently decided to let him live because so many others had been killed, and rabbis had been sent to Auschwitz, where he knew they would die. He gave me a copy of all the people who had ever been there and the dates when they had been deported or murdered. It may be that this copy, which I later gave to headquarters, was used to evacuate the liberated people, which happened very quickly. Many people had died of malnutrition because they were not able to steal food to supplement their normal rations, which could not sustain normal health. I went through the names and found my grandmother's. She had been there, and I found out from someone who knew her that she had starved to death.

—*Joseph Eaton; USHMM, RG-50.030*0581*

I was seven and my brother four when we escaped to the sewers from the Lvov ghetto. From the beginning we were scared, but you can get used to everything. We played with rats like you play with a dog or a cat. We watched them. They were very smart animals. They tried to bite us at the beginning, but we got used to them. They only bit our bread, but my father and the others stood guard and were constantly chasing them. It was very dangerous because the water rushed by. My uncle escaped to the sewers with us. He went to fetch water, but there was a storm and he drowned. He never came back.

—Kristine Keren; USHMM, funded by a grant from Carole and Maurice Berk, RG-50.030*0520

I was always scared at Leitmeritz concentration camp in Czechoslovakia because any day could be the last. I just didn't know how it would end. There were quite a few Yugoslavs in our barrack, and very often when we woke up in the morning, one of them would be hanging, the result of suicide. From my experience, the Yugoslavs were the nicest people in the camp. It might be because our languages were similar, but I never heard of suicides other than Yugoslavs at that camp. I promised myself to stay awake, and if I saw someone about to commit suicide, I would do the same. It's strange, but the next night I didn't fall asleep, but no one committed suicide. I figured that I must be a coward to have fallen asleep after hearing someone making sounds to commit suicide.

—Joseph Koplewicz; USHMM, RG-50.106*0121

Usually when transports arrived at Sobibór, we helped unload people from the train, but this time they locked us up. We heard a lot of shooting, and the following day, when we were separating their clothing, we found them soaked with blood. We always searched the pockets and in one pair of pants, I found a note saying they came from a camp at Bielitz, Poland. In Yiddish he had written, "Take Revenge." They had resisted and not gone like lambs to the slaughterhouse. But they had all been shot in the train.

—Chaim Engel in an interview with Sandra Bradley for the USHMM film Testimony, *RG-50.042*0009*

Starvation was so bad that cannibalism became stylish. I, myself, like many others, became what they called a muselmann—no flesh and no muscles on the body, and no desire to live. So we were hauled off to piles by the crematorium. This was already springtime of 1945 at Ebensee. There were several piles, but they were huge. They just piled them up one on top of the other. Some were moving but dying, and some were already dead. Many of us—hundreds. If this had lasted for another two or three hours, I would not have survived, and I didn't care. I didn't want to survive anymore. The American Army was getting closer and liberated the camp. That was May 6, 1945. My brother knew I had been taken there. He came looking for me. He shook me and said that the American Army had liberated the camp. I couldn't figure out what he was saying, so he pulled me off and told me, "I saw them with my own eyes!" They were Americans and we would get something to eat. He even told me that he went on top of an American tank and stepped on it to make sure that I believed him. At that time, I didn't try to think about it. But looking back, I said to myself, "Where in the world was I? Where was mankind?"

—Lou Dunst; USHMM, RG-50.544*0001

The impression of most people was that the Germans were brainwashed or crazy because at the Nuremberg war crimes trials, they said they had followed orders. They said the same thing when they killed my mother. They said they didn't have a choice, that they had followed orders. The world knew that they could have done something because they had the power and authority to do what they should have done, and they didn't. The worst of it was that they intimidated the entire population to do the same. No one acted on their own free will. It's unfortunate that only Adolf Eichmann was executed for the deaths of millions. To the end, he denied being responsible. But he and others had made the decision to impose the "Final Solution." Even though we say that God is the final judge, at that moment Eichmann's fate was in the hands of a human court. The majority of mankind was involved. To that extent, I think justice was done. Justice will eventually prevail. Hitler did not achieve what he wanted to do, so God was the final judge.

—Jacob Wiener; USHMM, RG-50.106*0112

You have people in politics today who say the Holocaust never happened. How can they reconcile that with the facts? In 1952 or 1953, I made a business trip down south where my clients were, and I went to a town, Crowley, Louisiana. A Catholic priest there was invited to my client's house for lunch. I was there and in the course of the conversation, he found out that I was Jewish. He said to me that the Holocaust never happened, and he had told his parishioners that the Holocaust never occurred. I told him, trying to be as polite as I could, that he was wrong. I was there and I saw it. He said, oh no, the Catholic church would never allow something like that; therefore, it never happened.

—George Pisik; USHMM, RG-50.106*0124

When the Americans came in, most of the Germans had already gone, but they caught a lot of them. They made them dig trenches and bury the dead. There were loads and loads of them. There was revenge by people who were able to do something. But not so many people were able-bodied enough to do anything. They would beat them up and point them out to the Americans. I would have wanted to beat them up, but I was in no shape to do anything. Why would anyone do that to anyone for no reason whatever?

—*Alan Kalish; USHMM/Jeff and Toby Initiative for Rescuing the Evidence, RG-50.562*0002*

A month after being in Auschwitz, none of us had our monthly periods. But I couldn't have any more children. I already had a daughter. I only found out why I couldn't conceive when we came to America in 1949. German doctors had experimented with my body. Mengele made visits, selecting one or two inmates for experiments, and on one of his calls, he picked me. I was tied to a bed and they shouted at me not to move. I couldn't move even if I wanted to. Things were taken from me without narcotics. I still don't know what parts were taken. I had to walk back to the barracks. It took me fifty years to be able to talk about that period. People were fortunate to start life again, marry, and have families. If I were a hateful person, I would only hurt myself because I could not live with hate. But the pain and agony doesn't go away. [Later, reunited with my daughter after the war] I wanted to hold her all the time. That's all I wanted to do, just go to bed and hold her all the time so she wouldn't go away.

—*Fanny Aizenberg; USHMM, RG-50.030*0621*

We were naked when we stood in front of Adolf Eichmann and his helpers during selection on arrival at Auschwitz. Can you imagine how we felt, especially a woman, in front of them? I was fifteen. We practically lost our minds. It did not matter who it was, but it was a man, and it was devastating, especially for a teenager who was modest. I didn't know what to do. He stood there with a dog and a thick leather horsewhip that was very thin at the end, which he pointed left or right. He took my mother to the other side. I cannot say I was brave. Perhaps it was inexperience, but I begged him, saying, "Please, she is the only person left in my life. I won't have anyone anymore." He struck me on the face with his whip so much that I swelled up like a balloon and could barely see through puffy eyes. He put me with my mother and that meant going to the crematorium. But I was desperate and there was a German girl there about my age. I pleaded with her in German, "You're the same age as I am, and I'm sure that you would want to know that your parents were safe. If something like this happened to you, wouldn't you want to save your mother?" I wouldn't want to say anything nice about Germans, but occasionally there was among them someone with feelings and compassion. She took my mother and I, and smuggled us to the other side. We survived.

—*Guta Blass Weintraub; USHMM, RG-50.030*0250*

I bought the cyanide capsule for about four rations of bread in Auschwitz and took it, and a small pocket knife, to Bergen-Belsen, where we arrived in January 1945. I wasn't going to go to the gas chamber. I was going to cut my veins. But I didn't have to. When we woke up one morning, there were no guards. I crawled out and saw people running toward the open wooden gates. There were no guards on the towers or anywhere else. We couldn't believe it. Then the first tank came in and they were British.

—*Anna Maxell Ware; USHMM, RG-50.030*0427*

I was sick when my depressed sister went over to an SS man, which was the biggest no-no, because you were not allowed to approach them. Luckily, we were out of Auschwitz and already in the moving train. He was eating an apple. She said, "Please, can I have a piece of apple for my sister?" He punched her so hard that she was thrown all the way to the other side of the of the cattle train. In a weak voice I begged her, saying, "Don't you ever do that again. Please, you know that you're not allowed to." I was lucky that he didn't do more to her.

—Cecilie Klein-Pollack in an interview with Sandra Bradley for the USHMM film Testimony, *RG-50.042*-0018*

When we got there, we undressed, and went into the shower. They cut our hair, tattooed us, and gave us clothes. You have to remember we came from a normal life. We had normal clothes on and here I got whatever they gave me. It was a navy blue, straight dress. I had to go to the bathroom and all the latrines had windows. I saw somebody standing in the reflection in the window. I turned around and was looking for the person. I thought maybe there was somebody in back of me. There wasn't. Suddenly I realized it was me. I didn't recognize myself because my hair was cut and I had this funny dress on. It was a shock because I didn't have a mirror.

—Ann Green; USHMM, RG-50.030*0509

The will to survive is very strong. The idea that I would survive and tell the world what happened was always a very, very important element in that feeling. And the feeling, or the statements of those who were taken to the gas chambers, "Don't forget us," was also very important. "Don't forget us." This was very important to me. That was what kept me going.

—Sigmund Strochlitz; USHMM, RG-50.030*0397

We were counted outside every morning and again at night when the prisoners came back from work. If one inmate was missing, the whole camp had to wait outside until he was found. Sometimes after he was found, they hanged him in front of all the prisoners. They pulled him up by the throat so everyone could see that he was killed for trying to escape.

—*Max Liebster; USHMM/Watchtower Bible and Tract Society,*
RG-50.028*0034

The transport from Belgium was horrible, just terrible. We were herded into cattle cars, and they gave us a ration of bread and the children got a can of milk. The cattle car that I ended up in with my aunt and uncle was a coal wagon, so the floor was black. I don't know how many people were in the cattle car. We had to stand up most of the time and couldn't move. They gave us two buckets on each side to relieve ourselves, and before we knew it, the pails were turned over until we arrived at the camp. There was a small window with wires over it so that nobody could escape. We went like that for three or four days. People got very restless and nervous, upset with one another because their patience was running out, so they started arguing noisily with one another and fighting. All of a sudden, a German put his rifle in the window and shot at people and then hollered for quiet. He shot two or three people that way. We settled down, naturally, because we were afraid that we were going to be shot. When we arrived, it was dawn. The camp was called Birkenau. We were so exhausted and tired. I had eaten only bread in the train. My aunt wouldn't let me drink the milk because she thought I should save it for later, but I had to leave all my packages and the milk on the side because they told us to drop all our belongings. They told us to go into a line. The Germans were everywhere, with dogs sniffing at us. I heard screams because dogs attacked people, and I would hear shots, but we stayed in line. I saw this tall man who directed us to the right or to the left. My aunt went to the left, and I had to go to the right. I didn't even have a chance to say good-bye to my aunt because I thought she was just going to register us, to give our names and identification. Afterward, I found out that she went to the left, which meant the ovens.

—*Lilly Appelbaum Malnik in an interview with Sandra Bradley for the USHMM film* Testimony, *RG-50.042*0020*

I was with a group of young girls, fifteen or sixteen years old, in Birkenau. We quickly found out that the horrible odor was from people being burned in the crematorium. It permeated the camp, and ash flew in the air day and night. We didn't have a towel, a toothbrush, a piece of paper, a watch, or a calendar. When it rained we had an additional problem because we got wet and had no way to get dry, so we huddled together, soaking in our bunks. After a few weeks some of the people around me had a vacant stare. They were closing out life. They were giving up. That terrified me even more than hunger. So I devised a survival skill. I remembered all the books I had read and all the movies I had seen. I told and retold the stories to my bunkmates and people around me. They would surround me and ask me to tell about this movie or that movie. Some of the girls had never seen a movie because they came from little villages. I tried to explain to them how a magical machine makes these people move and talk on a screen, but they couldn't quite imagine it. This was my lifesaving skill and a way to preserve my mind.

—*Judy Freeman; USHMM/Gratz College Hebrew Education Society, RG-50.462*0081*

I knew something was going on when the SS brought out tables with papers on them to a small yard in front of Auschwitz's kitchen. From the second floor, we saw about one hundred men, stripped to the waist, but apparently soldiers, judging from their trousers. Many were Russians, and it was after the invasion of their country in 1941. They were killed in a vicious manner. I saw some hit with spades that split their heads. Others were told to lie down with spades over their throats; then the SS stood on each end and suffocated them. Some stood on the edge of a pit and fell into it after being kicked in the groin. Then the SS threw large stones at them. They told prisoners to lie down, loaded wagons with sand, and then tipped them over and buried the men alive. That was the most horrible thing I ever saw. They probably killed half the men before noon; then they went to lunch. When they had eaten, they killed off the rest of them. None of the prisoners were shot. Instead, they were murdered in the most brutal way.

—*Leonard Zawacki; USHMM, RG-50.030*0271*

After a forced march over two days, we arrived late at night at Blech-hammer, a subcamp of Auschwitz. The SS men waiting at the gate laid into us because we did not sing as we went through the camp. Blows rained down on us. We tried to support each other. My friend put his arm up to protect his head and mine, but his arm was broken by the blows. I only received a violent hit on my back, but I had a very painful injury of the groin and could not walk anymore. I told the two friends who had supported me to go on alone because I could no longer lift my legs. I would rather die in the camp than on the road. The two friends said they would prefer to stay with me rather than go with the transport. We lay down on beds in another barrack and tried to sleep. Someone rushed in and shouted, "Quick, quick, get a move on, the SS are coming back!" We hid inside the latrine opposite. The Germans torched three barracks. Those who remained inside were burned alive. The SS men stationed themselves by machine guns and shot at anything that moved. We were afraid that the latrine would also catch fire or that the SS would come in and see us. We jumped into the pit, but it was the stupidest thing we could have done as we sank slowly. When I was deep in the mire, I felt solid ground beneath my feet. But the smell of crackling wood, and of those who had run out and were shot at, though not yet dead, was the worst thing I went through in the concentration camp. It was even worse than the moment I was sentenced to death. I don't know how long we hid there, but it was dusk when we heard people saying that all the camp gates were open and the SS had left. Several prisoners helped pull us out and we washed ourselves with snow because there was no water. Then the Russians liberated us and weighed me. I was 86 pounds.

—*Alfred Oppenheimer, Eichmann trial, session 68, 6/7/1961, Nizkor Project, League for Human Rights of B'nai Brith Canada*

On the first day we cut bushes, an SS guard with a huge German shepherd picked on me because I was tall, to show what would happen if we tried to run away. We had to cut away the bushes so if anyone tried to escape from Auschwitz or if there was an attack by partisans, they could not hide there. It was the hardest job I ever had. My hands were bleeding. The SS guard told his dog to bite my dress. I froze because I'm afraid of dogs, especially mean ones that bark and have big teeth, and I don't like to touch them. But this dog tore my dress to pieces. It never bit me, but my dress was in shreds. The SS man stopped him once and then told the dog to resume attacking my dress. I was very scared because I thought the dog would kill me, though I just stood still. We worked there for three months.

—*Anna Laks Wilson; USHMM, RG-50.030*0411*

I had probably just become a teenager when the block foreman asked mostly older people in our group of over one hundred, whether anyone could cook. I didn't know how to cook because our maid did everything at home. But in order to survive in Auschwitz, you had to lie and cheat. So I stepped forward and said I was a cook. He told me I would be his cook. Being a cook meant that I had access to food with protein, like eggs. I was able to help my father and friends because I could get them food. To get a dozen eggs, I traded seven loaves of bread. All the time, it meant bartering food. My father got all the food he needed, like meat, salami, eggs, and fruit. We never got any of this. Instead we were given some potato peels in water.

—Michael Finkelstein; USHMM/Gratz College Hebrew Education Society, RG-50.462*0078

I think Ohrdruf was the worst camp I saw on liberation. There were large pits with legs sticking out. The odor was very bad, and it was something you didn't want to get too close to or spend much time around, other than taking a picture [like these that I have]. I understand the civilian population claimed not to know anything about what was going on at that camp. Yet it was only one quarter or half a mile away from the civilian population. They could see it, but they claimed that there was nothing wrong going on in there. So you can see the elderly men of the village had been brought up, and they actually are digging the graves and are going to handle the bodies with their bare hands, to impress upon them what had taken place. I was commanding a US rifle company in the 260th infantry, 65th Division, that went through several camps. Ohrdruf was one that I remember distinctly.

—John Henry Baker, Jr.; USHMM/Fred Roberts Crawford Witness to the Holocaust Project, RG-50.010*0004

I was a GI, a lieutenant-colonel, in April 1945. I told the chief of staff that I would go to Buchenwald and find out about it. I got in the jeep, mounted with a radio, and got there about two hours after it had been discovered by our troops. The inmates looked like there was no flesh on their bones. The conditions I saw there would just turn your stomach. Some were leaning on the wall of the barracks. I couldn't tell whether those lying on the floor were dead or alive. Some were in their stacked bunks. If a man my size got in there, he'd have to get out if he wanted to turn over. None of them bothered to say anything. I presumed that people went by the chow line and got their little rations and then went out and ate it on the grounds somewhere. I didn't really know. I did see that there was no supply of food. Two big ovens I saw at the crematoriums had obviously been used. You could poke a body through it to the end of the doorway. They had apparently brought people into the room alive and yanked them up or tied them up by their feet because at about my eye line, somebody had clawed on the walls with fingernails. It obviously hadn't been done by any tool to make them even and smooth. Bodies were stacked up like cordwood, some clothed and some not. They were just stacked up out there. This shook me up. I figured I had enough. We had no idea that it was so horrible, that they were in such a state of horror. At no time had we encountered brutality, where people had been subjected to such inhumane treatment, where people were dying, where people were being killed as prisoners, as we did at Buchenwald and some other concentration camps. You never forget it. I can't describe it. Words won't permit. It was terrible. Such horror.

—*James Moncrief in an interview with Sandra Bradley for the USHMM exhibition "Liberation 1945," RG-50.470*0016*

Early in the morning of our January 1945 death march, I sensed I would be shot on the road. I was weak and tired, and it was tough trying to drag my feet. I thought if I tried to continue, they would shoot me. I thought of escaping. If there was only a 10 percent chance, I would take it. I told the inmates to stay together and help each other, but I couldn't continue any longer, and anyway I was of no use to them. It was really dark with no moon, when we came to a forest on both sides of the road. This was the moment. I slipped into a ditch by the side of the road and lay face down in the snow. A guard shot me under my arm and the bullet lodged in my ribs. Blood colored the snow, which was good because nobody else shot at me. When the column had passed, I had the strength to go into the forest and linked up with other prisoners who had escaped. We huddled together and slept sitting up. In the morning, we saw another camp from the top of a hill. The gate was open, but the watchtower was unoccupied, and prisoners were walking in and out. We not only walked but ran to the camp and asked what had happened. One of them said all the Germans had jumped into trucks before dawn and taken off. They didn't even have time to liquidate the inmates with machine guns and grenades. Russian tanks had broken through and they didn't want to be caught. That's why they had left in a hurry.

—*Edgar Krasa; USHMM, RG-50.030*0478*

I think my parents were born in Warsaw, but I'm not sure because I don't remember them. Both of them had black hair. At the start of the war, there was shooting, and people were running and shouting. I heard a gunshot and saw my Lassie dog lying on the floor with a hole in his head and something red was coming out. I crawled to him, but a big drunk came in and lifted me up. He had red cheeks and a horrible smell. My mother was screaming and he was laughing. My father, who was the only Jew to be awarded the army's highest decoration, had disappeared. My mother and I were taken away like cattle and given a cold shower with other women. She was very sick and died. A month before liberation, I left for Bergen-Belsen with a man who hit me and took my food rations, but many women took care of me. I remember walking for miles and then riding on a train which stopped. German soldiers were running away. Then the Americans came and gave me chocolate, which I had never had before. A woman with contacts in Palestine looked after me, and I arrived there in July 1945. I didn't want to talk about it, only when my granddaughters were at school. I always knew I had a secret. There are Holocaust survivors who talk and those who don't. But I don't judge. Many people ask why we didn't do this or that. They cannot grasp what happened there, so they cannot judge. When my son was small, I woke up and sat next to his bed, waiting for them to come and take him. That's when things came back, but I didn't talk about it. Who would I talk to? What would I say? They can read about the war. I chose to tell students how to live with that story, how to grow up and live life, and how to be a mother. I'm a survivor and know that whatever happened, I can stand on my own two feet.

—*Lily Cohen; USHMM, RG-50.030*0575*

I was standing in line to get bread in the Łódź ghetto, when the gestapo ordered me to get on the truck. I was still a teenager and screamed, "Mommy, where are you?" I was so young and knew something would happen to me. I was all alone. The train had a lot of cattle cars, crowded and very slow. There was nowhere to relieve ourselves. On the way, the train stopped and a woman took her baby bundled in a blanket and begged the gentile women watching us to take it. As she gave it to them she was crying and said she would come back later for it. She never came back.

—*Gina Beckerman; USHMM, RG-50.030*0259*

221

My sister was such an exceptional violinist that my father bought her a very good violin, though not a Stradivarius. She would have gone very far because it was the love of her life. When we had to live in the ghetto, my mother told us to take only clothing and what was special for us. The Germans wanted us to surrender all musical instruments, but she took the bow and violin out of their case, tied them together, and smuggled them in under her loose dress. Then my mother hid her with a farmer, but she took her violin. I heard two versions of her fate. Either the farmer betrayed her because he wanted the violin, or someone else exposed her, and she was paraded naked through the main street and then murdered. That is all my former neighbors told me.

—Charlene Schiff; USHMM, made possible by a grant from Jeff and
Toby Herr, RG-50.549.02*0068

When Auschwitz was not as prominent as it became later on, the Germans took Jews there and sent telegrams back to the families. You could hear the crying and screaming as the postman arrived. We knew he was coming with a telegram. They announced that someone had died of cancer, another person from pneumonia, or while trying to escape. About two weeks later, the same bereaved families got bills to pay for cremation and burial of the ashes.

—Norman Salsitz; USHMM, RG-50.233*0119

Many people died every night and didn't make it to the roll call, but they were accounted for by being bodies. After the grown-ups were marched out, a squadron of inmates pulled a horseless wagon around, came into the barracks, and took the corpses. The bodies lay in all directions. Two of the inmates would take the corpses, one by the feet and one by the hands, and toss them on top of the heap. This happened every day. I still have trouble with that.

—*Doriane Kurz; USHMM, RG-50.030*0120*

The most horrible transport to Auschwitz came from Będzin, Poland. They knew more or less where they were bound for. When the train arrived, we saw people hanging out of the barred windows. About one hundred fifty were crammed into each cattle car. They had all evidently taken off their clothes owing to the great heat inside. When the SS opened the cars, people fell out. They did not notice a declining slope and rolled down, to wild laughter from the SS. Remaining inside were those who had been trampled on and suffocated, emitting tremendous heat, and either dead or half dead. Fumes rose from the dead bodies. We stood aside until the order came, "Get inside, you filthy Jews!" Amid shouts and blows, we went into the cars to remove the dead. It was not easy. They were interlaced, hanging onto each other. Sometimes, when we pulled an arm or a leg, the skin would come off owing to the great heat. The SS men had drawn revolvers and shot enfeebled people. A girl, approximately ten years old, emerged from a pile of corpses and started walking and floundering until one of the SS men "took pity" on her and shot her in the back of the neck. There was a half-naked boy sitting down in the middle, with the dead lying on one side and the dying on the other. An older SS man we nicknamed Zeide, grandfather, came from behind and was about to shoot the boy in the neck when the child turned around and managed to call out Shema Yisrael [Hear, O Israel] before he was shot. The SS explained that they shot people to "spare their suffering." A young man recognized his brother, got on his knees, and pleaded for mercy and for him to be allowed to go into the camp. But he was told, "If you like, you can join him."

—*Gedalia Ben-Zvi, Eichmann trial, session 71, 6/8/1961, Nizkor Project, League for Human Rights of B'nai Brith Canada*

I was an officer with combat engineers supporting an infantry division at the liberation of Dachau. The first reaction was anger. The second reaction was to retaliate. That's probably the reason they let the prisoners get at the guards. I don't think there was anybody in command at that point. As weak as they were, they got them. They just overwhelmed them. All they could do was beat and pummel them and hit them with whatever they could find. That's why we held the guards, so that the prisoners could get to them. We felt like they were entitled. The first reaction was, let them have them. It was finally stopped. Bodies were piled up like cordwood in open-like coal cars of a train probably half a mile long. There were one hundred cars or more, with four hundred to six hundred bodies in each car. It bends your mind. Being a Christian, it's unbelievable to me how anybody could be involved in doing such a thing by one human being to another. I stood on a little knoll and looked at these people. Their eyes were black coals; their heads like skeletons; their hair half gone. People whose elbows stood out like big knobby things and their bodies swollen. There was a language problem. Most of them just said Jude, Jude. [Jewish, Jewish].

—*Harry Allen; USHMM/Fred Roberts Crawford Witness to the Holocaust Project/Manuscript, Archives, and Rare Book Library, Emory University, RG-50.010*0001.*

One lady came in from Theresienstadt and the chimneys were going—and the smell—I mean, when hair burns and when flesh burns, you smell it. And she thought it was a bakery because that's what she was told. But once you're there, you knew.

—*Ann Green; USHMM, RG-50.030*0509*

About a month after we got to Majdanek, my father and I were together, digging a ditch. Suddenly a Polish prisoner passed by, grabbed a stone, and threw it at my father. He must have broken my father's leg because he couldn't walk. He had to hold onto me when we went back at night. Somehow a friend and I dragged him back to the barrack. He lay down, but his foot swelled up. Someone said we should call a medic or a doctor. I didn't realize what would happen to someone who got sick. The medic wore a red cross and told my father he would have to go to the camp infirmary, though he would bring him back the next day. I never saw my father again.

—*Abraham Lewent; USHMM, RG-50.030*0130*

We were herded into a Polish jail and didn't know what was happening. After a few hours, we were loaded into buses and taken to the railroad station. In each car was a policeman. Nobody moved. We were very disciplined, frightened. They had no problem with us. One hardly dared go to the washroom. The train went all through the night at a slow pace. At about 4:00 a.m., the train stopped. Everybody rushed out instinctively; in fact I jumped out. The SS guards were waiting for us. Older people who couldn't get out fast enough were yanked out. We had to run in the rain to a huge gate. The sign read Sachsenhausen concentration camp. They chased us into the yard and made us stand for at least six hours without anything to eat. It was cold. Then a commandant came to scare us [to] no end. He asked everybody, "What is your profession?" One man was stupid enough to say, "I am a manufacturer." So the commandant said to one of his subordinates, "Make a note of it. This man will be cremated." The poor fellow lost consciousness and dropped to the ground. Somebody next to him wanted to help him, but the commandant said, "Let him lie there."

—*Herbert Prover; USHMM/Holocaust Memorial Foundation of Illinois, RG-50.031*0057*

As the Germans retreated before the Soviet Army, they exterminated Jews rather than allow them to be liberated. Many concentration camps and ghettos were set up in which Jews were incarcerated and tortured, starved, subjected to merciless atrocities, and finally exterminated.

—Captain V.V. Kuchin, assistant prosecutor for the USSR., Nuremberg trials, vol. 2, 11/20/45; The Avalon Project, Yale University

Some of the girls were working in the warehouse where they collected the looted possessions from the people who arrived in Auschwitz-Birkenau from all over Europe. They called it the Canada warehouse, the rich warehouse. Two thousand women prisoners worked there. Some of the people who arrived in Auschwitz-Birkenau had luggage. The rich carried suitcases with fortunes in them because they were told that they were going to be resettled in other places, and they brought all their valuable possessions to Auschwitz-Birkenau. The jewelry, gold, and other valuables were sent to the Third Reich's main bank, Deutsche Reichsbank, to help the German war effort. The clothes and other personal items were also sent to Germany. The perishable food was given to the SS and elite, influential prisoners. Some of the food and clothes were taken from the Canada warehouse by some prisoner workers for their siblings and friends. When they were caught stealing, they were severely punished. Even in Auschwitz-Birkenau, there were two classes of prisoners: those who had, and those who had nothing.

—Joyce Wagner, author of A Promise Kept To Bear Witness

We were three days on the train. It was horrible, unbelievable. People were dying. They opened the door and threw us a little bread and gave us water. My father said it was the end for us. At Auschwitz, Jewish inmates whispered to give the children to grandmothers. We knew they were meant to be killed. First my father was separated from us. Then Mengele separated me, twenty-eight, from my mother. I wanted to kiss my mother but he said, "No. You will see her. Don't worry." That was it. We were in a trance. Everybody was crying and going crazy. Crying for food, their fathers, mothers, sisters.

—*Lily Blayer; USHMM/Holocaust Memorial Foundation of Illinois, RG-50.030*0005*

Anne Frank's mother and two daughters were with us. I knew the mother but was unaware they had been arrested shortly before us. A woman offered to give the daughters soup every day if the mother exchanged her shoes for the other woman's. Mrs. Frank hesitated and then naively agreed. She never got a drop of soup. Very attractive young women tattooed us before stripping the females in front of soldiers with big dogs. The woman who undressed me yanked the wedding band off my finger. I forgot I had it; otherwise, I would have put it in my mouth or hidden it elsewhere. I still thought they were Germans, not realizing they were Jewish female prisoners. They tried to find jewelry hidden in other places, and shaved our heads and body hair. They left us with our wooden shoes only because footwear had not arrived that day.

—*Helen Waterford; USHMM, RG-50.030*0246*

I became a surgeon after the war, and have seen some pretty awful things in the operating room but nothing like Buchenwald. It was probably one of the worst things I've seen in my whole lifetime. I was a sergeant in a US observation battalion and saw a horrible situation that should never have been allowed to occur. The stench was overpowering. There were little children in the camp, and the only way we knew they were children was the size of their bodies piled up like everybody else's. We went to the crematorium and saw six or seven ovens. The fires had been turned off, but we saw bodies still there. A basement below the crematorium had big hooks on the wall where they hung people until they died, before an elevator would take them up to the crematoriums to be burned. People were lashed at posts stuck in a compound ground and sometimes left there to die overnight. Bodies were stacked outside the barracks, and you could see emaciated legs and arms. Several photos taken by me show burnt ashes from the crematoriums. People couldn't believe they were free, that it was happening to them. They all anticipated dying. We could not understand how some of the people survived as long as they did. It was just atrocious. People in nearby Weimar claimed they didn't know what was going on, but they had to know because you could smell it from miles away. The camps could hold only a certain amount of people, and they had to get rid of those displaced by new arrivals. You got a feeling of real loss. It was a relief to leave.

—John Bucur; USHMM, RG-50.106*0160

One particular form of torture we discovered at Dachau was a platform about six or eight feet long with a swivel chair at one end. At the other end stood a German interrogator. He had two handles with which he could swivel the chair from left to right. We noticed a hole on the floor about an inch deep on either side of the person seated, nude and freezing. There was a pedal on the floor. When it was stepped on, a spike went up the man's derriere and made a hole. This was one form of interrogation. There were so many forms it's hard to remember what they did. Teeth were knocked out and hair and fingernails pulled out. Anything you could imagine was used.

—*Jerome Goldman; USHMM/National Council of Jewish Women, Sarasota-Manatee section, RG-50.154*0013*

Soon after the war, when Jews were returning to Poland, my father and brother went to see our house in Kraków. They knocked on the door. Some Poles were living there and said, "You were supposed to be dead!" Then they slammed the door. Straight after that, the pogrom began, and they escaped by this much from being killed. They survived the war, but they were so scared that they came back to us in Hungary. My father told my mother, "There's nothing there for us."

—*Barbara Firestone; USHMM, RG-50.030*0570*

Not far from Katowice in upper Silesia, the train came to a halt. The doors were unsealed and SS guards with rifles acted like animals, yelling and shouting and hitting us with truncheons. They ordered everyone to jump out into the cold winter night. We were told to forget about the luggage and leave it where it was. Far more gruesome was the order to separate into groups of men, women, and females with children. This was the moment when I had to say good-bye to my wife and child. My wife had always been very courageous, very optimistic, and had been looking forward to the future. Now she said, "This is the moment I feared most, that they would separate us."

—*Norbert Wollheim; USHMM, RG-50.030*0267*

229

My parents, two younger sisters, and I lived underground in a hole for sixteen months after the Germans invaded our town of Ostrog, Poland. The poor gentile woman who hid us believed in God, who she said had sent us to her, and she was obliged to save us. In Europe people put potatoes in a hole during winter. She took them out, put straw in their place, a pole to hold boards on top, and then covered it with pumpkins. We couldn't stretch our legs. We had a pot for sanitation but didn't use it much because we ate so little. Once a day she brought a quart of water and a potato for each of us. She begged for bread and brought it to us. We tied it to the pole, in case we got hungry much later, and stared at it, wanting it so badly, but we kept it for later because we didn't know what tomorrow would bring. When it was quiet, she removed the pumpkins to give us more air. But she had to replace the pumpkins in winter with cow manure. We breathed through a hole, especially when everything was covered in snow. If the Germans had found us, they would have killed us, together with the gentiles. The woman, with three small children and a forester husband, just wanted to save us. Her four-year-old used to bring us carrots and say, "The Germans will not live long enough to find you." At night she would bring us the newspaper and a candle. My mother used to tell us, "Don't worry. We've made it so far. We'll make it." In 1942 I was seventeen and my sisters fifteen and eight. We just lay there and waited, not knowing what would happen. One day our protector said the Germans had left and the Russians were back. My parents went out to check. We heard people walking outside and I told my sisters not to cry and to stay still. Then I heard my mother say in Yiddish, "Children, we're here." I was in heaven!

—*Lisa Dawidowicz Murik; USHMM, RG-50.030*0168*

We saw the furnaces at Dachau. The dead were piled up, lying on top of each other. They were taking them and putting them in the fire and burning them. It made a terrible smell. I couldn't believe anyone could be so rotten. I had a German in my sight because three prisoners were chasing him after we opened the gates. I told my buddies to look at that German running away from those guys. He was in A-1 shape, but they were starved. I said they would never catch him as he was heading for the woods. So I got down on one knee, took the safety off of my rifle, and got the back of his head riding on the top of my front sight. They asked what I was going to do. I said, "I'm gonna knock that guy if it looks like he's gonna make it to the trees." I didn't think those guys were going to be able to make it. Anyhow, the gap was getting closer and they were gaining on him. They caught him before he got to the trees. One guy grabbed an arm, another held the other arm, and the third one took his pistol. The German was screaming his head off when all of a sudden you heard the bang. He shot the German in the head. I came pretty close to helping them but I didn't have to. They did a good job themselves. We were only there about maybe fifteen minutes at the most because, like I said, we were chasing the Germans.

—*Grant Shultheis; USHMM, RG-50.030*0589*

An official United States government report issued by the executive office of the president of the United States, war refugee board, on the German camps at Auschwitz and Birkenau, sets forth the number of Jews gassed in Birkenau in the two-year period between April 1942 and April 1944. The figure printed in this report is not a typographical error. The number is one million seven hundred and sixty five thousand.

—*Major William Walsh, assistant trial counsel for the US, Nuremberg trials, vol. 3, 12/14/45; The Avalon Project, Yale University*

My brother, Erik, twelve, was with my father as we walked into Płaszów concentration camp in 1943. There was a lot of crying, screaming, and pleading as they separated parents from children. I was fourteen but went with the women. Later, when I was in the barrack, I froze when I heard awful machine-gun fire. I thought our children were being killed. From the window I only said, "Erik," and my father answered, "I don't know." It was a nightmare. A few days later I saw my father who had been looking for me. He grabbed me, but I hardly recognized him. He had aged beyond recognition. I asked, "Erik?" and he replied, "He's not here." That's all he would say. A little while later I was herded to the railroad station to be taken somewhere else. My father managed to find me and embraced me. He pointed to a rock on a hill and said, "You see that hill? That's where Erik is." Later I found out that after shooting the children, they chose fifty men to bury them in a shallow grave, and my father was among them. He saw a hand and recognized Erik's ring.

—Edith Lowy; USHMM, RG-50.030*0584

Life was terrible for children in the Polish ghetto. They got half a glass of milk and one egg a week. The SS and Jewish police came for the children but didn't get all of them. I was hiding on the roof, where they didn't search. If I had given away my child, I would have lost my mind and gone crazy. We didn't go outside often with my boy because people would have noticed and said, "See, they have a child." When I was out at work, they took my mother away but left the boy because my sister said he was mine. I never saw my parents again. When I got back, my little boy was crying. We spent about twenty hours in a congested cattle car going to Auschwitz. My boy was with me but we could barely breathe, pressed against one another, and with only one very small window. I had made a sandwich, but my child would not eat it and it was left on the train.

232

I had also brought three pieces of bread for him. When we arrived at nighttime they opened the doors. I looked around and thought this was the end. They put up a board and we had to go down, leaving everything behind. We came down together, but the SS took my son and my sister's boy and gave them to an elderly woman. We were taken to another side. We had to stay outdoors until the morning. I saw a lady praying and I asked her what she thought they would do with our children. She told me not to worry and pray to God. She said we would see our children and husbands after the war. I found it very hard to believe her, but then I thought, well, she had been in Auschwitz longer than me, so maybe she knows better. One time I saw children marching to the accompaniment of music and told my sister they must have saved the children. But then again, they might be playing tricks to deceive us. If we saw children marching to the sound of music, we believed they must be alive.

—*Hannah Kalmanowicz Kalman; USHMM, RG-50.106*0118*

The latrines at Gurs internment camp, France, were big oil drums with the front open and the back covered with a wooden frame resembling a roof. There were about ten places to squat over the drums. Sometimes they made a little walkway by throwing on pieces of wood, but when it rained the clay soil turned to mud. You had to be very careful because you sank in the rain. The mud had a tendency to suck the shoes off our feet. It was unpleasant.

—*Kurt Julich; USHMM, RG-50.030*0511*

The first deportation from the smallest of our two Polish ghettos took place at night in August 1942. The SS troops, Polish police, and Ukrainians surrounded the ghettos. Ukrainians helped the Germans a lot. They were volunteers and very good executioners. They always loved Jewish blood. They completely emptied the small ghetto. Five percent were shot there and the rest deported in cattle cars. I was dragged out of bed, and with others had to put the bodies on buggies and take them out to mass graves. Younger people buried them, but I witnessed clothes being pulled off male and female corpses, which filled up the bottom of the trenches. Calcium was poured on top to prevent disease and the smell of decomposing bodies. Then they covered it with another layer and dirt. I saw Germans shooting people as I walked away to the large ghetto. A few weeks later, they carried out the same atrocities in the other ghetto. Huge lamps lit the area as if it was daytime, and hundreds of SS opened fire, even on babies. It was horrible. The small ghetto was gone and the large one was decimated, only to be extinguished a year later. The Germans called the remaining little area "Jewish Forced Labor Camp." We thought nothing worse could happen, but it did. They broke into houses, and if they found people who should have been working, they lined up ten or sixteen at a time and opened fire on them with machine guns. Ukrainians perpetrated much of this. I worked in a labor gun factory until a school friend arranged for me to work in the better electrical department. Later I was sent to Dachau and liberated by Americans across the border in Austria.

—*Jules Zaidenweber; USHMM/Jewish Community Relations Council, Anti-Defamation League of Minnesota and Dakotas, RG-50.156*0059*

We crossed the Rhine River and I happened to be downtown when a German woman ran across the street to me. Speaking perfect English she said she was from St. Louis. "You can't let those people out of there. They'll kill us!" I said, "That's tough. Anyway, what are you doing here?" She said her mother was ill before the war, and she was forced to stay, which I didn't believe. I told her, "These people have suffered, and you have to give them whatever they need. It's their turn now." She became hysterical when I left. The underfed laborers, who had got through a barbed wire fence to get to the town, were starved. All of them were looking for food. In the nearly five years I had been in the US service, I had taken eight hundred to nine hundred photographs. On the back of each, I had written the date and place and what happened there. People are amazed at them. Our commanding officer had told us, "You won't believe it until you see it. And after you see it, you still won't believe it."

—*Edmund Motzko; USHMM/Jewish Community Relations Council, Anti-Defamation League of Minnesota and the Dakotas, RG-50.156*0042*

We were shoved into showers. First they opened the hot water so we were scalded. As we ran out of the hot water, we were beaten back by the SS and the kapos. They opened ice-cold water which had the same effect. Finally we were out of the showers. Each of us was given one garment, which of course didn't fit. Some got something too small, others too large. We didn't get underwear or brassieres or panties, just that one dress. It was not a striped dress. It was just a dress that probably came from those killed before, and they had taken away their clothes. Finally we were ordered to line up. My sister was calling my name and I was calling her name. Even though we were standing next to each other, we didn't recognize one another.

—*Cecilie Klein-Pollack in an interview with Sandra Bradley for the USHMM film* Testimony, *RG-50.042*-0018*

My crime was being a Jew. I had lost my job in Berlin after our family business was destroyed. Then they torched synagogues and vandalized Jewish firms on November 9, 1938. Immediately they arrested my father and me in a three-day roundup. We spent twenty-four hours in police headquarters, where the gestapo was located, before they took us under armed guard in trucks to Buchenwald concentration camp. We had to jump out and run between double rows of cursing SS, who beat us and tried to trip us up. My dad was with me for five weeks and then released because he was over sixty. For seven days I didn't have anything to drink, but lots of things are possible. There were many Orthodox Jews and they didn't want to eat the food until the rabbis told them they could. Life wasn't easy during those nine weeks, but I was only twenty. We were punished for the slightest offense. They made innocent detainees stand on their tiptoes, with hands behind their heads, for as long as two and three hours. They called it *saxengrusse*, Saxon greeting. One prisoner escaped but was caught. The whole camp had to stand for a day in the courtyard while they built a gallows; then at nighttime we had to see him hang. If we as much as turned our heads, we were beaten. We were able to see a neighboring compound through the fence and watch the inmates bend over what looked like a saddle before getting fifty to seventy-five lashes. After it was over, the victim had to take the saddle back. I was afraid for my life because two thousand of the approximately ten thousand prisoners died while I was there. A lot of them died from heart attacks or suicide.

—*Manfred Klein; USHMM/Jewish Community Relations Council, Anti-Defamation League of Minnesota and Dakotas, RG-50.156*0029*

My colonel and I, a truck driver with the US 685th Ordnance Ammunition Company, paid a visit to Dachau a couple of days after liberation. We did find one storm trooper with his head cut off. One of the prisoners had been able to get a knife and relieve him of his head. I didn't go up to the bodies in the railroad cars because I didn't want to get involved with the smell or anything else. You could see a few cars sitting there with some bodies, maybe three or four high, just piled in the boxcars. I know they were bodies because you could see they were dead. Those out in the area were just lying around, not stacked in any order. They were all ragged. I guess they had taken [the striped, pajama-like clothing] off the dead ones. I don't see how they survived as long as they did in there. I think they were human beings in body only. I don't think their minds even knew what they were. It was a disgrace to see a human being in that condition.

—*Grady Barker; USHMM/Fred Roberts Crawford Witness to the Holocaust Project, RG-50.010*0005*

They gave me a tattoo. My number was A5143. They told us we should never answer by our name. From now on we are this number. This is our name. I don't have to tell you the terrible feeling I had in my heart when at my age, a girl of fifteen years old, you are told that your name is a number. Forget your name. You don't have a name anymore. You had your hair shaved off, you're hungry, you have no clothes, you're freezing, and your family is taken away. It was very hard for me to accept that, and I don't know how I made it. I got hold of myself and pushed all this behind me. I said I have to live. I have to be strong. At that young age I felt like I was ninety. I felt I had lived a lifetime.

—*Lilly Appelbaum Malnik in an interview with Sandra Bradley for the USHMM film* Testimony, *RG-50.042*0020*

237

When the soldiers of the Fourth Armored Division entered the camp [Ohrdruf, a subcamp of Buchenwald], they discovered piles of bodies, some covered with lime and others partially incinerated on pyres. The ghastly nature of their discovery led General Dwight D. Eisenhower, Supreme Commander of the Allied Forces in Europe, to visit the camp on April 12, 1945, with Generals George S. Patton and Omar Bradley. After his visit, Eisenhower cabled General George C. Marshall, the head of the Joint Chiefs of Staff in Washington, on April 15, 1945, describing his trip to Ohrdruf. [He said,] "The visual evidence and the verbal testimony of starvation, cruelty, and bestiality were so overpowering as to leave me a bit sick. In one room, where they were piled up twenty or thirty naked men, killed by starvation, George Patton would not even enter. He said that he would get sick if he did so. I made the visit deliberately, in order to be in a position to give firsthand evidence of these things if ever, in the future, there develops a tendency to charge these allegations merely to 'propaganda.' "

—US General Dwight D. Eisenhower; USHMM.org Holocaust
Encyclopedia entry on Ohdruf

They loaded us in open train cars and the only food was snow. We traveled for ten days. One time in Czechoslovakia they stopped the train, and people on an overpass threw loaves of bread at us. Some of it hit peoples' faces and they died. We arrived at Oranienburg, part of Sachsenhausen concentration camp. One day I heard my number called. I thought it was the end of me but ignored it. During lunch they yelled my number. I said it was mine, but I had been paying attention to others talking. They talked to me kindly, gave me a shower, shave, good clothes, and food. I didn't know what was going on. They took me in a limousine with SS on both sides. One of them said a friend in his office knew me from Auschwitz and they needed a tailor, so the commandant, Major [Reinhard] Heydrich, sent for me. He was a murderer. Everyone knew he killed a few prisoners before breakfast. He said the previous tailor was old and couldn't work anymore. He brought uniforms to be finished and fabrics to make coats for his wife and relatives. He was fair with me and gave me cigarettes and the same terrific food the SS ate—rice, goulash, and noodles. There were five of us, and I gave a bit to friends from Auschwitz to put more skin on them. I signaled them to come to the window and gave them shoes, boots, and pants, as if they were going to a wedding! In April there was an air alarm and I was wounded in the upper right thigh by a bullet from an American plane. They gave the commandant my number and he ran to the so-called hospital. The German doctor wanted to amputate my leg but the commandant said, "If you cut off his leg, I'll cut off your head!" I started to feel better, but they began evacuating the camp. A friend told me to hide. With torn sheets I hid in the attic for two days. The SS disappeared in jeeps, cars, and motorcycles. About twenty or thirty inmates came out of hiding and got water, rice, and tea from the kitchen for those with diarrhea. About two days later, Russians approached the camp.

—*Max Roisman; USHMM/Gratz College Hebrew Education Society,*
RG-50.462*0095

After the selection at Auschwitz, we were marched along the barbed wire fences and I saw a guard with a rifle over his shoulder. Naively, I asked him what the chimneys were for because sparks and flames were coming out in addition to the smoke. He said, "Oh, that's the bakery. They must have burned a whole load of bread."

—*Edgar Krasa; USHMM, RG-50.030*0478*

We undressed completely when we got to Mauthausen at night. We had to go on a chair or table and they looked all over our bodies, even in our rectums. They looked in our mouths to check if we'd hidden anything, like gold, diamonds, or coins. For two days we weren't given any clothes, and we were outdoors as they wouldn't give us a barrack. There was a latrine nearby. Some people tore a little piece off their shirts to wipe themselves. After a while they had no shirt. Then they gave us striped uniforms and we slept next to each other. A German banker next to me complained that he was not even Jewish, neither was his son, who was raised a Christian. But the banker said his own father was Jewish. He was such a nice-looking, sweet man. I was twenty-two, about the age of his son. Maybe that's why he talked to me, because he wanted his son to listen.

—Norman Belfer; USHMM, RG-50.030*0367

The first day Russian prisoners of war arrived at Sobibór, they wanted to escape. We explained the difficulties of mines planted outside, with a generally hostile population. But we met with them secretly every evening and decided the best time was before we returned to our quarters at 5:00 p.m., when a German guarded us. He would be killed and hidden. Then the uprising would start. Everyone was nervous and excited as the hour approached in October 1943. Wires and telephones were cut, and the camp commandant was away on vacation. Hidden inmates killed a few Germans; we knifed one, and about a dozen were dead, so we couldn't abort the uprising. Everyone started shouting and running in different directions. Some people died from exploding mines. Others gave up and sat down. Everyone at first stopped when an SS appeared with a machine gun, but some prisoners used weapons stolen from an arsenal. I took Selma, a Dutch woman who later became my wife, by the hand and we ran through the main gate. They shot everyone who remained and liquidated the camp, leaving no trace and even planting trees to cover up. We ran through the woods at night using the stars to guide us. We paid money saved from discarded clothing to pay a villager to hide us by day, but mostly we hid in the fields. Even though we offered pilfered gold coins and diamonds, few helped feed or take us in. Finally a farmer said he had a brother living in a more isolated place ten miles away. He dressed Selma like an old lady and covered me with branches. It was probably the most dangerous ten miles because if the Germans had caught us they would have killed us on the spot and then his entire family for helping Jews. The brother housed us for about eight months, giving us royal treatment until the Russians came. But we were really free from that moment.

—*Chaim Engel in an interview with Sandra Bradley for the USHMM film* Testimony, *RG-50.042*0009*

It was a major event and very meaningful when I became an American citizen in 1950. It was grandiose. The fact that I was a refugee before meant that I was the odd man out. I had no country that I could appeal to for protection. Nobody cared for me. Now I was a citizen of a big, free, and humane country. I was born under an emperor and I had been an Austrian citizen. Then the empire collapsed and I became a Czechoslovakian citizen. Then I was nothing because Czechoslovakia was no more, and nobody else wanted to recognize my nationality. What is a man who has no country? I am satisfied but not proud that I dared to make dangerous decisions. One was to go into hiding when our camp was evacuated. If the jittery SS had caught me they would have killed me because they were afraid.

—*Ernest Koenig; USHMM, made possible by a grant from Jeff and Toby Herr, RG-50.549.02*0003*

In mid-1938, two Nazis in full regalia waited with crossed arms for about two hours for my father to come home. It was a frightening experience. They told him to pack a toothbrush. They wanted to ask him questions. My father had gone to law school in Vienna, had represented me, and was a personal friend of the wealthy Sassoon family in England. People we knew had disappeared and we had no idea where they were going. He came back twenty-four hours later. They had beaten him up, but he refused to talk about it. We got an exit permit for England. The gestapo came to our house, carried away Persian rugs, and allowed us to take out two paintings, a ring of no great value, ten shillings each , and a change of clothing. Just before we left, my mother took my brother and I to the Schönbrunn Park. When we got to the gates, there was a huge sign that read, "JEWS AND DOGS ARE NOT ALLOWED IN THE PARK." She turned to us and said, "I purposely brought you here because I want you to remember that."

—Lisa Tyre; USHMM/Gratz College Hebrew Education Society,
RG-50.462*0124

We evacuated Kaufering labor camp and had walked about two hours toward Dachau, near the end of the war, when we looked back and saw our camp in flames. American bombers struck the camp and railroad to prevent the Germans from transporting things to Munich. They must have known all along that the labor camp was there but never touched it. Half of our guards vanished. Others removed their insignia and medals. Nobody cared about us any longer. Someone warned not to go to Dachau because they might kill us before surrendering, so five of us hid in a pit. A German woman passed by and told us the allies had arrived. We heard shooting in a village and saw soldiers smoking atop American tanks. Suddenly planes swept overhead and everyone took cover, but they were

American. They put us in a hospital with wounded German soldiers, but I don't think they knew who we were. The nurses took good care of us. We stayed about a week.

—*Ernst Weihs; USHMM, RG-50.030*0248*

In 1944 they ordered all Jews in our town, annexed by Hungary, to move to a cordoned-off ghetto guarded by armed Hungarians. They would beat us up if we went outside the perimeter. We took whatever they allowed. I walked away with the clothes I was in because we didn't know where we were going. The five hundred families left behind horses, cows, house, stables, and other animals, some of which they gave to others. We resigned ourselves to fate. Then there was an order that all Jews had to assemble in an airport hangar. We knew something was wrong when the rabbi arrived and they tugged at his beard and side-curls ripping his skin. We were trapped. The Hungarian guards were waiting to pick a fight and pushed people around and beat them up. We were frightened and were like animals taken to the slaughterhouse. We slept on the floor overnight and then were shoved into cattle cars. People were hungry and thirsty. Children were crying and screaming. My father grabbed a guard by the neck inside a car and would have done him in if someone had not said, "Hirsch, don't be a fool! They'll kill you!" It was bedlam. Very little air came through in the three days we were inside the closed cattle car. There was just a little window with iron bars. At nighttime the train stopped at Birkenau.

—*Mark Moskovitz; USHMM, made possible by a grant from Jeff and Toby Herr, RG-50.562*0005*

When the Germans marched into our city in Poland, they began to take away our rights. We were not allowed to listen to the radio. They didn't want us to hear what was going on in the rest of the world. If you didn't turn in the radio and they caught you, it might mean death. We had to stand in line, sometimes all day. Jews had to wear armbands. If a German walked on the sidewalk, Jews had to get off. They took away all Jewish businesses and properties. They confiscated apartments and settled Germans inside. All the Jews had to live together in a ghetto. We supported ourselves by smuggling in goods from outside. There was no freedom of movement. It was terrible. We were used to some discrimination from the Poles before the Germans invaded, but now it was much worse. And the Poles cooperated with the Germans. One day they chased us out of our homes and reduced the population by about three quarters, taking people to the Treblinka death camp. They hauled off my mother, both grandmothers, and others in my mother's family, whom we never saw again. That was when I saw people shot to death on the spot. One row was for the gas chamber, the other to continue living, but nobody knew for how long. We knew that sooner or later we would die.

—*Michael Finkelstein; USHMM/Gratz College Hebrew Education Society, RG-50.462*0078*

I was in Nuremberg working on a film on German war criminals when Kurt von Molo told me that all through the war, while working for the SS, he had hidden a Jewish film editor in the attic of his house. I took it with a grain of salt. It was a joke to us. From our first crossing into Germany we didn't meet a German who didn't have a Jew in the attic. Kurt said it was very precarious because he worked on those horrible SS films at the same time. I told him I was sick of hearing it and didn't believe him. He said the Jew had been seen a few days earlier in Berlin and was still alive. So on a Sunday morning, we took a jeep. The place was a total disaster. People were living in holes and doorways. We asked some girl and she said he was definitely there. She'd also heard it. There was an amazing word of mouth. People seemed to know where other people were. After a few hours, we found his own girlfriend, who had also survived. She said he was definitely in Berlin and told us where she thought he might be. We went there, and here comes this little Jewish guy, still in his concentration camp stripes. He saw Kurt, hugged him, and said, "This man saved my life. I lived in his attic." Finally, we had found a real Jew in the attic. Kurt had been telling the truth the whole time.

—*Budd Schulberg; USHMM, RG-50.030*0502*

We left Bergen-Belsen in a train, probably in cattle cars, when I heard booms and shooting. The train stopped and we ran under it. I looked at the woman next to me. She didn't move. She was dead. On a hill, I saw a German escaping. A young soldier said, "Don't blame us. We're not all the same," and ran off. Then the Americans came, chewing gum.

—*Lily Cohen; USHMM, RG-50.030*0575*

My brother was in Prostějov, Czechoslovakia, where he had a girlfriend he was fond of. He said someone tried to escape but was caught. They took people at random and she was one of them. They hanged his girlfriend and others. He said it could have been him or anyone, but they hanged her. I never saw him cry. He was a very brave person. I try not to think about these things.

—*Anna Ware; USHMM, RG-50.030*0427*

We children spent a lot of time looking for lice. We all had lice and combed our hair to try to catch them on combs and then squash them with our thumbs. Lice were horrible little gray things with a black spot in the middle. They had little white eggs, which they laid in our hair and we couldn't take off. They shaved our heads from time to time and I always tried to hide myself so my head wouldn't be shaved. The fleas were red and long, like little worms. They were carriers of a disease called spotty typhus. Everyone came down with it. Beside typhus, we had yellow jaundice. Eyes and skin turned yellow and people were nauseous with fever. I had it twice. Typhus was on a different level from yellow jaundice. If you made it through the crisis you survived. If you didn't make it, you didn't survive. After two weeks of typhus, we neared the end of the war. We heard bombardments very close by.

—*Doriane Kurz; USHMM, RG-50.030*0120*

Altov was the most horrible killer. He was the worst. I heard he was from a very famous circus family in Germany. I met someone in Auschwitz who must have been his mother because she had the same name, and said she was a gypsy from a circus family. Everybody was afraid of him. He must have been an acrobat because only an acrobat could kill from every position like him. He jumped over fences and would sit down, killing anyone who got in his way. I don't remember what his face looked like because when he came into the office, I froze, afraid to look up. If you walked by him you had to stand upright, so I kept my shoulders straight because I was afraid he would shoot me. He wasn't an SS, and he didn't have a uniform. Everybody was afraid of him and barely spoke to him.

—*Anna Laks Wilson; USHMM, RG-50.030*0411*

My fondest memories are of Sundays in Czechoslovakia, when my father walked with my younger brother, Erik, and myself to ponds and made us whistles while my mother cooked a delicious lunch. Then he bought us wonderful pastries. Or we would go to a nursery. My love for nurseries dates back to that time. In the afternoon, we went to my maternal grandfather's house, where he played cards with his sons-in-law while my mother's sisters came with their families. My grandfather had a lovely garden with lots of flowers, a brook, geese, and a little bridge leading to a meadow, where I picked lilies of the valley and forget-me-nots. Then in 1938, when I was ten and Erik [was] eight, the Nazis took the Sudetenland and Jews were exiled. We went to my grandfather's brother in Poland and then to a smaller community near Kraków. I survived many German concentration and labor camps, including Buchenwald, from which my father also came out alive. But my mother was probably killed in Belzec. Erik was slain in Płaszów.

—*Edith Lowy; USHMM, RG-50.030*0584*

I went out with the last transport from Buchenwald. We walked to Weimar by foot and were then five days on a cattle train. People died every day with neither food nor water. We threw out bodies. When there was more room, we used bodies for pillows or sat on them. On the fourth day, they stopped and gave us soup, which was pure salt. They probably meant to kill us off, so we threw it away. On the fifth day, they gave us some potatoes. Then two Russian planes strafed [stopped] the locomotive. Every five minutes, the two came back. Everybody ran because we were afraid of the bullets. The SS looked for us, but we walked all the way to Terezin. We were dirty, hungry, and eaten alive by lice. In the morning, a Russian soldier woke me up.

—*Morris Rosen; USHMM, RG-50.106*0119*

We got a tip there was a high-ranking Nazi living in Waidring, Austria, but we didn't know his name. From the description, I thought it was Heinrich Himmler. I was a major attached to the 101st Airborne Division and went with another guy's jeep to the chalet on a hill. With my .45 in hand, I went upstairs. A man was sitting on a chair with an easel on his right, painting the Alps opposite. He told me his name was Joseph Seeler. It was the name on the identification paper. I thought I had the wrong guy. He said he knew nothing about politics and was an artist. He had J.S. on his papers. I don't know why, but I said, "What about Julius Streicher?" He replied, "Yes, that's who I am." He and I were in the jeep on the way back and I had my gun riding his ribs so nothing would happen. He wasn't going to jump out or commit suicide. I had the opportunity to kill him, but I had two other people in the jeep and war or no war, you just don't kill people who've surrendered. The only interrogation he got from me was when I asked if he was the Julius Streicher who was against the Jews. Very calmly, he said, "Yes, that's who I am." He was arrogant to the very end, so much so that when we got to Berchtesgaden, as he was getting out of the jeep, I booted him a little bit to accelerate his departure. A reporter came up to me and said I had just killed the greatest story of the war. I asked how. He said, "Can you imagine if a guy named Cohen, or Goldberg, or Levy had captured this arch-anti-Semite. What a great story that would be!" I asked why. He said because a Jew would be doing this. I told him, "I'm Jewish." That's when the microphones came into my face and the cameras started clicking.

—Henry Plitt; USHMM, RG-50.030*0181

A soldier came over from his tank and asked if I was alright. I said yes, but I pleaded for wasser, wasser [water, water]. He gave me some and said, "I am a Jew." I replied, "I am a Jew too." Then he took off a mezuzah, put it on me, and said, "You're going to live." He took out a chocolate bar, which he gave me, and said in Yiddish that the war was still on and he couldn't take care of me. He told me he would leave me there, and somebody would come and look after me.

—Abraham Lewent; USHMM, RG-50.030*0130

Occasionally, there were rumors that they needed more people for the crematoriums because the transports were arriving infrequently. So what we shared with the children I didn't share with my mother: finding places to hide. They would find you under the blanket by stripping the beds. The hiding place which I thought was pretty smart of me was next door to our block, where they used to throw skeletons of dead people. When the block got full, they would come with a truck and take them to the crematoriums. A child and I tried to find a way to make a little hole in between those skeletons to see if we could get in there before the selection took place. This is the kind of place where we were playing and trying to find a hiding place among the corpses. There wasn't a stitch of clothing on them. They were just bones. We tried to arrange them in such a way that we would have a hiding place in case we needed it.

—Ruth Webber in an interview with Sandra Bradley for the USHMM film Testimony, *RG-50.042*0030*

I was in the infirmary with an infected leg and I thought it was raining. I opened my eyes and saw a Russian soldier holding me. The rain was tears from his eyes. He was crying. He gave me some vodka, trying to bring me back to life. He cried so terribly. We were liberated.

—Marianne Windholm; USHMM, funded by a grant from Carole and Maurice Berk, RG-50.030*0503

We were tired and hungry when we crossed the border into Poland at the end of the war when the little girl next to me touched a fat Polish woman. The woman screamed, "The Jews are back!" I was ready to kill her. I yelled at her in Polish, "You used to call us dirty Jews! You dirty Pole! I wish they would burn you like they burned all of us! Good people died and you're still alive!" This took place in front of Polish officers and soldiers going in the opposite direction to Berlin. A high-ranking Polish officer said I had a very coarse mouth. "Why did you go like sheep to the Nazis? They killed you." It was too much for me. I addressed him by title. "Herr general, don't you remember how the Polish Army crumbled in 1939? Who do you think made it possible for you to go to Berlin now? The Russians? The Americans?" My frightened mother thought he would do something to me, and yelled, "Eva, stop it! Stop!" I answered, "No! I'm going to tell him as it is!" The officer told us to get hold of ourselves. We should have got to Kielce in three hours, but it took us eighteen hours. They told us not to go outside as there had been a pogrom against Jews, whom they had killed the day before. It was the hometown of the parents of the little girl I was with. So we went on to Kozienice.

—*Eva Rosencwajig Stock; USHMM, RG-50.030*0225*

The German officer wanted me to arrange a Christmas party. I refused and ran away. He was so angry; he started hitting a woman I held onto. I hid on top of the bunk. He was like a wild man and was probably drunk. They were not supposed to have anything to do with Jewish girls. The law was that to have any relationship or sex with a Jewish girl was a disgrace to the German race. But they did it on the quiet. He came in and shouted, "Where did she go!" Everyone said I was not there. He picked on another girl and started hitting her. She refused to go. He was afraid. If the Germans found out, perhaps he would be punished. That was the law. The next day he took me and my girlfriend up to his room and made us clean up all the broken glass. We cut our fingers. For ten days, I had to polish his officer's boots. He didn't do anything wrong. He just made us work.

—*Sally Chase; USHMM, RG-50.029*0010*

The block leader always cautioned that nobody should ever volunteer because you don't know what you're volunteering for. I was so desperate that I decided to volunteer. They were looking for girls who still looked half decent, so I pinched my cheeks red and bit my lips to have color. I did the same to my sister and told her, "Let's go and line up." I had no idea what we were lining up for. They were selecting us as if we were horses. They even looked in our mouths and touched us up. It was very odd. They said we would be going to work, but my sister was not selected. All of a sudden, I saw my sister walking back to the block and this was when I knew either we will both die, or . . . anyway, I didn't want to live without her. So I decided to run after her. I expected if it would have been me, I would have gone to a different line, but my sister had no fight. She didn't know how to fight her way into anything. So, I just ran out. I decided if they shoot me, they shoot me. To this day it was like a miracle that nobody shot me. When I ran into the block, it was one of the most exhilarating moments of my life when I embraced my sister. I expected that she would be just as happy, but she was in such a depressed mood that she couldn't react to anything. Then the block leader came over to me and said, "You don't know what you ran away from. Didn't I caution that you should never volunteer for anything? These girls, they were selected to be prostitutes."

—*Cecilie Klein-Pollack in an interview with Sandra Bradley for the USHMM film* Testimony, *RG-50.042*0018*

At the age of twelve, I became a tailor's apprentice and then a tailor. I survived Auschwitz and was one of six children, the only one alive after the Holocaust. But I liked challenge. My son finished law school at Hofstra and said he was going to open up his office. I asked what he was talking about. He'd just finished law school. He should first get experience. He asked if there was anything wrong in following in a father's footsteps. He said I was a tailor and he was a lawyer. All my life, whether at the table or with my friends, they had asked how I accomplished what I did. I had always replied that it was a little bit of knowledge and ambition, applied to work. He said he had a little bit of knowledge and ambition. He didn't have any expenses living at home, and he had money in the bank. Why was I against it? He said he always used to hear me say I could always get a job. I had taken the chance to better myself. I couldn't say anything to him. I had to agree. And it worked out.

—*Nathan Krieger; William B. Helmreich's book* Against All Odds: Holocaust Survivors and the Successful Lives They Made in America, *USHMM, RG-50.165*0058*

I was liberated at Salzwedel, where I was a laborer in an ammunition factory. All the guards from [nearby] came to our camp and tore off their insignia. I have to say that the Americans treated them with kid gloves. It was absolutely revolting to watch. Revolting in a way, in another way admirable. The only incident happened when the cook, who was a German soldier, ran and was shot from the turret. They let him lie there for a couple of days. That was the only incident that took place. But it was just absolutely disgusting to watch how they were treated. I mean they weren't even treated as prisoners or anything. They were handled almost as if they were guests. It was disgusting to watch. As the troops were going through, I said it was so American. I mean, they were young kids. They must have found food in farms or wherever. They threw cartons of eggs at us [hoping] we would catch them as the trucks were going very slowly. All the eggs broke. Then they fed us and made chicken soup with rice. It was more fat than soup, and I would say 99 percent of the inmates got jaundice. Everybody was yellow. It wasn't funny—but it was funny.

—Ann Green; USHMM, RG-50.030*0509

We defied rules that said we would be beaten or deprived of food if we spoke to prisoners of war and others, and that's how we learned that the Germans were losing the war. I realized that things must be very bad for the Nazis when an elderly factory foreman asked my mother, who spoke German fluently, if she would write in his notebook, and sign, "I treated you well and never hit you. I treated you with as much humanity as I was allowed to." He wanted to present proof of his humanity to the allies! If a German could be that scared, the war must be close to an end. I could also tell they were scared because their brutality toward us was even worse than before. The closer it got to the end of the war, the more vicious they became. In Belsen, they stopped distributing that disgusting food, and we went for days without eating. My mother died in Belsen because I had no water or medical care for her. I doubted very much that my father, fifty-two, would survive hard physical labor. Unfortunately, I was right.

—Felicia Weingarten; USHMM/Jewish Community Relations Council, Anti-Defamation League of Minnesota and Dakotas, RG-50.156*0056

They sent about one thousand of us to a concentration camp somewhere in Bavaria, which was the worst of them all. I can't imagine how I survived. There wasn't a thing I didn't do for something extra to eat. You couldn't go out, you couldn't scrounge, you couldn't beg, but you had to work. Sanitary conditions were unbearable. The place was full of mud. If anybody was weak and had to walk to the latrine, they sank in the mud and couldn't get out. They died there on the spot. People with all kinds of diseases had to go to the latrine. It was like a wheelbarrow with handles, but no wheels. For an extra piece of bread, I volunteered to dump the human waste. That was how I survived. Jewish doctors had to perform operations without anesthetics or surgical instruments but with real butchers' knives. Lice crawled all over us. There were deaths every single day and night. They brought more and more people into the barrack. There were a lot of nationalities, but people died like flies.

—*Harry Tabrys; USHMM, RG-50.233*0134*

Inmates escaped from Auschwitz, many of whom knew the Polish language of the locals. But if they caught someone, they made us watch the hanging. You couldn't put your head down; otherwise, they would knock out your teeth. You had to look straight up during the hanging. We had to wait until the victim turned blue and could not look away until they declared him dead. Then they let us go about our business, to shower or get food. One night they hanged three or four inmates.

—*Bernard Pasternak; USHMM, RG-50.030*0177*

I was in Buffalo, New York, when my mother wrote from Germany about Kristallnacht. She said what happened to my father and her "is really beyond description." She wrote, "I won't go into it here, but suffice to say that we all acquired a set of mini-furniture in a hurry." She meant that they had come into the house and smashed all the furniture. We later found out from other relatives who had left Germany after Kristallnacht, that a gang of SA [Sturmabteilung] storm troopers had invaded my elderly parents' home that night [November 9, 1938]. They were led by a former classmate of mine, who had been in and out of our home, who had eaten at our table, and in whose house I had spent some time. They had lined my parents up against the wall and made ominous threats against them. Then they had vandalized the home and destroyed most of their possessions. They arrested my father and hauled him off to the jail, which was better than the fate that befell most men. Maybe my father was not sent to a concentration camp because of his advanced age. Subsequent letters from my parents reported that there had been no news yet from a husband, or that a family had been reunited. They themselves were alright. Eventually most of the men arrested on Kristallnacht were sent home, but some never made it out of the concentration camps.

—Kurt Klein; USHMM, RG-50.042*0015

I made the mistake at Mauthausen of taking out a packet of cigarettes a day after liberation, and I was practically mobbed. The ones that could walk smelled the smoke and saw the cigarettes. I gave them the pack and didn't pull another pack because I think they probably would've killed me to get a cigarette.

—Donald Dean; USHMM/Jewish Community Relations Council, Anti-Defamation League of Minnesota and the Dakotas, RG-50.156*0009

When the train stopped in Auschwitz, I saw unusual scenes, dogs barking and straining at the leash, and SS men shouting and shooting. People were ordered to jump out of the train. It was complete chaos. Mothers looking for children, and we looking for our fathers. I jumped out of the train and like everyone else was brought before the SS officer, who looked high-ranking. He was directing people to the right and to the left. To one side, older people and women with children. To the other side, young people. An inmate walked over to us and we asked where the older people were going. He pointed to the chimney and said, "See that smoke coming out from both chimneys? Your parents, children, and older people will be in that smoke." At that point, I realized that older people and children were going to an immediate death. I'll never forget that.

—*Sigmund Strochlitz; USHMM, RG-50.030*0397*

After a week crammed in cattle cars with the dead and then delousing and showers, it must have been midnight when we got to the barrack at Auschwitz. People were sleeping on the floor, wall-to-wall, but we stepped over them. Then we were woken at 4:00 a.m. for a head count outside. It was freezing, and we didn't have a toilet, showers, water, or food. My mother recognized a childhood friend of hers who was like a manager of the barrack. The woman gave us all kinds of information: where we were, the name of the concentration camp, what they did to inmates, and told us to volunteer for a group so we could work away from the camp, which only happened four or five months later. This friend gave us a little bit of food whenever she could spare it, so we had a bit more than everyone else. Even though we were emaciated, we were young and healthy, could walk, and had the will to live.

—*Alice Ruda; USHMM/National Council of Jewish Women,*
*Sarasota-Manatee section, RG-50.154*0023*

Nobody knew that the lady was pregnant when she hid with us in the sewers under Lvov as she always wore a big black coat. Sometimes she couldn't squeeze through the narrow pipes, so we pushed her through. Later on, only the adults knew she was pregnant, and they did not tell my brother or I. But I suspected something was going on because they whispered and spoke Yiddish among themselves. Shortly before the delivery, they told our contact outside that she was pregnant. He said it was impossible, that no baby could survive down there, and its cries might lead to our discovery. He said it was very dangerous; then he left. A day or two later, she gave birth to a boy and my father acted as midwife. He had a pair of rusty scissors and tied the umbilical cord with shoelaces. My mother tried to give the newborn sugar and water, but the lady pushed her away and held her baby close to her chest. I heard the baby cry; then all was silent. My exhausted mother fell asleep. When she woke up, she saw that the baby had been suffocated. The lady had decided there was no way the infant boy could survive in the sewers, so she had sacrificed it. The next day our contact was very upset to learn what had happened. He had wanted nuns to take care of the baby. The lady never knew about that.

—Kristine Keren; USHMM, funded by a grant from Carole and Maurice Berk, RG-50.030*0520

The SS used to shoot people for entertainment. In the fields they would take off a person's cap, throw it down, and order him to pick it up. Then he would tell us to lie down and shoot the inmate. These are the games they used to play. So I never stood on the outside, next to the SS. I always stood inside the group because it was easier for him to grab someone from the exterior.

—Jack Bass; USHMM, RG-50.562*0001

Two days after the liberation of Dachau I was there and saw what a horrible place it was. I saw one building that had obviously been torched with people locked inside, who then tried to dig their way out underneath it. That was the worst. I actually saw one person die. He was too weak to talk. That was devastating. I didn't want to see much more of it. I saw corpses of people who had been starved. Even a prisoner who committed murder should not have been treated the way these people had been treated, the way they looked. Inhumanity was evident. At first I thought it was a prison camp where the prisoners were not properly treated. We honestly were very naive. I have a weak stomach and am a softy who certainly doesn't like to see people suffer. I'm a lot like other people who would rather not have looked at it if they didn't have to. We were there for less than a couple of hours.

—*John Dolibois; USHMM, RG-50.030*0408*

Our family was very religious and my favorite holiday was Sukkot, when we children loved to go in the backyard where we had built a beautiful Sukkah. Where we lived, in a small town outside Cologne, there were many Jewish families, but no such thing as a Jewish neighborhood. On November 9, 1938, when I was eight, I went to school but was told by the gestapo, with German shepherds, to go home as there wouldn't be any classes that day. The roof of the beautiful adjacent synagogue was burned out. I took the train home. A friend of my uncle came to our house and said on no account to leave home that day, whatever we saw or heard. In mid-afternoon we saw flames coming from the synagogue and fire engines on their way. My grandfather had been president of the congregation for over twenty years and his natural instinct was to run and save the Torah scrolls and books, but my father and uncle wouldn't let him leave. Other Jews who ran to the synagogue were picked up and sent to concentration camps. A non-Jewish man drove us to Cologne with the children on the floor, where they were prevented from looking out the window. When the gentile drove back, he was severely beaten for taking Jews to Cologne. After Kristallnacht, the Jews were told to clean up the mess. My mother, who had gone back, said she would never do that. Persian carpets were on a heap of manure, and prayer books were soiled with eggs. We still have some of them. America wouldn't let us in, but through contacts we arrived in Kenya three months before the outbreak of war.

—*Inge Katzenstein; USHMM, RG-50.106*0144*

We hated the Jewish committee for leaving us in the Belgian orphanage during the war. Staff at the seashore home weren't particularly fond of Jews. I hated it there and was under a lot of stress. I became physically ill and used to throw up all the time, and they made me eat the vomit. They humiliated the kids, not just me. When they wet their beds, they would parade them around and make them put their bed sheets on their heads. They were extremely mean and almost like sadists. We spent nine months there, but when we got to Brussels, we didn't have those experiences. After the Germans decreed that Jews couldn't go to school, authorities at the Brussels orphanage abided by it. We spent most of our days pasting ration stamps in huge books for sixty girls in each of the four or five homes. We also had to clean the dishes, mend clothes, babysit, and keep our home clean. There was no open hostility from the other Belgian kids. However, had we not been there, I wouldn't be here today.

—*Leni Eckmann Hoffman; USHMM, RG-50.030*0653*

The gestapo and city police took my father and all Jewish men from Celle, northern Germany, into "protective custody" after Kristallnacht. Word came that they were sent to Oranienburg concentration camp near Berlin. When he came back, he sat down and cried. He was in his seventies and I had never seen him cry before. His head was completely shaved, and his body smelled because his clothes had been disinfected. I can still smell it today. Then he related the tortures they had endured. He was very nearsighted, but they had taken his glasses away, so he was like a blind man. He didn't see, but he heard. They had to stand at attention in the cold of December for six hours, and if someone dropped, they were not allowed to help him. They were humiliated. If anyone broke a rule, they were strung up and whipped in front of everybody. People collapsed from watching it. Luckily, my father was unable to see well. At the railroad station on the way back, they had paid for tickets after a younger friend used his hat to beg for money for the blind man. My father never talked about anything else. Who could listen to that? He'd break down and cry.

—*Kurt Roberg; USHMM, RG-50.106*0141*

Two or three men pointed out somebody who looked like one of them, but he was younger and healthy looking. He was one of the guards. We searched him and he was screaming, "No! No!" But they all claimed he was one of the brutal guards. They took him into one of the barracks and killed him with their bare hands. I heard the scream. Many of them had changed into civilian clothes and many of them got away. But others that were pointed out were taken by the military police. I don't know what happened to them.

—*George Pisik; USHMM, RG-50.106*0124*

Most people who study the Holocaust cannot come to grips with it. They ask why people didn't revolt or fight. It is hard for them to understand that hope existed, that somehow we would survive; that as long as people lived, no matter how weak they were, how hard they worked, or how many beatings or cruelties they suffered, they would survive. People ask why they didn't rebel when they went to the gas chambers. The answer is that there was always a belief that something would happen before the final hour—that there would be an end to their suffering. You have to bear in mind the punishment. If an inmate ran away they would kill fifty other inmates. How can you accept that responsibility? Conversely, if an American soldier ran away they would not kill fifty Americans. I think it's a very hard judgment on concentration camp inmates to ask why they didn't resist. Most of the Jews were not trained in anything. It's hard to agree, but if you accept it as a reality, it's not hard to understand. If you know that fifty people will be killed if you struck a German officer or soldier, you'd think a long time before doing it.

—*Herbert Finder; USHMM/Gratz College Hebrew Education Society, RG-50.462*0035*

My mother, brother, and I decided we were going to live. My grandparents never made it. We were separated from my brother, who eventually did not survive. We were pushed into a building. I was sixteen and had two beautiful, thick braids. They shaved them off! God, I wanted to die when they took off my hair! For a teenage girl... I looked for my mother and couldn't find her. She was standing next to me all the time. I didn't recognize her because they had shaved our heads.

—*Alice Ruda; USHMM/National Council of Jewish Women, Sarasota-Manatee section, RG-50.154*0023*

One Sunday, in my final camp, a Hungarian gypsy offered to tell my fortune by reading my hand. This was against Jewish tradition, but I thought to myself that I had nothing to lose, so I opened my hand. She looked at it and said, "I want you to know that you're going to get out of here. You're going to meet a young man, someone you knew from early childhood, and you'll marry him. And you're going to have a son and a daughter." I couldn't pay her so I said, "From God's ear to your mouth." That's all I could tell her. It happened. It really did happen. I don't know how, but it happened. It was a very strange thing, but I'll never forget it. I always remember the gypsy who told my fortune.

—*Carola Stern Steinhardt; USHMM, RG-50.030*0368*

I believe it was Rosh Hashana when we were told that no one should go home that night because the Germans would round up all the Jews. At that time, there were about six thousand Jews in Copenhagen. The Germans had got all their names and addresses, even business locations, from the Jewish community. By then they had already taken away all the Danish police and soldiers. Everyone was scared, and most people believed it. A small percentage did not, and they were taken away but came back after the war. We went to our grocer, a gentile and a bachelor, who said, "Come to my house and I'll take care of you." In his store he had bread, butter, cheese, eggs, and milk, anything we needed. He took care of us for a week, until we found out how to flee the country. Everybody went to Sweden because at its narrowest point it was only three or four miles across the water. We were six: my parents, a sister, two brothers, and me. The grocer didn't know if his telephone was tapped, so he spoke to someone in the Resistance and said, "I have six tons of potatoes; can you pick them up?" The day before Yom Kippur, we were covered by a blanket, like sick people, and went by taxi for the thirty- to forty-minute ride to a house. At night a member of the Resistance took us to the pier, but we discovered that the fishing boat we were supposed to go on had been taken by a man who paid a huge sum of money to take him across alone. The next day we went across in a larger boat holding two hundred to three hundred people, all of whom went below deck. About midnight, a ship approached. We thought they were Germans, but they were Swedes. They gave us candy and coffee; then we went to Sweden. We were saved.

—Niels Bamberger; USHMM, RG-50.030*0013

British prisoners of war at Auschwitz had to be very careful because if the SS saw you talking to the inmates, they'd kill the Jew in front. We'd expect to see at least two or three murdered every day just because the Germans didn't like Jews. If they were caught talking to us, that was the end of them. We found out about the gas chambers within about two days of being there because you could smell it in the air. And the Jews that we managed to talk to told us.

—Arthur Gifford-England; USHMM, RG-50.030*0710

My father had been going to a Viennese coffeehouse for twenty to thirty years, sitting at a specific table and served by the same waiter. The day after the Anschluss, my father went to his coffee house as usual. He greeted the waiter by name, but he pretended not to know my father. He looked my father up and down, turned over the lapel of his coat, and showed a long-time Nazi membership button. Then he said, "I don't wait on dirty Jews!"

—Lisa Tyre; USHMM/Gratz College Hebrew Education Society,
RG-50.462*0124

The Poles called us *zhidki*, and the Germans, of course, called us *saujuden*. Even when the whole camp moved around after roll call, we were still forced to stand outside, and we were let into our rooms at nine or ten o'clock in the evening when it was dark. It was called sport. There were steps leading to this building and after people were exhausted from a day's labor in building synthetic rubber factories near Auschwitz, they shouted, "Hinlegen! Auf! Rollen! Huepfen!" [Lie down! Get up! Roll over! Jump!] We had to hop with our hands on our hips, making short jumps. The SS men stood on the steps angrily lashing us with whips and truncheons. This was the way we entered our rooms.

—*Gedalia Ben-Zvi, Eichmann trial, session 71, 6/8/1961, Nizkor Project, League for Human Rights of B'nai Brith Canada*

I was arrested in March of 1943 and beaten up eleven times by the gestapo. I cut my own wrist because I did not think I would be able to survive. I was taken unconscious to a hospital in Vienna, but the doctor said I would be alright. Because of my strength and my nose and green eyes, I was thought to be a Christian. They had said circumcision did not mean I was a Jew because people got circumcised for other reasons. I was taken to three jails and to many different camps, before Auschwitz, in September of 1943. Then we went to Sachsenhausen, where a factory printed counterfeit money. The Germans asked us, "Where are the Jews?" We said that we are the Jews. They did not believe that we were Jewish because we looked just like them. They were taught that Jews looked like the devil. I was there for two weeks. Then we went to Dachau and other camps before I was liberated on April 27, 1945, by the Seventh American Army.

—*Mark Weinberg; USHMM/Holocaust Memorial Foundation of Illinois, RG-50.031*0075*

I was drafted while a student at Morehouse College and was a sergeant with the 183rd Engineering Combat Battalion when we got orders to go to Buchenwald. I can understand why people say it didn't happen because this is what I would have said as we drove into the camp. I would be telling people they wouldn't believe it. But it was worse. It was unbelievable. It was worse than a dream. I actually saw it. Bodies were piled by the side of an incinerator. There were some children. I saw one cross section of a brain sliced down the middle. I couldn't understand what kind of sharp instrument could cut a brain down the middle. The situation was unbelievable. I told my wife I saw lampshades made from skins. I was told by some survivors that they were trying to kill everybody before we got there. They said over thirty thousand people were killed in two weeks. I saw them beat to death a German who may have wanted to die because he remained there. I was a survivor. I was walking around just as they were, in a trance.

— *William Scott; USHMM/International Liberators Conference/US Holocaust Memorial Council, RG-50.234.0025*

A German got one of the female inmates to take over from him, even to beat us, in exchange for a large piece of bread. She was Jewish and worse. She wanted to show him how well she did her job, and her punishments doubled. We made a vow to each other that we would hang her before we left. At the end of the war, when we were still in the barracks, about two or three of our strongest inmates lifted her up and hanged her for what she had done to us.

— *Gina Beckerman; USHMM, RG-50.030*0259*

They always made selections in Auschwitz. They got a note that three thousand people had to be killed, so they took them from the place where we were standing. I came back to the barracks on Hanukkah 1943. Only three came back from one thousand. Each time there was a selection someone asked me how I survived. I always said the same thing. I was the last in line. That's the only way—not because we were smart or healthy. That didn't matter. They had to burn so many people. It was even worse for people coming from a transport. They didn't know what was going on. It was at night. When they took people from the camp, we knew where they were going. That was very sad. There was crying and hollering. They sang Hatikvah. They put people on trucks and didn't offload them gently. Like potatoes, they rolled down on the ground. That's the way they treated people.

—Lonia Mosak; USHMM, made possible by grant from Jeff and Toby Herr, RG-50.549.02*0045

The Germans were marching a whole bunch of Jews like cattle to Treblinka. I was twelve and my sister, Etta, walked on the sidewalk posing as a Christian. I protested to the Germans that I was not Jewish, what was I doing there, and what did they want from me. "I'm a gentile! I'm a gentile! Please, let me go!" I don't know who watches over us, but they let me go, and I left with my sister. My uncle was among those taken to the railroad tracks. I spent the whole night in a cement mixer, wondering what would happen to me in the morning when the workers arrived, switched on the cement mixer, and made soup out of me. I didn't give them a chance. As soon as the sun came up, I climbed out and went back to the town of Dęblin in Poland. I jumped over the corpses of at least five hundred Jews who had been shot. The town was now totally empty of Jews. The labor camp was on the outskirts of Dęblin, so that night I smuggled myself in because my uncle and my cousin were there. By then I had separated myself from my four sisters. I ran into a latrine, knowing that if a German had seen me, he would have shot me on the spot. The whole night I waited for the German to come in, but it never happened.

—*Mark Mandel; USHMM, RG-50.156*0035*

They threw only one piece of clothing at us after the shower, either a dress, a rag, or a house robe. One woman got a pair of Dutch wooden clogs. In the evening there was supposed to be soup, but we were not given any utensils. So Alice, who came from Vienna and who had been in a ghetto, took off her wooden clogs. We filled them with soup, drank some, and handed it to the next in line. But we guarded the clogs as if they were Fort Knox. We were afraid somebody would steal them and run.

—*Lucille Eichengreen; USHMM, RG-50.030*0417*

Our boss was a very young junior squad leader, equivalent to a corporal. When he came in, even though no one was in his office, he saluted a large picture of Hitler. One day he went to the window and saw mini-buses full of gentile Polish men. They had come from jails and we knew they were to be executed in Auschwitz. He looked out of the window and put on his gloves; then he shot them in a crematorium not in use. He came back and laughed as if nothing had happened.

—*Else Turteltaub; USHMM/Gratz College Hebrew Education Society, RG-50.462*0072*

They took us by truck from Auschwitz to Gleiwitz, where there was nothing but mountains and wilderness and a barracks and electric fences patrolled by SS. We worked in shifts, mixing cement by hand. I was young, energetic, and a farm boy, so after work, I polished the boots of the SS and cleaned their floors for extra soup. I survived because I was a fast runner. Those they overtook on runs around the central barrack went to the gas chamber. One day I volunteered to wash the container of soup because the best stuff was at the bottom. As I had already received soup, the SS man called me a swine and hit me so hard that he punctured my eardrum. Since then it has pained me. After liberation, a doctor in Washington, DC, said it had deteriorated too much and would affect my brain unless I had an operation. He removed the mastoid and replaced it with a plastic one. I don't hear in my left ear, but thank God the operation was successful.

—*David Yegher; USHMM, RG-50.233*0142*

I remember Kristallnacht in 1938 so well. They came for my father in the morning and took him to Buchenwald with other men. My mother took my younger brother and I into the attic of our three-story building. She cautioned us to be "very quiet when they come here." They barged in, but not above the second floor. They threw all our furniture, porcelain, and crystal out the windows and demolished our living and dining rooms. But physically we were untouched because they never knew we were above them. My father came back after about a month later smelling terrible. We had only a flush toilet and no bathroom, so she washed him from top to toe with hot water in the sink. We continued to live in Freiburg but went to school in Frankfurt, which my parents visited sometimes to see how we were doing. In September 1942, they sent us to Theresienstadt.

—*Gisela Zamora; USHMM, RG-50.030*0476*

They put us into what I would call a standing coffin, a box. Small, dark, and I could only stand. That's where they put me for hours. I heard men scream, "Let me out, let me out! I'll tell you what you want!" I imagined I was in a meadow with sunshine and this is where I was. Little is known of that concentration camp called Fuhlsbüttel. It was really the Hamburg prison. There were lots of other people brought in that night, but I was the only one who was put in solitary. Part of it is because I think I was considered an intellectual, a political, *and* a Jew. The SS guard was a bit younger than me, twenty-six. He stood in front of me using dirty words that I had hardly ever heard. He yelled at me to stand up straight. I imagined I wore a raincoat and his words dripped down. That's the way I felt. The worst treatment was reserved for women.

—Gisela Konopka; USHMM/Jewish Community Relations Council, Anti-Defamation League of Minnesota and Dakotas, RG-50.156*0030

On a Hanukkah night in Birkenau, the curfew was very clearly explained to us. However, I heard very tender little voices and wondered what was going on. So I sneaked out of the barrack and went to where I heard the voices. There were long trenches and I saw nurses with white uniforms and hoods bearing a red cross. They were leading toddlers, from two to maybe four years old, on a little walk. But they were tricked by the fire they saw in the trenches. The nurses, or whomever they were, pushed them in and the kids were burned alive.

—Bart Stern in an interview with Sandra Bradley for the USHMM film Testimony, *RG-50.042*0025*

I lost my parents and brothers in the war and am not sure about my birth date. I think it was March, but I love May because my little brother was born then, and it is a way of remembering little things about them. So I put down May. Afterward, I was registered at a displaced persons camp as being born in 1933. The baby was born in a Ukrainian ghetto, but there was fear, not only for his survival, but for our lives because the gestapo and Ukrainians had killed Jews on a previous Jewish holiday. My mother cried and had to be forcibly restrained as we left the baby on a bed with pillows and went down to the cellar. His cries would have jeopardized us down below. At nighttime we went up and found him dead. The next day a horse and cart arrived to pick up the dead. My mother was so distraught that she gave me the baby, which I wrapped in a blanket and put in the cart. I don't know where he was buried. Either on Purim or Passover, they lined up hundreds of Jews, massacred them, and dumped the corpses in a mass grave. The peasants talked about the grave bubbling with blood. I went to the Jewish cemetery to see it. It was big, almost half a block long. After that mass shooting, there were not many Jews left in the Borschiv ghetto.

—*Feiga Hollenberg Connors; USHMM, RG-50.030*0543*

None of my parents, brother, and three sisters survived after we got to Birkenau. I was sixteen. After the Day of Atonement, I tried to take an additional ration of food, but I didn't succeed. They put the upper part of my body in an oven and struck me on the lower part of my body with a thick pole, like the poles with which they used to carry food. First they gave me ten blows. I fainted. They poured water over me; then they added another ten blows. Again I fainted, and they poured water over me until they completed the twenty-fifth blow. Thereafter, I was unable to move. I was left there for a whole day. No bones were broken, but I still have a red mark on my flesh, like a wound, to this day. I ask the court's pardon; I have to sit on one side. I cannot sit on my right side as a result of these floggings.

—*Nachum Hoch, Eichmann trial, session 71, 6/8/1961, Nizkor Project, League for Human Rights of B'nai Brith Canada*

We left Drancy, outside of Paris, in March 1944 for Auschwitz. We were herded out of the cattle cars and an SS man just pointed. My parents went this way, and I went that way. Whoosh. They got loaded on a truck, and of course it went straight to the gas chambers. Nobody had to tell me anything. I smelled it. It was sickening.

—*Emanuel Munzer; USHMM, RG-50.233*0095*

I don't like to talk about the experience at Auschwitz. I saw the crematorium and smelled people burning. Brutality was so unexpected. The soldiers ripped our earrings off and stepped on my father's picture. They took our clothing and gave us some rags to wear. I had no shoes. All the beautiful girls had their long hair cut. I never remember seeing any women molested by the soldiers. They had no need to as we were unkempt and dirty. Twice daily there was roll call. At 4:00 a.m., we were woken and stood in the courtyard for three hours. We were given one scoop of soup each day and one slice of bread. I used to comb all the German women's hair for an additional slice of bread. The heat in the summer of 1944 was parching and we sat crouched between the barracks to avoid it.

—*Magda Rebitser; USHMM/Holocaust Memorial Foundation of Illinois, RG-50.031*0059*

My father had a wholesale wine business in Germany until Kristallnacht, when they poured out all the wine. His business was destroyed, and he couldn't work anymore. I was rabbi of the Worms Synagogue, under an hour away from my parents, when I was told our eleventh-century synagogue was on fire. I hurried on my bike and saw a small fire that was burning the pulpit. I called the fire department, but they said they were busy. I didn't know this was happening all over Germany. When it was extinguished, I saw beds and sheets stuck between the windows and the ground of a Jewish home. It fascinated the Nazis to throw out closets with china and glassware, anything that could be broken noisily. My congregants had their furniture ejected. A woman had just cleaned her house when they tossed out everything. Another man had a case of liquor smashed when chucked out a window. Kitchens were emptied, and people didn't know how to make meals for their children. My rabbinical and doctor's diplomas, which hung on the walls, went out the window with many other papers. Then we were ordered to clean up the streets because traffic was blocked, and that would not be tolerated in Germany—as if it would help to bring back a broken dish or typewriter. The non-Jewish population looked on but was silent. It took us all afternoon to clean up. About midnight, they put us in three trucks while a huge crowd gathered to clap and show their happiness at our being carted off. They drove us to Buchenwald, where I was a prisoner for a month, though some stayed much longer. They shaved us, just to make fun of the Jews. The Nazis prefaced each surname with the words, "The Jew." I can never forget victims coming back with bloodied heads. Quite a lot of our people committed suicide by running to the electric wire, but the guards shot many before they could burn themselves at the fence. We saw the dead just lying there.

—*Helmut Frank; USHMM/Gratz College Hebrew Education Society,*
RG-50.462*0080

My late husband always remembered one young man who was very religious and believed deeply in God. He even believed that whatever was happening now could not be blamed on God, who had a purpose. He believed there was a purpose to everything. He was with my husband when the train pulled in and they chased them out. They sat in the snow to rest. They expected to get buses or something, but then they decided that the trains were going to continue. So the Germans told them to run, and whoever ran into the train was going to live. Whoever didn't make it was shot on the spot, so they had less people. My husband was already on the train and gave him a hand to pull him in, but because he didn't make it on the train, he was killed. They shot him. My husband always lit a candle for this man because you never know who has family left or who doesn't, because families were wiped out.

—*Cecilie Klein-Pollack in an interview with Sandra Bradley for the USHMM film* Testimony, *RG-50.042*-0018*

I was in a room with the block leader and a few others when a very drunk SS man came in. He took off his cap and gun and said he was going to stay with us—sleeping on the floor or on a bunk. The assistant block leader spat on his head. Then he said he was worthless and didn't want to live, having killed so many "beautiful" Dutch girls by throwing Zyklon B into the gas chamber. We were frightened, so I went to an SS officer and told them [they] had a drunk colleague there, and we were scared of his gun. One of them followed me back and took him and his gun away. I wouldn't recognize the drunk again. The SS all looked the same.

—*Alice Jakubovic; USHMM, RG-50.030*0469*

People ask why the Jews went like sheep to be slaughtered. They didn't. But there were people who became paralyzed; that's the only way I can describe it. They didn't know where to go. A panic set in that made them inert. There was also disbelief. Belgium was a very free country. You could walk down the street and say, "I'm a Jew." People were very tolerant. The Belgian government paid for parochial schools whether they were Catholic, Protestant, Jewish, or whatever. Even though there were fascists, the country was a comfortable place for people of any religion to live in. Consequently, a lot of people were immobilized by events. We knew we had to go into hiding or else they would kill us. If we made a noise or disobeyed, these terrible things would happen to us. It was September 1943. I was thirteen years old and had to make sure that my sisters, ten and seven, didn't give their real name, or say they weren't Christian. It wasn't that the gestapo would take us away to be gassed, but bad things would happen. Nobody at that time knew when. A lot of Jews were in the Resistance, from which people got their information like a grapevine. We couldn't even hug mother good-bye. We had to pretend she was a stranger. We couldn't even look at her, touch her, or wave good-bye from the train. A poor Christian woman waited until we were far from the station; then she wrapped her arms around us and said, "I'm taking you to a safe place." She took us to a farm with an orchard and boarding house. It was a convent.

—*Flora Mendelowitz Singer; USHMM, RG-50.030*0356*

There were fathers and sons, and the father would say to his son, "My stomach is hurting me. Here, you take the little food I have received." He gave it to his son just to make sure that the offspring would survive. The father didn't care about himself, but he worried about his son. So he gave him his food, hoping he would survive.

—*Lou Dunst; USHMM, RG-50.544*0001*

After distributing K-ration biscuits, we visited Dachau soon after it had been liberated by infantry units of the US Seventh Army. Near the eight furnaces was a large room with an estimated several thousand bodies. It looked like they had just been taken, grabbed by the legs, and thrown up in large piles as soon as they were gassed. The odor was unbelievable. What a traumatic experience for these inmates to burn some of their own people day by day. Is it any wonder that some of them had lost their whole sense of being? Their personalities seemed to have disappeared. It's just beyond any imagination what they had suffered. We found thirty-nine open boxcars and saw dozens of people who had been on that siding for several days. Some had frozen to death. Some had died from starvation. Some had been gunned down by German guards when the Americans were approaching. The very purpose of this whole camp was the destruction of the Israel people. I will never forget it as long as I live. You had to be there to really understand how much these people had suffered. Their eyes had sunk back into their heads. There was a dump and I saw them pick up garbage by the handful and eat it. You could reach around their waists with two hands. It is beyond my comprehension how man could be so inhuman to his own kind. Things that we don't even see in the world of nature.

—*Nick White in an interview with Sandra Bradley for the USHMM exhibition "Liberation 1945," RG-50.470*0024*

My mother had taken a beet from the kitchen and looked for her cousins in the block but didn't find them. She got scared and ran to the selection line where she saw them. She told them to rub the beet on their cheeks, so they would look good when walking up to the doctor. So that's what they did and suddenly they looked so healthy. They went to a train and that day, October 26, 1944, they were taken from Auschwitz to Landsberg.

—*Lucia Franco; USHMM, RG-50.030*0452*

I was nine years old when I got to Auschwitz and was for some time in a children's barrack, perhaps kept there for medical experiments by Mengele. A female kapo took me to bed a few times. She offered me extra meals from the bread and salami on the lower shelf of a round table. That is typical of a so-called pedophile or child molester or a person desperate for male companionship. But she was not actually forcing herself on me—just being playful. I didn't really know the implications of it all. She must have been in her forties. Someone told me she survived the war. I was more attracted to the girl who washed me and fondled my private parts than to the woman who took me to bed.

I lost my wife, my parents, and two sisters who were taken to the gas chambers. I did not say Kaddish for them because I was taught that the prayer of Kaddish is a reaffirmation of life. Could I at that point praise God and reaffirm that life is beautiful? I couldn't. I don't have any guilt feelings about it. We lost faith in ourselves after they ordered us to wear yellow bands and the Juden sign. It was difficult for us to understand. After arriving in Auschwitz, we lost faith in man and in God when we saw what was happening. People who were from my town, who I knew were very pious, started to mock God. Maybe mocking is too strong a word. Conversely, friends who were atheists all of a sudden became believers. Why? I think they blamed themselves for creating the situation and forcing the wrath of God. The religious group couldn't understand why God was not intervening. They learned from Jewish history that God had intervened in many instances, in Egypt, Persia, or whatever. If I am guilty, fine. But how can you permit small children to be thrown into the fire? I couldn't believe that a merciful, compassionate God would let things like that happen to his Chosen People. So anger was the right reaction. A change overcame me later on. I realized that without faith in God or faith in a human, it's very difficult.

—*Sigmund Strochlitz; USHMM, RG-50.030*0397*

In 1938 an SS man, whom I later fought in a boxing match, arrested me and sent me with other Jews in Germany by cattle car to Poland. I had started boxing twelve years earlier in a Hanover club because the Jewish sports club did not have such a sport. I did fairly well as a junior featherweight. Then I was paired against a boy who went to the same school but was not friendly toward me because he was a Nazi. I fought him and won. About a year later, when I was still allowed to box there, I fought him a second time, and again I won. Later, I saw him in an SS uniform and we boxed against each other for the last time. I could not restrain myself and punched him with all I had, knocking him out. He was the same person who arrested me afterward in a concert hall and sent me away to no-man's land. That was the end of my boxing career.

—*Bert Fleming; USHMM, RG-50.030*0365*

The war was ending when a colonel told me about 120 Jewish girls who had been dumped by their SS guards in an abandoned factory in Czechoslovakia. We would have to see what could be done. I saw a young woman leaning against a doorway in slightly better condition than the others. We spoke German, went inside, and saw a scene of devastation that nobody who has ever seen it will forget. Young women close to death or in various stages of disease, were lying on scraps of straw. Living skeletons were walking around. It shattered me. She pointed at them and quoted some lines from

Goethe ... "Noble be man, merciful and good." I spoke to one of them and tried to reassure her she was alright, but she said in English, "Too late, too late." She died a few hours later. I was in the US Third Army when we evacuated all the Germans from the hospital, and American doctors cared for the women. I wanted to see the girl I had met first and found she had collapsed on admittance to the hospital. The doctors wanted to amputate her legs, but she wouldn't let them, and she was right. Despite the fact that she was ill, we carried on quite a lively conversation. She was an unusual person with a certain aura about her. I just knew that I had to know her better, and I was able to visit her later. Even after I was transferred from the area, I would still come back and made it possible for her to be nearer. After the war I found her and a friend some lodging in Munich where I had been transferred. About a year later, we got married in Paris.

—*Kurt Klein; USHMM, RG-50.030*0106*

When there was no longer a line to the train's toilet, I saw a girl go in. I thought she had opened the glass window, but there were soldiers with machine guns on the roof. I thought she was trying to escape, so I stood at the door as if I would be next in line. I thought I'd give her a chance. At one point we went through a wooded area of occupied Holland and the train slowed down. I said a prayer for her safety; then I went inside. I didn't need to go, but I had given her a chance. When we were in the woods near Vught concentration camp, they made a count and discovered eight prisoners had escaped. I hope she survived. We arrived at 2:00 a.m. and had to get out. There were furious soldiers with helmets and bayonets, shouting at eighty of us, who were told we would be punished. They pushed us toward the camp's barracks. It happened to be the day of the Allied landings in France. We didn't have a hope of escaping because of their big Dobermen dogs.

—*Berendina Diet Eman; USHMM, RG-50.030*0481*

My husband decided to go to the village where he had vacationed with his father and where there was a non-Jew called Bolek, a shoemaker. He might be able to help us. We ate corn seeds for three days in his attic without telling him we were there. He had known the shoemaker, a very religious man, from childhood. He fed us for five weeks, but he got scared and asked us to find another place—but said his door would never be locked to us. We alternated between living in a hole in the fields and returning to Bolek's house where he gave us baked potatoes, bread, and milk. My husband wanted to give him his mother's ring in exchange for bread, but Bolek refused, saying it belonged to my husband's mother and he should wear it. We stayed in a widow's attic while Germans fleeing the Russians stayed at Bolek's. We got water from snow falling through the straw roof, but we were thin like skeletons. We were in her house when Russians came and advised us to flee because the fight between them and the Germans might come our way. It was March 24, 1944, when the Russians finally liberated us.

—*Luba Margulies; USHMM/Gratz College Hebrew Education Society, RG-50.462*0091*

279

We [partisans] saw burned-out tanks in the fields. I was a machinist so I took the machine guns out and brought them to the forest. I would heat them up and wrap them in oil. Sometimes I succeeded. That's the way we used to make machine guns work. We had to hit and run because we couldn't maintain a long fight with the Germans. I had fifty bullets. How long could I fight? We burned down bridges and trucks, cut telephone lines and then targeted trains. Anti-Sem-itism rose in the woods, but a Russian major, a communist, had many Jews with him from Russia. When he heard about the anti-Semitism, he assembled all the partisans and issued an order. He said if they killed one Jew, he would kill every partisan. They had to kill Germans. They were the enemy. Then it receded.

—*Aaron Laro; USHMM, RG-50.233*0065*

A young Polish woman came up to me at Ravensbrück and said we French could go back to our country, but they would be killed. She said they had something the world had to know. Every month the Germans took ten young schoolgirls to the infirmary, and when they came back they had terrible scars. They were experimenting on their legs. "They won't keep them alive. You French must learn the names of the girls so you can speak about them when you get back." They were so sure they were going to be killed that one schoolgirl stole a camera [shows a picture of a leg with the muscle missing]. We knew the Ger-mans wanted to kill them, so we hid them among the tens of thou-sands of inmates. But they had mutilated legs for the rest of their lives.

—*Anise Postel-Vinay; USHMM, RG-50.027*0007*

I have purposely forgotten a great deal because you can't live with all those memories, but there are some things that stand out. There was a woman at Auschwitz called Irma Grese, who was frightening to be around. She was always with an enormous German shepherd and a whip. She would sic her dog on a poor inmate for no reason at all, and it would almost demolish that person. She was extremely cruel and looked human, but she wasn't. Normal people couldn't behave in that manner. She had a predisposition to be evil. She could do anything, to anybody, at any time. She killed an awful lot of women and tortured thousands. But she was apparently a lesbian. She was extremely beautiful, like a vision, with blond hair and boots so shiny that you could see your face in them. She never abused me but took a liking to me, and one day I was summoned to her little office. She wore a yellow coat and smiled at me. She touched my cheek and said she'd been told I looked a lot like her. I told her I didn't see any resemblance. Then she made me stand guard in front of the barracks while she made love to the most beautiful Jewish girls. After the war and a trial, she was hanged.

—*Nina Kaleska; USHMM, RG-50.030*0101*

It did not take the Germans long to take out the Jews of Vengrov, Poland. Jews were not allowed to be out in the early morning or after evening. My father came back from morning prayers about seven thirty and they caught him. He would not let them cut off his beard, so they beat him up and he died. On Yom Kippur they surrounded the synagogue. Where to go? Where to hide? We scattered and rushed home. We sat, prayed, and talked. I had to take care of my elderly mother, who walked with difficulty. I took her up to the attic and covered her with clothing. I went to another nearby place so one of us would live. My mother insisted on going about ten blocks to see her oldest son. They caught her in an alley, killed her, and we never found the body. Then they started rounding us up to go to Treblinka.

—*Norma Schneiderman; USHMM, RG-50.030*0287*

In our German office you didn't say good morning, but "Heil Hitler." As an apprentice I passed the difficult examination on commerce, but a Nazi examiner said he was surprised a Jew was allowed to take it. In 1935 the trade union insisted I be fired; otherwise, no one else would be allowed to be dismissed, so I was out. That year I went skiing in the Black Forest where I liked skiing, hiking, and swimming alone since the Nazis came to power. But I saw a sign which read, "No Jews Allowed." Nobody at that time believed the Nazis would stay in power. Younger people tried to leave, but the older ones either didn't believe it would last or they went to Palestine. Then I decided to go to Athens, Greece, where my sister was living. An official at the Frankfurt office thought I was an archaeology student going there to study. My father had already lost his pharmacy, but was allowed to join me a year later.

—Frederick Wohl; USHMM, made possible by a grant from Jeff and
Toby Herr, RG-50.549.02*0077

Things were revealed here which are so monstrous and abysmally degrading that a normal brain would reject even the possibility of their existence. In so saying, I am not thinking of the prepared human skin or the pieces of soap made out of human fat, which were shown to us. I am not thinking of the systematic way in which millions of innocent people were tormented, tortured, beaten, shot, hanged, or gassed. No, I am thinking of the many touching individual pictures which have made the deepest impression on me personally and probably also on everyone else. Auschwitz alone has swallowed up three and a half million people: men, women, and children.

—Dr. Gustav Steinbauer, counsel for defendant Seyss-Inquart,
Nuremberg trials, vol. 19, 7/19/46; The Avalon Project,
Yale University

I don't buy German products and I will not go to Germany. It has nothing to do with forgive and forget. I just don't like them. I don't want to have anything to do with them. I think they would do it all over again at the first opportunity. I know it's a terrible thing to say. It's a prejudice. I try very hard not to be like that. Yet I saw a wonderful bag on sale but gave it back saying it was made in Germany. I love sales and bargains, but I put it down and walked out. It's crazy; that's what it is. I haven't listened to Wagner. I was listening to a fellow being interviewed on the radio, and he said he had a big problem with people objecting to Wagner because of his political views and that they should listen to the music and forget about the rest. I don't know. It depends who I want to argue with. It's like Vanessa Redgrave. She's a wonderful actress, but I don't like her political views. On the other hand, I don't have to force my political views on anyone, nor do they have to, so I can separate the two. My problem is with the whole concept of Germany. When I took my grandchildren to Disneyworld, we didn't have restaurant reservations and couldn't be seated at a few … so we ended up at a German eatery. They played the Oom-pa-pa and had this wurst and that wurst. One of my grandsons said, "Grandma, I can't believe we're having dinner here." I said I couldn't believe it either, but they were all hungry, "So here we are." But I definitely did not like eating there.

—Eva Cooper; USHMM, made possible by a grant from Jeff and Toby Herr, RG-50.549.02*0047

Some Ashkenazi Jews, in Birkenau for two or three years, made a candle on Friday night. They took the little bit of margarine they received, melted it down, and ripped little threads of blankets for the wick. Then they lit it and cried, amazed that they were doing that.

—Lucia Franco; USHMM, RG-50.030*0452

I saw how they separated children from their mothers. And I saw the children go away in a little row. One of the kapos saw me standing there. "Why are you looking there? Do you want to go there too?" she said. And then she beat me. Even today, when I see a row of children, I start to cry. When my children were small, they were in kindergarten. When I see them in a row I cry because I always have this picture before me.

—*Betti Frank; USHMM/Gratz College Hebrew Education Society,*
RG-50.462*0059

I knew that cod liver oil was very good for frozen nipples, toes, and other affected areas. Non-Jewish prisoners received packages from home, but the SS threw out bottles of cod liver oil and vitamins. In the early morning, cleaners collected them and put them in the garbage. As the package room was next to our barrack, I went out every morning to collect the cod liver oil. I drank a bottle a day and was stinking. But I think it saved my life. I even supplied my doctor friends at the infirmary, so they could treat my friends and other patients with frozen nipples and toes.

—*Helen Spitzer Tichauer; USHMM, RG-50.030*0462*

When the Nazi party gained control of the German state, a new and terrible weapon against the Jews was placed within their grasp: the power to apply the force of the state against them. This was done by the issuance of decrees. Jewish immigrants were denaturalized. Native Jews were precluded from citizenship. Jews were forbidden to live in marriage or to have extramarital relations with persons of German blood. Jews were denied the right to vote. Jews were denied the right to hold public office or civil service positions. They were denied access to certain city areas, sidewalks, transportation, places of amusement, restaurants. They were excluded from the practice of dentistry. The practice of law was denied. The practice of medicine was denied. They were denied employment by press and radio, from stock exchanges and stock brokerage, and even from farming. They were excluded from business in general, and from the economic life of Germany. The Jews were forced to pay discriminatory taxes and huge atonement fines. Their homes, bank accounts, real estate, and intangibles were expropriated. I quote the defendant [Hermann] Goering: "German Jewry shall, as punishment for their abominable crimes, et cetera, et cetera, have to make a contribution of one billion [marks]. The pigs won't commit another murder in a hurry. I would not like to be a Jew in Germany." Finally, in 1943, the Jews were placed beyond the protection of any judicial process, and the police became the sole arbiters of punishment and death.

—*Major William Walsh, assistant trial counsel for the US, Nuremberg trials, vol. 3, 12/13/45; The Avalon Project, Yale University*

At Auschwitz there was a person from our town in Poland. He was a Sonderkommando, a special detail charged with working in the crematoriums. When things got out of hand near the end of the war, prisoners were allowed to mingle with the Sonderkommando. He told me my mother was among those burned. Others said the same thing. I still continued to check at the Red Cross, Yad Vashem, and other places just in case they were wrong. You never give up hope. Unfortunately, I pretty much knew it was the truth. But she vanished in Auschwitz.

—*Fred Bachner; USHMM, made possible by a grant from Jeff and Toby Herr, RG-50.549.02*0032*

After Hitler came to power, it didn't take long for an atmosphere of fear to set in. In Bochum, Germany, a country where the family went back several generations, we had blackout drills. Lights had to be switched off and blankets put over the windows. Headlights of cars had to be painted blue. Once a week we had to have the meal prepared in a single pot. The Nazis would come in and peek in the pots and collect the leftovers. To this day I do not like eating pea or lentil soup for that reason. Young people in our building swaggered in their Nazi uniformed and pushed people around. My father, a lawyer, saw the way things were moving and tried to persuade others that it wasn't just a passing fad. Then he was arrested, forbidden to practice law, and fired because he was Jewish. His partner was beaten up in an alley and left for dead. That was when my father said it was time to get out. We were more fortunate than most because my mother's sister went to live in the United States after World War I, making it possible for us to go. Others were not so fortunate. The families of both my parents were lost.

—Lore Koppel Schneider; USHMM, RG-50.106*0161

Some months after the German invasion of Warsaw, they told my grandfather he could keep several dozen shoes and said the remainder, together with his shoe store, were being confiscated. He, my father, and strangers rounded up on the streets were forced to load the shoes in trucks, like a bucket brigade. Economic strangulation of the Warsaw ghetto was not working fast enough for them, so they began a reign of terror to paralyze the will of the people for what was in store for them. The SS men rode in rickshaws, firing randomly at crowds and residents watching by windows. We literally dodged bullets coming back from work. They posted notices telling people to report to the train station, deceptively promising bread, jam, and safety in the east. Someone escaped from the train and reported the real destination was the extermination camp at Treblinka. I was told I would be interned and realized I would have to part from my family. I said good-bye to my mother, who was packing for me, and to my sweet brothers, Meir and Szymon. My father was praying; then he gave me his blessing. It was the only time I saw him cry. He was a very self-possessed individual, confident that we would get through this ordeal, and a very steadying influence on me. I don't know what was going through his mind, but even if I did not realize it, he must have known that we were parting forever. I haven't seen my parents or my brothers since. After the war, a tracing bureau discovered that my father died at Majdanek in 1942, the same year my mother and younger brother, Meir, were killed at Treblinka. To this day I don't know what happened to my brother Szymon.

*—George Topas; USHMM, RG-50.233*0136*

We didn't even know the war had started. We saw planes flying overhead and thought they were Polish. My older brother was meant to come home that day, but we thought he had been killed. When he did arrive a couple of weeks later, it was a miracle. He told us Polish soldiers had been drinking coffee when they suddenly saw tanks emerge from the woods. They thought they were Polish, not realizing that war had broken out with Germany. That day, the Germans came into our town, ten miles from their border. Across the river was our beautiful synagogue. We peeked through the windows and saw it burning. My mother told us to keep silent, while the Germans laughed in the street. They were boasting, "We will make it hot for the Jews."

—Jack Fuchs; USHMM/National Council of Jewish Women,
*Sarasota-Manatee section, RG-50.154*0011*

On July 17, 1941, I witnessed a large pogrom in Vilna. The gestapo and others drove all the men into the street and ordered them to take off their belts and put their hands on their heads. When the Jews marched off, their trousers fell down and they couldn't walk. Those who tried to hold up their trousers with their hands were shot there and then. When we walked in a column down the street, I saw with my own eyes the bodies of about one hundred or 150 people who had been shot. Blood streamed through the street as if a red rain had fallen.

—*Abram Suzkever, Nuremberg trials, vol. 8, 2/27/1946;*
The Avalon Project, Yale University

I was horrified when young Nazis took my father, uncle, and grandfather to the Austrian police station, where they were manhandled and my father's glasses were broken. I was a preteen and it shocked me. I was frightened because my bed had to be pushed up against the wall, away from the windows, which were all broken by the stones they threw. At school, Aryan children sat in the front; then there were some rows where nobody sat, to prevent contamination from Jewish kids in the back. Eventually the Aryan children were sent to another school. One understands the meanness of anti-Semitism, but when a regime mandates it, then you get hell on earth. They put ladders up against my grandfather's house, and even though some had gone to school with my mother and uncles, they sat on the windowsills and then helped themselves to whatever was in the house. They emptied his store of everything sellable and had it closed down. These same people, who had grown up with my mother and uncles, had written "Don't Buy From The Jew," in blood-red letters on the outside of houses and windows and on sidewalks. The Nazis kept turning the lights on and off, as practical jokes against those over whom they had power. They'd taken our apartment and we had nowhere to live, so we went to Vienna, where we lived apart from one another. One day my father picked me up and said I was going to England. I didn't want to leave, so he took me to a burned-out synagogue to see the fallen lumber while people waited to be processed on stairs leading to the women's gallery. He told me I was going to England on a Kindertransport.

—Lore Segal; USHMM, funded by a grant from the Lerner Family Foundation, RG-50.030*0522

I was fourteen years old, to my way of thinking already a grown-up person. When they put us in those cattle cars, it was almost impossible to survive. It was so packed you could hardly breathe. When the train stopped after a day or so, a few people were dead. There was no water to drink, and it was in the heat of summer in Poland. Elderly people were dying. I'm so ashamed when I think of it. How could I ever have done that, saying "Thank God they died, there'll be more room for us." That's how I felt then, but I wasn't human any more. How can a human being think like that? To be that selfish? But unfortunately that's how it is.

—Zygmund Shipper; USHMM, funded by a grant from the Lerner Family Foundation, RG-50.030*0526

I was standing in formation next to a friend when I asked what he was praying for. He had already said the morning and evening prayers. He said, "I'm thanking God." I was bewildered. Thanking Him for what? For the misery we were in? For the terrible situation? For being forsaken by God? He said I didn't understand. He was thanking God for only one thing, that He didn't make him like the murderers around him.

—Norbert Wollheim; USHMM, RG-50.030*0267

My father was very orthodox, very religious, and on the Sabbath was reading in Płaszów with two other people, probably from a prayer book. A young SS man, perhaps in his twenties, took them outside, made them undress, and whipped them. He ripped their clothes apart and then shot all three. Just like that. My family and I witnessed this from not far away. I was so upset I wanted to kill the murderer. I didn't care if they killed me. But my mother and sister held me back. They argued that if I did it, they would kill all of us. So I stayed put and we went back to work. They dug a hole where the execution had taken place and dumped the bodies inside. My brother, brother-in-law, and I measured off the exact burial spot by striding from nearby trees. We wanted to give them a proper burial when the war was over. I was later in Italy with my brother, Maurice, when we both decided we wanted to return to Kraków to carry this out. That night I had a dream that my father was burned with the others. My brother said it was only a dream. Then I had another dream, that my father told me not to look for him because he was on fire. However, my brother-in-law had the same idea of going back, and he did, but learned they had been exhumed and burned. It's hard for me to believe, but it happened.

—*Norman Belfer; USHMM, RG-50.030*0367*

I went to a Catholic school in Debrecen, Hungary, where I had always lived, because there was no Jewish high school for girls. I used to walk home from school with one of the girls. But in 1944, when we walked in the middle of the road to be deported to Austria, this same girl thought nothing of picking up a stone and throwing it at me. A lot of Jews converted to Catholicism, hoping it would save them, but nothing did. You had to prove that you lived in Hungary for centuries and that you were not Jewish. It didn't help. A young female doctor deported with us never knew she was Jewish because her parents converted and she was born a Christian. Yet she was considered a Jewess. After liberation, I walked back to the house and it was totally empty. Everything had been taken away. Everything was in chaos. There was no future. I decided to leave [for France].

—*Agnes Vogel; USHMM/made possible by a grant from Jeff and Toby Herr, RG-50.549.02*0006*

At Mauthausen we had to strip and lie like sardines against the wall. Prisoners had to put their legs between our legs, then another, and another. Three hundred of us. It was cold, and we had to urinate a lot. But if you got up, you had to step on other people and you got beaten up. If you really had to go, you would jump up and step on other people. You'd have to be nice to others who would hold the place you had left. But it was horrible because some people couldn't wait, so they urinated, and in the morning it was wet all over.

—*Boleslaw Brodecki; USHMM, made possible by a grant from Jeff and Toby Herr, RG-50.549.02*0070*

During the evacuation march from Buna, one of the Nazi guards gave me his shoulder bag to carry because it was too heavy for him. We reached Gleiwitz, a subcamp of Auschwitz, and I found treasure in this rucksack. All kinds of food. There was cake, bread, salami, and schnapps. We had a ball! Late at night we heard someone walking around calling for his rucksack. I did not say anything and he never got it back.

—*Max Roisman; USHMM/Gratz College Hebrew Education Society, RG-50.462*0095*

I was studying at Brooklyn College [in] New York and had just finished my army basic training when we entered Dachau in May 1945. When our troops, tanks, and half-tracks entered, we couldn't believe what we saw. I was a naive kid, about to turn twenty. When I saw the bodies lying around, it really got to me. Some were just thrown in the corner and some were piled in blocks of five, like cordwood. There were some bodies in the ovens, and I couldn't believe it. A young lady came up to me. I thought she was in her thirties but it turned out she was nineteen. The Germans, I learned through an interpreter, had kept her alive because she was a plaything for them. In return they kept her out of the ovens and gave her food. She kept pointing to a mezuzah that I was wearing around my neck, given to me by my grandmother. I gave it to her and she opened it. On paper in a small cylinder was Hebrew. She started to cry and grabbed me around the legs and was hysterical. We weren't prepared for this. I was there maybe four or five hours when we had to mount up, get back on our tanks, and continue further on. That night I wrote my mother to forgive me because I had given away the mezuzah in a concentration camp. She told me that she had told a neighbor, and that neighbor had told another, and before I knew it I began to receive shoeboxes full of mezuzahs from all over New York City. So I gave them to the chaplains and they said they would distribute them. But I still had a whole bunch of mezuzahs left. So I went to my southern soldiers who were mostly from Alabama, Mississippi, and Georgia and gave them the mezuzahs. I told them they were good luck charms and not to put them on until they got home; otherwise, they would have endless erections. I said, if you take more than one you should put it on the door to the entrance to your house and it will bring you good luck. For all I know there may still be some mezuzahs up on the doorways in the backwoods of Alabama, Mississippi, and Georgia.

—*George Pisik; USHMM, RG-50.106*0124*

After liberation I looked for my brother, who was with me in the beginning at Buchenwald and Buna. I didn't know whether he was still alive or where he was. I went to Bergen-Belsen. I stopped in so many German towns and cities, looking for him and asking around, but I couldn't find anything. After the war, three or four people were in the car, returning to Bad Reichenhall camp, when one of them, whom I knew from Buchenwald, asked my name. "Sure," he said. "I know an Avraham Schwartz. He lives not far from here." I was already tired, but he said he would go and check. He told my brother I was alive, so he came to the camp to see me and we stayed together. My younger brother was taken straight to the gas chamber. I think my father and grandfather also went to the gas chamber. That's what I hear. I wasn't there. That's what I'm told.

—*Max Schwartz; USHMM/Jewish Community Relations Council, Anti-Defamation League of Minnesota and Dakotas, RG-50.156*0052*

We fashioned a menorah out of our evening meal of potatoes. We cut it very carefully but had a dilemma. We had no candles. But then we thought that even if we had candles it would be more symbolic to sort of light the flame of hope within us, without seeing it. We sang a song about Hanukkah, but we reworked it to a modern version of this new hopeful menorah and of the defiance of the Maccabees. We compared ourselves to the little bit of oil that lasted for seven days when it was supposed to last only one night. We felt very strongly about that. On Yom Kippur everyone fasted, even though it was difficult under normal circumstances. There was a feeling of almost holiness and tranquility. It was a very important victory for us. It was also a victory over the Nazis.

—*Gerda Weissmann Klein; USHMM, RG-50.042*0001*

I was close to dying in the infirmary when the Americans liberated us at Ebensee. They gave us hospital food, which was better than the yellow pea soup I had once. I was always looking around, scrounging for anything. I saw a cart loaded with food containers being pulled to the infirmary. German discipline and organization had already vanished. The containers were no longer closed and the lids and rubber gaskets were missing. Nobody cared about anything. While the food sloshed in the containers, I collected some in my bowl and downed it. At least it was something I could take. There was only one catch. The same cart on which they were hauling food had been used the day before to carry dead bodies. Nobody had washed the cart. Feces may have come out of the corpses. What I had taken was probably their excrement. I got diarrhea and was closer to death than ever before. It continued even when I got to Prague, and nobody could stop it until I was given cocoa. Finally the diarrhea stopped.

—George Havas; USHMM, RG-50.030*0378

My dad owned three clothing stores and two apartment buildings in Vienna and was also the director of Jewish affairs when the Nazis took over Austria in 1938. He had gone to the same barber for thirty years, but after Hitler came in, he said he didn't shave Jews. Then a business manager in one of our stores told my father, "As of today you get the same salary that you paid your best-paid employee." The next day I went there as usual and the business manager told me, "Come in the store one more time and I will blow your head off!" I was eighteen and he pointed a gun at me. I will never forget that. Things got worse. The Austrian Nazis picked me up at 2:00 a.m. to work for them. Another time they took my dad and I at 4:00 a.m. to a police station to sign over the house and business to them. He refused, even though they said they would beat him to a pulp. Fortunately they didn't touch him. An unidentified Nazi tipped him off in August 1938 that we had better leave within half an hour or they would send us to a concentration camp. We immediately caught the train to Germany but had valid Austrian passports that were useless there. A cousin went to a judge on our behalf but was told he didn't give passports to "lousy Jews," and we should go to gestapo headquarters for advice on crossing the border to France or Switzerland. A man there told us, "We give you half an hour. Get out, or get shot!" But, at the same time, he told us to take the train to Switzerland and when it slowed down at a particular place, we should jump off. When we got there, the Swiss man must have felt sorry for us because he let us board the train to Zurich.

—*John Lampel; USHMM/National Council of Jewish Women,*
Sarasota-Manatee section, RG-50.154*0016

We were marched to the police station in Cluj, Romania, and at one point my mother said, "Come on Eva, sneak off." I was frozen. I couldn't move. A short time later we heard shots. I never saw her again. Maybe if I had moved, my mother would be alive today. She was twenty-eight. I was crying and wanted her to hold me to make me feel safe. There was bombing going on and I just couldn't believe it. How could my mother leave me? There was a woman working at the Red Cross and she said she would take care of me. I was with her until we got to Ravensbrück. One morning her arms were around me in the bunk, but she wouldn't move. I tried to tell her to wake up, saying we had to get out of bed. Some women must have seen what I was doing because one said, "Oh my God, she's dead!" I also wanted to die, but the women wouldn't let me. They pulled me away.

—*Eva Brettler; USHMM, RG-50.030*0546*

At that time we didn't know it was Auschwitz. Some people in striped uniforms came on the train and started to yell at us to get out and leave everything behind. Everybody was terribly frightened because we didn't know what was going to happen to us. My brother-in- law asked a man, "Please tell me, what's going on here?" Outside we heard a lot of barking and shouting and a lot of commotion. He didn't want to say anything. When my brother-in-law slipped him a watch, he said, "If you have children, give the children away, and if you have a wife and she has a child, then she'll be killed unless you give the child to somebody else, to older people, because they are going to be killed anyway." My mother was standing next to me and my brother-in-law. My sister had already jumped down because she was glad to be able to get out of the cattle train, so that the child could get some air after this terrible journey. As soon as my mother heard that, she ran over to my sister, removed the child from her arms, and told her, "Darling, I just found out that women with children will have it easy. All they will do is take care of the children, but young people will go on hard labor, and I am not so young and I am not so well. I'll never survive. So I'll take good care of your child, and you take care of your sister." She had the child in her arms and was pushed to where all the women with children and older people were standing. My mother only had time to yell out, "Cecilie, please take care of your sister!" She knew the pain my sister would feel when she found out where she took her young son. We had no time to reflect on the separation because everything was done with such brutality, with such screaming and yelling. Kapos and block elders started to beat us into line, and the dogs were barking. They were trained to tear anybody to pieces if we did not obey their orders.

—*Cecilie Klein-Pollack in an interview with Sandra Bradley for the USHMM film* Testimony, *RG-50.042*-0018*

I fainted from malnutrition or hunger as we miserable-looking human wretches were counted at roll call. The Germans had large German shepherds, trained to attack people. They let one go as I was lying down. The dog came up to me and licked my face, and I came to. I adore dogs and animals, and I don't know if the dog sensed this. It didn't touch me, apart from licking my face. My friends picked me up and once more I was only a number. That was Ravensbrück.

—*Blanka Rothschild; USHMM, RG-50.030*0281*

In the two days we waited for boxcars on the German/Polish border, we were so hungry that we stripped bark off the trees and ate the branches and grass in the pouring rain. They stuffed about one hundred of us into each boxcar, standing very close to one another without water, food, air, or sanitation. The little windows had been boarded up. We wanted to die and tried to kill ourselves, but we couldn't. People collapsed and died. Others choked. The smell was horrendous. When we finally arrived at Dachau death camp, seven of us emerged. The rest of some one hundred were either dead or nearing it. The SS kept pulling us and slamming us with rifle butts. I was crawling when they continued to strike me with weapons. We saw dozens of walking skeletons, their lips black as they moaned. I worked at hard labor for ten hours daily, building an ammunition factory at nearby Landsberg. One man collapsed carrying a sack of cement, and they beat him with rifles before putting him headfirst into a cement mixer. When I got back from work, friends told me a colleague had been put in the death barrack. Anxious to check on him, I went there and saw forty or fifty dead bodies. He was hanging upside down but signaled that he was still alive. We couldn't go close because there was typhus, which I didn't want to pick up. I went away brokenhearted, thinking I could be next.

—*Irving Schaffer; USHMM, RG-50.106*0122*

We asked the inmates where we were. They told us Auschwitz. We didn't know what Auschwitz was or what it meant. In Yiddish they said, "You see the chimneys? You see the smoke? Can you smell it?" It smelled like burnt hair. They said, "If you take hair and burn it, that's what it smells like." They told us some were going to be gassed and cremated. We did not believe them. After the selection, we were marched to the top of a huge pile of clothing and were told to undress. They inquired, "What happened to the people who once wore this clothing?" They were told they went through the chimney. They took off all their clothes. The Germans picked out strong young men and took them to the Sonderkommando. The Sonderkommando dragged the bodies from the gas chambers to the crematoriums or to the fire pits.

—*Lou Dunst; USHMM, RG-50.544*0001*

It's the orderliness of the Germans that is so terrifying. Unfortunately, the demeaning of people has happened. There are a lot of things we should learn. One is not to raise children to be obedient. If you see a child too rigidly overbehaving, you sense something is wrong. When I look at the delinquency institutions, all they do is train them to be obedient. One day they will be obedient to anybody who sings the piper's song. If someone over them happens to have an authoritarian position, they will obey. Adolf Eichmann said at his trial, "I have always believed that one has to be obedient." They believed that! Secondly, we have to learn that people must be informed. A free press is the greatest guarantee of a free society. We must keep it alive. We have to tolerate obnoxious opinions. But I don't want only opinions. I want facts. Thirdly, we have to raise human beings with a philosophy of ethics. If it's Judaism, wonderful, because it has a basic ethic. If it's Christianity, it has a basic ethic. But we have to raise people with a conscience. Don't press values on them. Just let them think. That's what helped me. When my father argued with me, I said, "I don't believe this and that." It was possible for me to think these things through. We have to be very watchful when these things start up again.

—*Gisela Konopka; USHMM/Jewish Community Relations Council, Anti-Defamation League of Minnesota and Dakotas, RG-50.156*0030*

A lot of people in Samarkand, Uzbekistan, got packages from soldiers on the front. One day I went to the market and bought soap. I came home and washed the clothes, but the soap had a peculiar smell, and there were no suds. I asked myself what could it be? Someone discovered that it was pure Jewish fat. It was made at a concentration camp and was soap made from dead human beings. I don't know what they put in it. Then Jews bought up whatever they could and buried it.

—*Lola Krause; USHMM/Gratz College Hebrew Education Society, RG-50.462*0088*

We passed through the bombarded city of Dresden and had one ceramic bowl for the three or four of us but nothing to eat. We thought we would get soup, but we didn't. Then we had to defecate, but everyone would get soiled, so we took it in turns to use the bowl and then threw the contents out. Half an hour later, the soup came. We poured it in the bowl and ate it. I remember it vividly. Later we arrived at Bergen-Belsen.

—*Betti Frank; USHMM/Gratz College Hebrew Education Society, RG-50.462*0059*

While the Americans went on to the front, we came to a house with a German woman inside. She saw both of us in striped uniforms and started running away. We walked into that beautiful house with clothes in the closet. I took out a shirt and put it on. It was the first time in more than three years that I had a shirt on my back. I found pants and rubber shoes and put them on. She looked at me and I told her I needed to eat. She gave us food, but I noticed her looking outside. And there was a dog house, and hiding inside was a little girl, maybe four years old. I went out to her and asked if I would really harm a little girl. Did she think I would be just like they were? I told her I would not harm her and she didn't have to hide in the kennel. She didn't say a word. She was hiding because she thought I would do to her what they had done to us.

—Abraham Lewent; USHMM, RG-50.030*0130

The day after I was in Buchenwald, we brought townspeople in groups to see the camp. "You did this," we told them. "Look at the remains of what you did." They answered, "No, no, it was Hitler." We countered, "You allowed it to happen. You are responsible." They defied us. "No, no. We did not even know the camp was here." The prisoners said it was a lie. They had been taken in slave work gangs through the town to fix roads and repair buildings. They said many villagers had taunted them and thrown stones. How could they not have known the concentration camp was there? I wondered, how could the townspeople not have at least smelled it? After the war, we were asked to be silent. We were told it had all passed. They did not want to dwell on the past. They said, "We want to forget all that. Do not remind us." So we were silent. Now some say the Holocaust was fiction, that it never really happened. Now we have been unsilenced because we could never forget. We must take the journey again and again. Even though it is a difficult journey, it must be remembered. How could there ever have been a Buchenwald? Or a

Dachau? Or an Auschwitz? Or any of the other concentration camps? How could they have possibly come to pass? We must bear witness.

—*Kay Bonner Nee; USHMM/Jewish Community Relations Council, Anti-Defamation League of Minnesota and Dakotas, RG-50.156*0043*

My [Polish] father had nightmares till the day he died. He would not talk. If we talked about the Holocaust, he would leave the room. He wouldn't stay. He'd go and lie down, and for good measure, he would put the pillow over his head, turn toward the wall, and want nothing to do with us. He had endured a lot. He could have told us stories of how he had to take care of four children. What were his thoughts, trying to shelter and keep these children alive? He never talked.

—*Bozenna Gilbride; USHMM, RG-50.233*0032*

In the late 1930s, a friend of my brother came from Warsaw, saw me, and asked who was that cute little girl? My brother said I was his sister. He took us out to dinner and fell in love with me. We were engaged when the war broke out. He was wounded in the military and sent to a hospital. My father, a builder, sent a gentile employee to bring him back. They covered his face so they wouldn't recognize a Jew. Even the Germans carried him from one train to another. We married in 1940 during the war. I wasn't crazy about marrying, but he was wounded, and he didn't want to live unless I married him. My mother said all of us would die anyway; therefore, I should marry him. So I did. I got pregnant the following year and gave birth to a daughter, but she died after seven months from diarrhea as we were not allowed to go to doctors.

—*Rose Szywic Warner; USHMM, RG-50.030*0270*

I helped load people who had typhus onto trucks going to the gas chamber. In this way I wound up unloading them, and from there to the crematoriums. There were about thirty of us in isolation. Every time they came with inmates, we worked on them. After they died in the gas chamber, we put them on conveyors and they went into the ovens. I escaped by loading some equipment onto a returning truck and then later jumping off. A few people had done the same thing before me. When you work in the crematoriums or the gas chambers, you never came out. After a period of time they replaced you with other people so that no one who worked there would ever come out alive. But some people were very fortunate to survive.

—*Sam Bankhalter in an interview with Sandra Bradley for the USHMM film* Testimony, *RG-50.042*0005*

In 1944 the Kovno ghetto was going to be emptied, with the Jews herded together for transportation to the unknown. It could have been to the death camps or to oblivion. We had no idea. Many thousands were assembled in a big, open field. My uncle, a medical doctor, and his wife, decided that it was not for them. He had a poisoned capsule but only for one person. It wasn't enough for two. Of course they both ran around in circles, demented. His colleagues tried to subdue them, but they didn't succeed. A German quickly put him out of his misery by shooting him dead in front of us. The wife, however, was helped, and she survived the camps and later returned to Latvia, remarried, and died a normal death.

—*Manfred Simon; USHMM/National Council of Jewish Women, Sarasota-Manatee section, RG-50.154*0025*

302

I was recalled from Dora to Buchenwald because they learned that I was a specialist and they wanted me for the manufacture of vaccines. However, I was unaware of it until the very last moment. My pity was very great, but it was not a question of having pity or not. One had to carry out to the letter the orders that were given or be killed. Human beings were recruited for experiments. They were not volunteers. We counted six hundred victims sacrificed for the sole purpose of supplying typhus germs. They were literally murdered to keep typhus germs alive. Straitjackets were used for those who refused to be inoculated. Certain bombs dropped on Germany had burned civilians and soldiers, and their wounds were difficult to heal. The Germans tried to find drugs to quicken their healing. Experiments were carried out on Russian prisoners, who were artificially burned with phosphorus products and then treated with different drugs supplied by the German chemical industry. All these experiments resulted in death.

—*Alfred Balachowsky, Nuremberg trials, vol. 6, 1/29/4; The Avalon Project, Yale University*

I'm totally deaf in my right ear as the result of a beating at Auschwitz, probably from the wood of a rifle butt. I still have the marks on it. Luckily, I've got good hearing in my left ear so you don't notice I'm half deaf. If you were in the presence of German SS, you had a fairly good chance of making it to work. But if the SS in charge were Ukrainians, Croatians, or Austrians, your probabilities were greatly diminished. The worst overseers were the Ukrainians, followed by the Austrians.

—*Gert Silberbard Silver; USHMM, RG-50.562*0010*

The minute they opened the door at Treblinka, I was facing about two stories of dead people. Corpses in the trains were shoved out because another train came in and there was no time to haul away the dead. I saw boys dragging dead bodies to their grave, and I jumped right in and pulled those bodies as if I was one of them. When night rolled around, I hid between the bodies. By morning two or three had been killed so I did the same thing again, joining the group and becoming one of the inmates. I broke into the crew and became one of them.

—*Isadore Helfing in an interview with Sandra Bradley for the USHMM film* Testimony, *RG-50.042*0014*

I knew that my brother was friendly with a very rich gentile who owned a restaurant and lived on part of a farm, so I went looking for the man. It was about Christmas 1943 in Poland when I went barefoot through the snow. His wife said he would return after midnight. Everyone in my family had been sent to Treblinka and were not alive, so what did I have to live for? I told her I would return to my town, but she warned me not to go because they would kill me. I had heard they were hunting for Jews. Finally he came, held my hand, and asked if I really wanted to see him. I said he was the only family member left. He led me to a hiding place behind a door in the corridor. My brother was sleeping on the floor under a blanket. He was sick with kidney trouble, but we woke him up. He thought the Germans had come and couldn't believe it was his sister, especially since it wasn't so long since the train had left for Treblinka. In the morning, the host told me my brother would stay there, but what did I want to do? I was speechless. I told him whatever he decided was alright with me. I couldn't go back to my town. If he wanted to kill me, so be it. He said he'd make the tunnel larger and both of us could stay, "as long as I'm alive and can do something for you." In the daytime, we came out into the room and read or prayed, but the curtains were closed so we could see out, but no one could look in. They wanted so much to save us. On Passover she said she knew we weren't allowed to eat bread so we baked matzos. But my brother's health deteriorated so she went to her doctor to get medication replenished. She lied, telling him her father was so sick he couldn't come himself, and the prescription had expired. The doctor said she didn't have a father and must be hiding a Jew. She fled, telling us what had happened. My brother got worse and died a few weeks later. Earlier he had told them that if anything happened to him, he wanted to be buried under a specific tree. I dug the grave with my bare hands in an orchard behind the house. It was under the pear tree which he had selected.

—*Norma Schneiderman; USHMM, RG-50.030*0287*

When the Germans invaded Poland, they went from house to house, flushing out anyone hiding. We were concealed in my father's office on the second floor of a building in Łódź, but the manager had a child who cried. They heard him, took us out, and locked us in cattle trains for Auschwitz. We stopped once and told Polish workmen under the train that we were Jews from Łódź and asked where we were going. All they would say was, "If you have any valuables, make a hole in the floor and throw it to us." They didn't offer food, water, or information. They knew we were going to Auschwitz because they worked on the railways and had seen the trains passing by. At Auschwitz the bolted doors were opened by strange-looking men in striped clothes and shaven heads. Someone found a piece of paper stuck between the slats and read it aloud. It was in Yiddish and warned, "Brothers, save yourselves! This is death. Death awaits you." But it was too late. We had already arrived.

—*Felicia Weingarten; USHMM/University of Wisconsin and a summer teachers' workshop, RG-50.043*0010*

305

We dreamed of things we would do when we got liberated. I never thought for a minute that I would die. It just did not sink in. With all these horrors around me, I always dreamed of doing this and that when I got home. I wanted to live for the day when the Germans would be defeated—never to lose hope. That kept us alive. If you lost hope, that was the end of it. It was so easy to lose hope in Auschwitz. All you had to do was reach out for the electrified barbed wire. We would not do them that favor. We said if they wanted to kill us they would have to do it themselves. If we knew that our parents were alive we would not kill ourselves. We would fight. We could do it. We would stay alive.

—*Kate Bernath; USHMM, RG-50.030*0023*

One cold night I went to the latrines and suddenly got hit over the head. The kapo was there and shouted, "Get out, you son of a bitch!" He threw me out, but I figure since I was already at the toilet I might as well empty myself completely. So I sit down. All of a sudden, I feel something touching me on the shoulder. I look up. There's a guy hanging on the blankets. Hung himself. He was dancing on my shoulder when I was sitting. It did not faze me because it was a natural thing. I mean if you go in the swimming pool, you expect to get wet. When you're there, you expect to see hangings.

—*Jack Bass; USHMM, RG-50.562*0001*

I think it's a crime to miss [Holocaust movies]. They ask me, "How can you watch that? I can't watch it." I replied, "If you don't watch it, you commit a crime. How would people in those closed-up trains feel, who gave kids urine to drink, and you can't even watch it? And you sit on a comfortable couch, and you're not hungry?" I never missed anything. I always watch, and call my friends to watch it. I think if I don't watch it I commit a crime. That's the way I feel. I didn't talk about it, but I'm glad now that they show certain things on television. One time they showed how they put people in the crematorium. They didn't show how the bodies fell out. I never miss it. Those people suffered, and other people can't even watch it? I think that's a crime. People tell me, "You shouldn't watch it." I couldn't do that. I never miss it. Never.

—*Lonia Mosak; USHMM, made possible by grant from Jeff and Toby Herr, RG-50.549.02*0045*

Laborers were running in a certain direction, but I still had the survival instinct, even though I was very tired and my life was ebbing. I followed and came to an area where the latrines were, a special area where prisoners went to die, for some strange reason. There were mountains of bodies. I saw prisoners yelling and screaming, jumping and dancing. Standing among them were seven giants, young American soldiers who must have been eighteen or nineteen. They were bewildered by us, wild, unkempt, dirty, and smelly, trying to embrace and kiss them. I also joined the crowd and yelled and screamed and somehow knew that the day of liberation had come. It was a strange feeling. I had been under German control from the age of eleven and their prisoner since fourteen. During that time, I had been in ten concentration or labor camps. Now I was free.

—*George Salton in an interview with Sandra Bradley for the USHMM exhibition "Liberation 1945", RG-50.470*0018*

They would shoot us as if we were dogs, and we had no weapons. We were weak and couldn't fight an army with bare hands. But I feel that every day that we lived in the concentration camp and survived, was heroic by itself because we made it and survived a terrible life. In this way we resisted Hitler and showed him that we were here to stay, that he could not finish the Jewish people. In that manner, we resisted. It was heroism right there. We tried to fight for our lives.

—Lilly Appelbaum Malnik in an interview with Sandra Bradley for the USHMM film Testimony, *RG-50.042*0020*

They didn't have any trains to spare, so we left Auschwitz in the snow on a death march near the end of the war. Those who couldn't keep up were shot by the SS. We rested in a large factory at a camp where I dreamed that my mother told me, "Sam, don't leave this place." I argued with her and asked how I could not leave since we were about to be liberated. The factory was shelled about midnight and they chased us out. We were at the gate when my dream came back to me, and I figured I would not leave. One friend said, "Sam, we're almost liberated. I'm going with them." The other friend was a bit younger and I had taken care of him in Auschwitz. I smacked him in the face and we ran back to the camp, crawled through a crater made by a shell, rolled in the snow down a ravine, and ran into the woods. For about eight days we survived, even with frozen toes, by drinking snow, and stealing and eating raw potatoes when the sun came up. Then the Russians came and liberated us.

—Sam Spiegel; USHMM, RG-50.030*0324

Four or five days after liberation from Sachsenhausen, I went with my father across a field and saw a trunk covered in blood. I opened it and there must have been more than a million Reichsmarks inside. I told my father it was not worth anything because I thought the Reichsmark would not be worth anything after the war, when there would be a new currency. If I had have known that these Reichsmarks would be good and valid until 1948, I would have been a millionaire. I could have bought entire blocks of houses. But I didn't even touch it, and I walked off with my violin.

—Bert Fleming; USHMM, RG-50.030*0365

I was a young teenager working strenuous fourteen-hour shifts in the airplane factory in Saxony, Germany, where it was so cold that I couldn't stand it. Every week we were given little pieces of paper, torn from newspapers and magazines, to go to the latrine. It was freezing so much that I wound the paper around my legs. When we got a blanket, the first thing we did was unravel the border and put the thread aside for when it was needed. But I used a bit of it to hold the paper on my legs. Sleep was impossible because of the bed bugs. The midnight shift was hard to take, but you got used to it. The windows were open in the factory where I worked using a pressure hammer on the planes' rudders. When the air raid sirens wailed, the SS shut the factory's windows, locked us inside, and scampered down to the shelters. The factory was never bombed, though we heard the explosions at nearby Leipzig, an industrial town the allies wanted to hit hard.

—Friedel Treitel; USHMM/National Council of Jewish Women, Sarasota-Manatee section, RG-50.154*0027

At roll call in Auschwitz, they shouted, "Attention! At ease! Attention! At ease! Caps off! Caps on! Caps off! Caps on!" If, God forbid, anyone was tardy in obeying, the whole group received blows. And we had to act like frogs for half an hour. In other words, kneel on all fours on the ground and hop like a frog, in the rain, during a storm, in the mud, in all conditions. There were roll calls every day, morning, and afternoon.

—Alfred Oppenheimer, Eichmann trial, session 68, 6/7/1961, Nizkor Project, League for Human Rights of B'nai Brith Canada

Auschwitz was like hell. Neo-Nazis who say that the Holocaust never happened, that it's simply the imagination of the Jewish community, should know what a dangerous pack they are. The Holocaust not only happened, but it's a living reality. Auschwitz was the deepest you can plumb for hell. It was the final apocalypse. It cannot really be described. Even I, who was there for twenty-four months, have difficulty. I don't think I could function as a human being, and be as accomplished in many ways, and continue on with life, if I had to remember what happened to me there. The mind works miracles. It's like having a baby. You remember the beauty, but you don't remember the pain; otherwise, no woman would ever have a baby. Auschwitz was the cradle of death. It gave people who were deranged the perfect opportunity to exercise their wildest, macabre behavior. When people ask me how I survived, I haven't got the foggiest idea. Maybe it was to bear witness.

*—Nina Kaleska; USHMM, RG-50.030*0101*

My brother and I were chased for four weeks by the Germans, from Buchenwald to the Alps on the border with Austria, to keep clear of the Americans. When we got to a forest we thought this was it; they would kill all of us. But we were put in an empty barrack after we were slammed on the head with a truncheon. We had no idea what was happening, especially when the Germans started to flee. Anyway, many of us were sick. At that stage we numbered 158 prisoners. Then we asked a gentile woman what time it was and she said, "In five minutes." We thought it was the end. Then American soldiers appeared! One of them was a former Pole who found his cousin I knew from a previous transport. They immediately went off and an hour later came back with a lot of food. But many people, who hadn't eaten well in three or four years, stuffed themselves with fatty foods in cans and packages and got sick. After a week I came down with typhus, but the doctors looked after us.

—*Max Schwartz; USHMM/Jewish Community Relations Council, Anti-Defamation League of Minnesota and Dakotas, RG-50.156*0052*

On Yom Kippur in Auschwitz, they said it's the day you fast, so you don't need any food. So they didn't give us anything to eat. But we still had to work. You learned to survive in the concentration camp. You learned to steal. You tried everything to stay alive. If you saw something, you looked around, and if there was no one there, you took it. At 6:00 a.m. I would run to the kitchen to look for potato peels. You tried everything. Should you eat your bread? If you kept it for later, it would be stolen. We worked very hard. Once we were marching and an SS woman put her foot in front of me and I fell and broke my nose. She held her foot on my hand and it became badly infected. Look at it now. When we were liberated, I was known as a muselmann, which means I was skin and bones. I weighed 92 pounds.

—*Marianne Windholm; USHMM, funded by a grant from Carole and Maurice Berk, RG-50.030*0503*

My pregnant mother had been told by the obstetrician to abort me because it would be immoral to bring another Jewish child into the world. But my mother turned to the Bible and read the story of Hannah, who desperately wanted to have children but was barren. Later she told me she couldn't possibly have an abortion, so I was born at home on November 23, 1941, and the obstetrician refused to have anything more to do with her. My parents' friends advised strongly against circumcision because it would identify me as Jewish, but the pediatrician said there was a medical need for it, so it was done. Six months later the Jews went into hiding as they began to be deported. My parents decided we would be hidden in different places to ensure survival of at least someone from the family. My two sisters went with very close neighbors who were Catholics, but later the parents fought; the father denounced them to the Germans, and they were deported to Auschwitz, where both siblings died. I was hidden with an Indonesian married to a Dutch woman with their three children who had played with my sisters. I never went out the front door or into the streets but played in the back yard. They concocted a story that I was the Indonesian's illegitimate child of a former wife, whose boyfriend didn't want me. They called me Bobby and I thought I had the same name as the dog, so when anyone called me, others would think the dog was being summoned. Only later did I find out the dog's name was Teddy! To this day I am still their younger sibling. I was told my father died shortly after liberation at Ebensee, apparently from tuberculosis. My mother survived Auschwitz, and I was reunited with her three months after the war ended.

—*Alfred Münzer; USHMM, RG-50.106*0156*

A miracle happened to me while working at the Janina coal mine about eight kilometers from Auschwitz. I was sixteen when an SS officer came in. If someone was too weak, he sent them to the crematorium. He made this selection every three months. When we met I made a sour face. He asked if I was unhappy. "You want to go?" I said sure. I thought he was telling me there would be easier, better work. Immediately a Czech doctor, a Jew called Dr. Orlich, came between us and told the SS to leave me alone. "He is the only Hungarian Jew who has never been in an infirmary. He has never been sick and he can work." He saved my life. He knew it because he was an insider. He could do this because he was like a family doctor to the German families.

—*Andrei Rosenberg; USHMM, RG-50.030*0416*

It was very traumatic at Stutthof concentration camp. We women had to strip until we were completely naked and then go into a room with male and female guards and an SS man in a white coat. My mother, sister, and I held onto one another. I cannot even describe how we felt. We were searched everywhere. We had to spread our fingers, and that's when we lost cutouts of snapshots wrapped in paper, so that everyone would have faces of the rest of the family. Then we lay spread-eagled while they looked through every orifice in our bodies in full view of everybody. We lived through it, although we were in total shock because we didn't know what would happen from one moment to the next. After a shower under a trickle of water, an orderly gave us rags for clothing. Finally we were given our numbers in black on white backgrounds, which had to be sewn onto our sleeves.

—*Hinda Kibort; USHMM/Jewish Community Relations Council, Anti-Defamation League of Minnesota and Dakotas, RG-50.156*0028*

At liberation the fellow next to me was half dead, and I didn't know whether he had been a doctor before. When we got a package, he told me not to eat anything; otherwise, I would die. If I had sugar, I should suck on it and throw everything else away. I should not eat chocolate or milk. And I should not eat meat because it would be from a can of spam, from which I would die. He said people who ate this stuff died from diarrhea. So I sucked on tiny pieces of sugar. I was so hungry I could have eaten an elephant. Well, this fellow died the next day, not from eating but because his heart stopped. After a while the Americans gave us pieces of brad and, like babies, nudged us back to normality as if we were children.

—*Abraham Lewent; USHMM, RG-50.030*0130*

After five days in Dachau we were taken by truck to Berlin, except that every time the allies dropped a carpet bomb, we had to run to the bunkers. At a labor camp there was a bunker next to ours with only SS. One of the bombs really hit hard. The bunker next to ours got a direct hit. I felt the impact of the sudden air pressure rushing in. When they got the bodies out, the gun of one was turned around and looked like one of those French horns. They dropped a lot of incendiary bombs that never exploded. They looked like gigantic pencils with a pin. When the pin got pushed in, a flame came out. They had us pick up those things to get the stuff out and neutralize them. No one was killed doing that.

—*Emanuel Munzer; USHMM, RG-50.233*0095*

The Germans began seizing people in Sosnowiec, Poland, and sending them off to Germany. They would go in a closed van and round up anyone found in the streets, much as they would catch dogs, and send them off to labor camps in Germany. Later they insisted that the Jewish Community Council should deal with this. The man in the Jewish Community Council who handled labor affairs was Max Bejeski. He threw away his Jewish Council labor card and said, "I am not prepared to send my brethren to Germany, to an unknown fate." Later he was deported to Auschwitz. Eyewitnesses related to me that Bejeski told the Germans at roll call, "You won't kill me. I will kill myself." Then he ran to the barbed wire fence and was electrocuted.

—Frieda Masia, Eichmann trial, session 27, 5/4/1961, Nizkor Project, League for Human Rights of B'nai Brith Canada

ACKNOWLEDGMENTS

◆

I WAS VERY FORTUNATE TO have my friend Michlean "Miki" Lowy Amir as reference coordinator at the Holocaust Survivors and Victims Resource Center of the USHMM. She was invaluable in steering me to the right people among her colleagues in various departments and saved me endless time in this gargantuan effort. She also alerted me to the heartbreaking interview with survivor Ruth Elias.

James Gilmore, an archives specialist in the oral history department of the USHMM, was exceptionally reliable in checking the interviews to see that no restrictions applied for their reproductive use and in helping me with so many other quandaries, including credits for images and interviews. Vincent Slatt, reference librarian at the USHMM, assisted with the text and citation for Eisenhower's remarks after visiting Ohrdruf concentration camp. Janet Benson Forville, an attorney at USHMM, gave her time and advice on the wording of the disclaimer and other issues that only a skilled lawyer could field.

Jennifer Weintraub, former digital collections specialist at Yale University and now digital archivist/librarian at the Schlesinger Library at Harvard University, successfully ended a search for the right person to ask whether permission was required for Yale University's Avalon Project, which publicized testimonies given at the International Military Tribunal in Nuremberg. She named Scott Matheson, associate librarian for technical services at the Lillian Goldman Law Library, part of Yale Law School, as the point man. He was a writer's dream in replying after having done much research and finally put my concerns to rest. Michael VanderHeijden, faculty services librarian at Yale Law School, provided me with the results of his extensive research into the same dilemma. John Quentin Heywood, international law librarian at the American University Washington College of Law, enumerated where even more volumes of testimonies were available.

I am deeply grateful to Judith Cohen, director, and Nancy Hartman and Caroline Waddell, photo archivists, all of the Photographic Reference Section, Curatorial Affairs, at the USHMM. They were patient and extremely helpful, even as I altered my selections from their huge collection. Marshall Keith George, production manager at Dodge-Chrome, Inc., in Silver Spring, Maryland, sent me the digital images with admirable speed.

My profound thanks go to Martha Gluck and Susan Rosenberg, both in Israel, for their instant approval to use photographic images of drawings by Martha's late husband, Israel Alfred "Freddie" Gluck, a Holocaust survivor. The drawings will be a lasting tribute to Freddie and Martha's unimaginable ordeals during the barbaric rule of the Nazis.

With a thoroughness that is his hallmark, Brian McLaughlin, reference librarian at the US Senate Library in Washington, DC, tracked down Holocaust survivor Leo Bretholz's dramatic account of his escape from a French train bound for Auschwitz when he testified before the US House of Representatives' Foreign Affairs Committee. Even though no images were used from the repository at Yad Vashem in Israel, much time was spent in contacting them and receiving the benefit of their holdings. Particular mention should be made of Lital Beer, director of the Reference and Information Department's Archives Division; Maaty Frenkelzon, photo archivist; Yehudit Inbar, director of the Museums Division, and Dina Levine, of Chevy Chase, Maryland, for facilitating contact with them.

It is not often that an author can expect a foreword to be written by such an illustrious figure as Dr. Michael Berenbaum, an internationally acclaimed Holocaust scholar. Many years ago I was in a very small group honored with a private tour by him of the United States Holocaust Memorial Museum. He brought as much insight and emotion into that endeavor as he has done with the foreword to this book, for which I am humbled.

My son, Michael, saved the text on countless occasions from being garbled or destroyed as he fixed every computer problem that arose. I was fortunate to be able to draw on his expertise every time a problem confronted me. My daughter, Nomi, eased my path by locating an individual in Israel's Ministry of Justice who would be able to help with the use of testimony given at the trial of Adolf Eichmann in Jerusalem, later publicized by the Nizkor Project. Finally the Nizkor Project, League for Human Rights of B'nai Brith Canada was traced, and the B'nai Brith CEO, Dr. Frank Dimant, and his executive assistant, Linda Fleischer, were marvelously forthcoming in handling my request and in giving permission for its use. Maya Rabanyan, in the public relations division of the Israel State Archives, helped immeasurably, by sending videos of the same trial. My wife, Marion, translated text of the interview with Ruth Elias, and then of Cyla (Tsilah) Nikori, after the latter's daughter, Luta Goldman, supplied original disks of her mother's reminiscences of bondage in concentration camps. I also gratefully acknowledge Georgiana Gomez, access supervisor of the University of Southern California Shoah Foundation's Institute for Visual History and Education, Los Angeles, for allowing me to use excerpts from this wrenching transcript.

My appreciation is deep and I am humbled for the back cover comments of Ambassador Stuart Eizenstat, who has done so much in successfully negotiating reparations for Holocaust victims; Professor Emeritus Steven J. Fenves, a survivor of Auschwitz and Buchenwald; and Colonel Maxwell S. Colon, a national commander of the Jewish War Veterans of the USA.

No acknowledgements would be complete without a sincere tribute to my agent, Ron Goldfarb, and his colleague, Gerrie Sturman, of Goldfarb and Associates. Their dedication and belief in this book led to its swift publication.

And finally, sincerest thanks to my editor, Julia Abramoff, who vastly improved the raw text with her accomplished skills.

PERMISSIONS

❖

THE AUTHOR WISHES TO THANK the following institutions and individuals for granting permission to use excerpts from interviews and books listed below.

Janet Benson Forville, attorney, and James Gilmore, archives specialist in oral history, both at USHMM, for their permission to use the excerpted interviews held at their institution, with the proviso that the views or opinions expressed in this book, and the context in which the text and images are used, do not necessarily reflect the views or policy of, nor imply approval or endorsement by, the USHMM.

Dr. Frank Dimant, CEO of B'nai B'rith Canada, for permission to use extracts from the Nizkor Project, League for Human Rights of B'nai Brith Canada, which embraced testimonies from the Adolf Eichmann trial in Jerusalem.

Sara Logue, research and public services librarian in the Manuscript, Archives, and Rare Book Library of the Robert W. Woodruff Library at Emory University, for excerpts from interviews with Ari Falik, Roy Dodd, and Harry Allen.

Jenny Seabrook, rights assistant at Polity Press, in association with the USHMM, for extracts from the book *Inside the Gas Chambers: Eight Months in the Sonnderkommando of Auschwitz,* by Shlomo Venezia and translated by Andrew Brown.

Joyce Wagner, Gilda Ross, and Rod Ross, for extracts from the book, *A Promise Kept to Bear Witness,* by Joyce Wagner, published by AuthorHouse.

Bill Wolfsthal, associate publisher of Skyhorse Publishing, for an extract from the book *Auschwitz: A Doctor's Eyewitness Account,* by Dr. Miklos Nyiszli, translated by Tibere Kremer and Richard Seaver and published by Arcade Publishing.

Patricia Zline, rights and permissions assistant at Rowman and Littlefield for extracts from the book *A Typical Extraordinary Jew: From Tarnow to Jerusalem,* by Calvin Goldscheider and Jeffrey M. Green and published by Hamilton Books.

The University of Southern California Shoah Foundation's Institute for Visual History and Education, for excerpts from their interview with Cyla (Tsilah) Kinori. For more information, http://sfi.usc.edu.

Images

The author gratefully acknowledges permission from the following institutions and individuals for the use of images.

Judith Cohen, director, and Nancy Hartman and Caroline Waddell, photo archivists, of the Photographic Reference Collection,

Curatorial Affairs division of the USHMM, for the majority of images used.

Martha Gluck and Susan Rosenberg, of Israel, for the use of images of drawings by the late Israel Alfred Glück, a Holocaust survivor.

Szymon Kowalski, deputy head of archives at the Auschwitz-Birkenau State Museum in Poland, for the image of Rudolf Höess, former commandant of Auschwitz, about to be hanged.